"*Making Myths and Magic* has all the tools, tips, and tricks beginning writers need—and some for veteran writers too! I wish I'd had it when I was starting out."

— Mur Lafferty, author of *Six Wakes*, host of *I Should Be Writing*

"What I loved about this book is that it was nonjudgemental about the writing process. It explained the ins and outs of all levels and types of storytelling—from plotting to pantsing, from the hero's journey to the seven-act scene structure... It doesn't try to drown you with verbose language that leaves you yearning for the point, nor does it bury you in superfluous narrative. AND it comes complete with examples! Many other books tell you how to improve your writing but this one has a great balance of both show and tell... Highly recommend if you want a no-bullshit guide to writing."

— Dakota Rayne, Editor of *What Remains*, Co-Founder of WriteHive

Praise for Making Myths and Magic

"Comprehensive yet concise! Unlike other worldbuilding books that merely present advice in a vacuum, *Making Myths and Magic* shows the practical way to take foggy ideas and turn them into concrete action. This is an easy pick up for all speculative fiction authors and writers out there."

— Antoine Bandele, author of *TJ Young & The Orishas*

"*Making Myths and Magic* is a thoughtful and in-depth guide that covers everything the aspiring fantasy or sci-fi author will need, and then some. Not only does this field guide provide the building blocks for a book, but it offers suggestions on how to do so with care and originality. This guide is perfect for beginners, and as a welcome reference for more experienced writers."

— Trudie Skies, author of *The Cruel Gods*

"*Making Myths and Magic* is a master class in storytelling. Using accessible examples, we get concrete direction on how to shape everything from characterization to worldbuilding in order to write an immersive book that, above all else, embodies an author's voice authentically."

— Bharat Krishnan, author of *Privilege*

"*Making Myths and Magic* is an indispensable resource for every storyteller. This book encourages readers to have fun with their stories first, and then it equips them to send those stories into the world. It's relatable and uses familiar worlds and narratives to teach new and veteran writers alike how to take the tropes of genre fiction and turn them on their heads so that they can craft refreshing, unique tales that engage audiences. Whether you're writing for yourself or publication, *Making Myths and Magic* will keep your writing fun while honing your craft."

— Giles Hash, Co-Host and Production Director at *Beyond the Trope* Podcast

"Whether you're an aspiring speculative fiction writer or a multi-published author, you'll find *Making Myths and Magic* an invaluable resource! From structure to characterization to worldbuilding, all the essentials are here, broken down with such clarity and freshness, it all clicks into place. Replete with diverse examples from classic and contemporary sci-fi and fantasy, *Making Myths and Magic* will guide you as you translate your vision from your head to the page."

— Julie Eshbaugh, author of *Ivory and Bone*

"This book is a must-have for anyone considering the path of a fiction author; it contains everything you need to know, from brainstorming methods to story structure, character arcs, and developing cultures. This book alone can cut years from the learning curve to writing high-quality fiction."

— C.R. Rowenson, author of *The Magic System Blueprint*

Making Myths and Magic

A Field Guide to Writing Sci-Fi and Fantasy Novels

Shelly Campbell

Allison Alexander

Copyright © 2023 by Shelly Campbell and Allison Alexander.

All rights reserved.

No part of this book may be reproduced in any form or by any electronic or mechanical means, including information storage and retrieval systems, without written permission from the authors, except for the use of brief quotations in a book review or critical study.

Cover design by A.E. Alexander.

ISBN 978-1-7781943-1-3 (softcover), 978-1-7781943-2-0 (ebook)

Phoenix Quill Press
Winnipeg, Manitoba, Canada
www.aealexander.com

Contents

Introduction ix

Part One
Building a Novel Skeleton

1. At Dawn... We Plan 3
   Brainstorming and Outlining
2. Structure is a Superpower 21
   How to Tell a Story in Three Acts

Part Two
Hooking Readers

3. In a Hole in the Ground 33
   The First Chapter
4. I Have a Bad Feeling About This 45
   Conflict and Tension
5. We'll Make a Gonnagle Out of Ye 59
   Riveting Dialogue
6. Our Princess is in Another Castle 73
   20 Fantasy Tropes to Reimagine
7. I'm Afraid I Can't Do That, Dave 87
   20 Sci-Fi Tropes to Revitalize
8. It is a Great Misfortune to Be Alone 105
   Genres and Target Audiences

Part Three
Character Creation

9. We All Know I'm the Funny One 121
   Character Roles and Archetypes
10. We Are Open to the Greatest Change 131
    Character Arcs
11. To Be Human Is to Be Complex 145
    Diversifying Your Novel

Part Four
Worldbuilding

12. Hey, Listen! — 177
Creation Stories and Mythology

13. We Will Shake the World for Our Beliefs — 187
Deities and Religions

14. Even NASA Can't Improve on Duct Tape — 199
Science and Technology

15. Higitus Figitus Migitus Mum — 217
Magic and Superpowers

16. What Has it Got in Its Future, Precious? — 233
Riddles and Prophecies

17. So Sing We All — 251
Lyrics and Poetry

18. Avoid the Gaze of the Ravenous Bugblatter — 267
Creatures and Monsters

19. This Weapon Is Your Life — 279
Arms and Armour

20. Bow Ties Are Cool — 293
Clothing and Costumes

21. Mae Govannen, quSDaq ba'lu"a'? — 303
Languages and Communication

22. The King is Dead — 313
Politics and Economics

23. Spitting on Tables is a Compliment — 327
Society and Culture

Conclusion — 341
Endnotes — 343
Acknowledgments — 351
About Shelly Campbell — 353
About Allison Alexander — 355
Also by the Authors — 357

Introduction

Dear writers and worldbuilders,

    I'm so glad you picked up this book, because it means, in some small way, Shelly and I get to be a part of your writing journey. We've tried to include everything you need to write a sci-fi or fantasy novel—right from the brainstorming process to typing those glorious words: "The End."

    While the less glamourous parts of my job as a book editor involved scribbling those dreaded red notes over writers' manuscripts and potentially crushing dreams by rejecting queries (sob), my favourite part was cheering authors on, reading amazing speculative fiction, and helping writers shape their creations. Science fiction and fantasy are powerful genres because they delight our imaginations, ask "what if?", and examine life through a unique lens. You get to create whole worlds and universes—how amazing is that? I hope this book functions as both an encouragement and a helpful resource for bringing your imagination to the page.

    I also want to stress that there is no correct way to write a novel. As an editor and author team, Shelly and I point to things that have worked from our experiences in publishing and from our bleary-eyed nights of research. We also pull examples from all corners of our favourite sci-fi and fantasy media for your inspiration (beware spoilers).

In the end, only you can tell your story. You don't need this book to do it, but you might find it challenges you to level up your writing, asks helpful questions about your novel, and points you in useful directions. I hope you enjoy reading it as much as we did writing it.

—Allison Alexander

Part One

Building a Novel Skeleton

Chapter 1

At Dawn... We Plan

Brainstorming and Outlining

Writers are often divided into two camps—plotters (those who meticulously outline and make notes) and pantsers (those who discover the story as they go). But here's a secret: all writers are both.

The difference is when you do your planning. Some people like to meticulously plot out their book before they start writing and use that skeleton to shape their story as they write. Some prefer to start with a blank page and a few vague ideas. Others are somewhere in between, doing some preparation beforehand, but not entirely sure where their story will end up.

Whatever works for you—great! There is no "right" way to write. Plotters do a lot of work beforehand and less structural editing later, while pantsers do a lot of editing afterwards to get their manuscript in shape. The in-betweeners do a little bit of both.

The information in this chapter should be useful regardless of when you apply it. Use these tips to kickstart creativity, map out your plot, and keep readers turning pages.

Here are twenty questions, in no particular order, that might help you in the process of writing your sci-fi or fantasy novel:

1. What are three things you appreciate about your chosen genre?

Do you love pirates in fantasy? Faster-than-light travel in sci-fi? Animal protagonists? Intricate magic or science? Reminding yourself of your favourite themes or topics can inspire further brainstorming *and* get you excited about your story.

2. Who is your readership?

Deciding whether your book is for young children, middle grade children, young adults, or adults will impact your choices about tone, style, length, and more. Writing a picture book is very different from writing a middle grade novel. Young adult novels have a different tone and subject matter than adult novels, and so on. (See Chapter Eight for more information on target audiences.)

3. What fantasy/sci-fi tropes do you love and might want to include in this story?

If you love wizarding schools, quest stories, or sentient spaceships—great! Jot that down. Don't worry if it's been done before. There are always new ways to spin old stories (stay tuned for Chapters Six and Seven, which are about sci-fi and fantasy tropes).

4. What fantasy/sci-fi tropes do you dislike and want to avoid?

Bored with the "chosen one"? Tired of time travel? Jot these down, too. No need to use a trope, even if it's super popular, if you don't like it. This is your story.

5. Who is your main character?

What's their name? What do they look like? How old are they? Where do they live? What has their life looked like before the start of the novel? Who are the important people in their life?

6. What does your main character want? What do they need?

Your protagonist should always want something. Usually, that thing isn't actually what they *need*. The thing they want is almost always something external, something that they think will make them happy or improve their life. And the thing that they need is usually character growth. (See Chapter Ten for an in-depth look at character arcs.)

7. What is stopping your main character from achieving their goal?

Conflict is what makes a story interesting. There should be barriers in the way of your character's goal. (See Chapter Four for more tips on conflict and tension.)

8. What are three major problems or anxieties your character faces in their life?

Consider both external and internal problems that your character might face. Are they part of an oppressed minority? Are they battling literal demons? Have they never experienced real love before? Everyone's got problems—the options are endless.

9. What are the stakes? What happens if your protagonist fails?

The stakes don't have to be world-ending. *The Golem and the Jinni* by Helene Wecker is about two magical creatures who travel to America in the early 1900s and become friends. Universes won't collapse if humans discover them, but their story is still captivating because we care about what happens to them.

10. What is expected of your story's genre?

Are there ways you can subvert expectations or use tropes to your advantage? Make note of what's expected from your story, and then brainstorm a list of what's unexpected. For example, Veronica Roth does something new with the "Chosen One" trope in her book *Chosen Ones*; the story takes place *after* five teenagers have defeated an otherworldly enemy named the Dark One. No one even knows which one of the five was "the" Chosen One. The characters are now adults and have to deal with their celebrity status and past trauma.

11. What are your villain's motivations?

Think beyond a villain who is evil for evil's sake. Why are they opposing your protagonist? What do they want? What's their backstory?

12. How will characters change by the end of the story?

Characters don't *have* to change (see flat character arcs in Chapter Ten). But, in sci-fi and fantasy, they often do. They may mature, becoming better people; they may regress, becoming disenfranchised or villainous. Where do you want your character to be at the end of the story? What needs to happen to get them there?

13. Where does the story take place? Why? Could it take place somewhere else?

Your setting can be a character itself. What role does it play? How does it enhance your story? *The Fifth Season* by N.K. Jemisin takes place in a ruthless world, where earthquakes and volcano eruptions are common. On this planet, an apocalypse occurs every few centuries. The book is about how society survives these conditions and how the characters react to the end of the world. The story wouldn't work in any other setting.

14. What is your world's history?

If your story takes place on Earth, is history the same as we know it? If you're building another world, how was it created? Who lives there? What wars and conflicts occurred? Is there mythology or a creation story that people believe?

15. What technology and/or magic exists in your world?

Even if your world's society is primitive, some sort of technology exists. What do people use for lighting, cooking, and building? What kinds of weapons do people use? Has the printing press been invented? Is there advanced technology like teleporters and faster-than-light travel? Are there magic-users and, if so, what can they do? (See Chapters Fourteen and Fifteen for discussions on technology and magic.)

16. How does your society work?

What do people do to survive? Are there high-class and low-class jobs? Is there a government? How are resources and services distributed? (See Chapters Twenty-Two and Twenty-Three for more on culture, politics, and economy.)

17. Are there species, aliens, or other beings besides humans?

If you have other beings in your story, don't make them carbon-copies of humanity. Is their biology different than humans'? What is their culture like? Do they use other languages or methods of communication?

18. What sort of art and architecture exist in your world?

Is art celebrated or is it considered a waste of time? What do buildings look like?

19. What if?

If you feel stuck, ask yourself "What if…?" These can be general questions as you brainstorm your novel's premise; for example, what if the world we live in is actually a computer simulation? (*The Matrix*); what if humans discovered a portal to other worlds in the galaxy? (*Stargate*); or what if dinosaurs were brought back? (*Jurassic Park*). You can also ask yourself questions as you get into your story's nitty gritty details; for example, what if my protagonist's magic doesn't work the way they think it does? What if the sibling is actually the betrayer? What if my narrator is unreliable? Let the ideas roll.

20. What is your book about?

Try crafting a one-sentence response for when someone asks you what your story's about. This can be helpful to focus your novel even before you start writing it.

SUPPLEMENTAL MATERIALS FOR BRAINSTORMING

You can tap all sorts of resources during the brainstorming process! Here are a few suggestions.

Maps

Drawing a map of your world or galaxy can be helpful for worldbuilding. In addition to adding cities, towns, and terrain (mountains, hills, lakes, etc.) to your map, you can kickstart your world and its history by adding other elements. When you're creating your map, try out some of these ideas:

1. If your story has different races or aliens, drop them onto specific areas of your map and consider what their civilization might look like based on their location. Are they near water? Perhaps they evolved to live within it or became known for trade goods and ships. Are they located on a planet far from any other world? Perhaps they're lacking in technology that other civilizations have gained from trade and proximity.
2. Consider how races might divide into subraces—perhaps a group of surface elves founded a city beneath a nearby mountain and became deep elves. Perhaps aliens were genetically experimented on and became a subrace of their predecessors.
3. Choose a city. Decide on something it's known for—maybe a wonder they've built, a wall, a school, a tower, an army, a type of magic, a skill, or a specific trade good.
4. Pick an area of your map at random. A natural disaster happened there at some point in your story's history. This could be a drought, plague, famine, hurricane,

volcanic eruption, tsunami, or earthquake. How did that event shape the history of that area?
5. Choose a city or town and create a group within it. This could be a guild, a religious sect, a band of pirates, a sect of shipbuilders, an order of warriors—whatever you can think of. What has this organization done over your world's history? Are they feared? Respected? Unknown? Are they only located in that city or have they expanded over time?
6. Pick an area on your map. A major historical figure was born there. What did they grow up to do? Where did they travel throughout their lifetime?
7. Destroy one of your cities. What happened there—war? An earthquake? A deity's wrath? A mystery?
8. Two of your cities are in conflict with each other. Why? How does this impact your world's history?

Your map might evolve as you work on it, demonstrating hundreds or even thousands of years passing by. Make sure to keep notes as you brainstorm with it.

Photos and Art

Some writers love keeping folders of pictures to inspire their descriptions. If you know your city has Mayan-type architecture, find a photo and save it for reference. If you've decided your main character looks like a specific actor, save a photo with the character's bio.

You can also find art for almost anything. Looking for a three-headed, blue skinned alien? You can probably find a drawing for inspiration. Wondering what a steampunk monk might wear? Someone's probably drawn that. (While it's fine to look at art for personal use, don't publish it or post it without the artist's permission.)

Some writers, like Shelly, are also artists and draw their own characters (including dragons!) for inspiration. You can also hire artists to do this for you. But don't get too distracted with all these extras before you actually start writing—details might change by the time you're done.

Writers and Worldbuilders

Some people *love* worldbuilding. They love it so much that they make worlds during their free time just to enjoy the brainstorming process, even though they have no intention of adding a narrative. If you are friends with one of these people, ask them to be a soundboard for you.

Writing partners, critique groups, and writing communities can also be useful resources to start taking your novel seriously. Another writer might be willing to talk with you about your book ideas if you do the same for them. Discord, Facebook, Reddit, and other social media platforms can be great places to search for writing groups and ask for critique partners.

Media

Take inspiration from books, movies, TV shows, and video games you love. Analyze their structure, dialogue, plot, setting, and characters. Just remember, plagiarism isn't cool. Be cool.

For example, if you like Han Solo's cocky attitude, there's nothing stopping you from including an arrogant space pirate in your novel. But it might be too on the nose if your character wears a black vest, has a furry best friend, and uses the catchphrase "I know" (unless you're intentionally spoofing Star Wars).

In particular, read books from your genre, especially those that have been published in the last five years. Publishing is an ever-changing industry, and many books that were published years ago would be a tougher sell now. You can emulate J.R.R. Tolkien's pages of poetry if you want, but it will be difficult to market.

Reading with a critical eye and paying attention to a story's craft is very different from reading for pleasure. When you become engrossed in a novel, stop and look at what the author has done to get you invested.

When you get bored, stop and ask what's missing. Particularly note how your favourite authors handle dialogue, pacing, and tension—those are areas many new writers need extra work in.

Mind Map

Mind maps are visual representations of your ideas and how they relate to each other. Start with one idea in the middle, then branch that out into other ideas, and branch those out into sub-ideas.

For a novel, you might start with your book idea or title in the middle, then branch out into characters, settings, scenes, or whatever sub-topics you want to brainstorm (see the diagram for *Snow White* on the next page as an example).

Plot Embryo

Attributed to Dan Harmon, the creator of *Community* and *Rick and Morty*, this method uses a simple outline with eight points, and may appeal to visual learners due to its circular design.

To make a plot embryo, divide your circle or page into eight pie slice-shaped segments; then, starting at the top and working your way around, follow this plot progression: "You need to go search for something, find it, take it, and then return changed."[1] (See the diagram for Harmon's use of *Rick and Morty* as an example).

1. You: Who is the protagonist, why do we identify with them, and what is their normal life like before it gets turned upside-down?

MIND MAP EXAMPLE

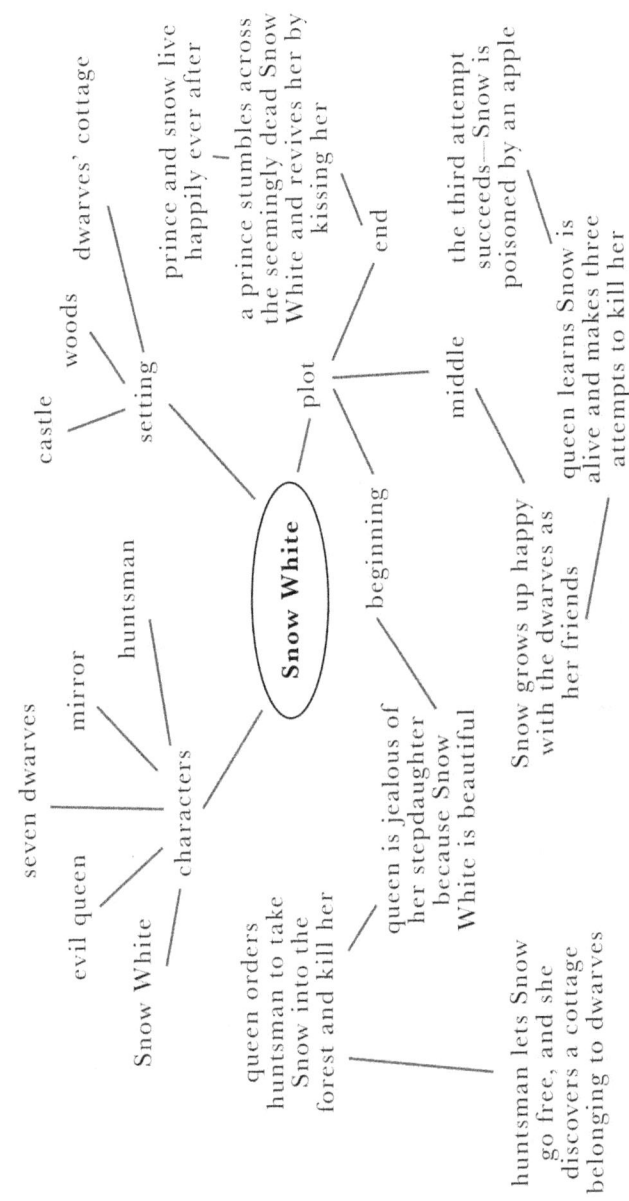

14 Making Myths and Magic

PLOT EMBRYO
Rick and Morty, S2E2, "Mortynight Run"

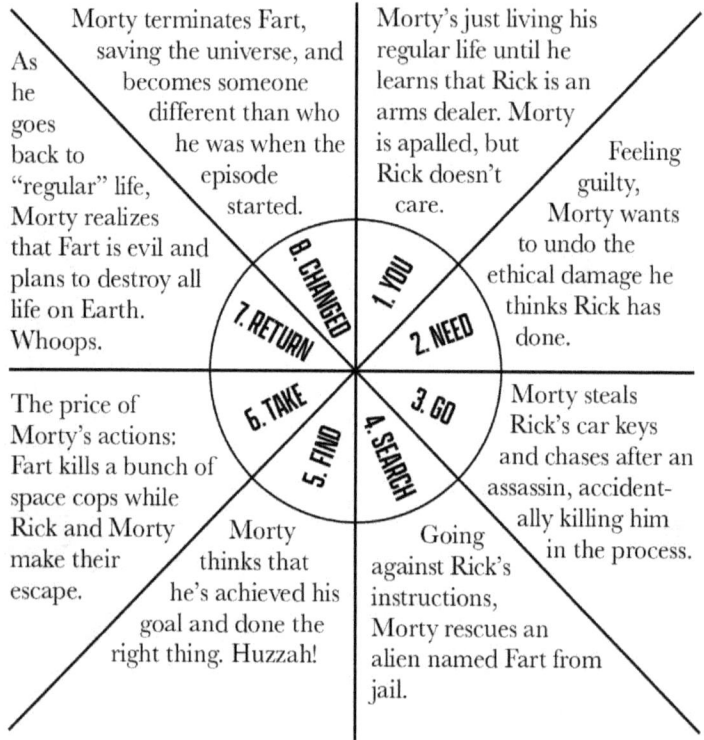

  2. **Need:** What does the character want? What calls them out of their normal world into the unknown?

  3. **Go:** What is the "new world" your protagonist steps into? How does the story change direction?

  4. **Search:** What trials do they face on the way to their goal?

  5. **Find:** What's an experience the character goes through, a revelation they have, or an answer they find that propels them through the rest of the story? Sometimes, at this point, they get what they originally wanted, but discover it's not what they want anymore. Note, this section occurs at the very bottom of

your circle; the hero has basically been propelled downwards to this point, in which things they have little control over are happening to them. But after this, they have to swing up through the next events on their own power.

6. Take: If the protagonist gets what they want, what is the price they pay? How does their attitude change as they realize what they need is different from what they want? You may start to notice how the events in your circle reflect each other. Just like #1 and #5 are related as vulnerable moments, #2 and #6 are linked, as they are action-filled moments during which the hero realizes they aren't content.

7. Return: How does the protagonist incorporate what they have learned to achieve their new goal? This point links to #3, because the new world they stepped into has changed them. They also may literally return to the old world and find it is not the same, because they have changed.

8. Changed: How does the hero demonstrate they have changed? Can you mirror the story's opening image to create a sense of closure?

Back Cover Copy

One way to check your plot for problems is to write a short summary—what you imagine the back cover on the published copy would read like—either before you start writing or before you start editing. Seeing the plot condensed into a short space can narrow your focus and help you organize your draft.

For example, here is the back cover copy for *Rust and Water*, a graphic novel by Justin Currie and GMB Chomichuk:

> When mermaid Nara discovers an inert, giant robot on the ocean floor, she accidentally activates it. Communicating with the robot is difficult, and even more frustrating—he seems determined to venture into the most dangerous parts of the ocean! Nara realizes he's trying to

get home and accompanies him on an adventure that takes them past glowing jellyfish, through the darkest parts of the ocean, and across molten fields of lava. What they find at the end of their journey will test their newfound friendship and threaten the beautiful world they just explored."

This summary clearly states who the story is about, where it takes place, and what the stakes are—all important things to know about your story!

Plot and Subplot Table

In this method, make a table with columns for your chapter number, plot, subplots, and character arcs. If you use a sheet like this, you can note if there are too many blank spaces between chapters so you don't leave a subplot dangling for too long.

For example, a sample of the table for Shelly's debut fantasy novel, *Under the Lesser Moon*, is on the next page. The "main plot" column is for the basic events that move the story forward. There are also five subplots integral to the story—Akrist's relationship with his father, his visions and dreams, his relationship with Tanar, the appearance of dragons throughout the story, and his romance with Yara.

The main plot column is always filled in, but not every subplot is referenced in every chapter; in fact, the romance column has no entries, because Akrist does not meet his love interest, Yara, until much later in the book.

If you plot your book this way, you may be able to fit your subplots into your novel like a jigsaw puzzle. It's best if they're not simply side stories, but elements that fit into the mystery or events of the main plot.

PLOT AND SUBPLOT TABLE
UNDER THE LESSER MOON BY SHELLY CAMPBELL

Ch.	Main Plot	Akrist/Father	Visions	Tanar	Dragons	Romance
1	Akrist listens to his parents argue about how he "killed" his sister when she was in the womb because he's cursed.	Akrist's father forces him to tell the Creation Story over and over again.	Akrist dreams of a wurm eating him alive.			
2	Akrist finds a dragon scale and is punished, because dragons are sacred and not to be touched by daeson.	Akrist's father warns him not to show emotion when he's whipped.	Akrist has a vision he finds a dragon scale and feels an earthshake.		Akrist sees a dragon in the sky.	
3	Another tribe joins Akrist's camp.			Akrist meets Tanar.		
4	Akrist struggles to accept that daeson are sacrificed.	Akrist confronts his father to ask the truth.		Akrist and Tanar decide to run away.		

Other ideas for subplots:

- a parallel story that only converges with the main plot later.
- two or more stories that only interweave further into the story (writing in multiple points of view allows for this).
- a series of vignettes (preferably united by a character, theme, or setting).
- a subplot that is only referred to again at the end of the story (like bookends).

Subplots can be used for a variety of effects: slowing pace, increasing tension, revealing plot, defining characters, adding conflict, or foreshadowing. You will likely want to include several subplots in your story.

Subplots commonly focus on a relationship between characters, whether it's a friendship, romance, rivalry, or mentorship.

The best subplots also drive the main story. For example, Luke's relationship with Obi-Wan in *Star Wars: A New Hope* is pivotal to the plot—Luke decides to go with Obi-Wan after his aunt and uncle die, Luke is heavily influenced by Obi-Wan's training, and he is devastated by Obi-Wan's death, which triggers future decisions and events that shape Luke's character arc.

Here are some basic ideas for subplots you may want to include in your own novel:

- a romance
- a friendship
- a rivalry
- an activity, pastime, or skill (e.g. a sport, game, weapon, art form, magical ability, etc.)
- a mystery
- a crime
- a lie

- an emotional issue that needs working through
- a secret
- a dysfunctional family relationship
- a contest or trial
- school / exams
- the past coming back to haunt a character
- financial difficulty
- a prophecy
- a side character's problems
- an argument
- a side goal
- a grudge
- a child
- a death
- learning a new skill
- a sacrifice

Relationship Arcs

In addition to asking how your characters change by the end of the story, you can also ask how characters' relationships with *each other* change. Figure out what scenes need to happen between these characters to get them from point A to point B, and weave those scenes into your main plot.

For example, in the second campaign of *Critical Role* (a show in which a cast of voice actors play Dungeons & Dragons), adventurers Caleb and Beauregard don't like each other. Beau doesn't appreciate Caleb's habits of keeping secrets and trying to direct the group's decisions. Caleb doesn't like Beau's abrasive attitude. However, they begin to trust each other as they open up to each other about their pasts.

Their burgeoning friendship is challenged during later missions—arguments and tension ensue. But they work through their issues and become friends, which is shown in subtle ways: Caleb puts his hand on Beau's shoulder when his senses transfer to his familiar, Beau usually goes to Caleb first when she has a problem, and the pair often does research together.

Arcs between various characters in your story will enrich and direct your plot. Thinking about these relationships might even give you ideas about where the main plot could go.

Scene Lists

If you are the type of writer who envisions various scenes that will take place in your novel, write them down! Put them on note cards, writing whatever scenes come to you, and then try arranging them into a logical order. Once you get enough scenes, you can insert them into the story's main structure and have a decent working outline.

Three-Act Beat Sheets

Beat sheets are a useful way to brainstorm a novel if you're a planner and like to shape your story before you start writing. But if you prefer to write first and add formal structure later, you can apply beat sheets to a completed draft.

Any of the other outlining methods on this list can work in conjunction with a beat sheet. Turn to the next chapter for the rundown on beat sheets and an overview of three-act story structure.

Chapter 2

Structure is a Superpower

How to Tell a Story in Three Acts

An understanding of story structure can make your novel shine. This elusive word—*structure*—simply refers to plot elements that are put together in a certain order. Structure can go a long way towards creating a strong story that people enjoy reading.

While structure may seem similar to an outline, outlining is a process (in which you brainstorm your story and its specifics), and structuring is a technique (in which you string your scenes together to create a specific reaction from your readers). Clear as tea leaves? Cool.

DOES STRUCTURE MATTER?

If your end goal is to get published and you want to write fiction that engages readers, then plot and structure can be helpful. Structure is an answer to the reader's question, "Why should I care about this story?" Structure gives writers a roadmap to distill what they're promising to their readers and ensure they deliver. In essence, structure helps sell books.

You might find your writing improves when you understand and apply structure to your stories. Ultimately, of course, you're free to break all these guidelines! We're not the structure police. But we find it useful to understand the rules of structure before break them, because then we know exactly what we're doing and why.

Some writers assume that applying structure means you'll end up with a cookie-cutter story that is the same as everyone else's. But, just like flour, salt, baking soda, and spices can be used to make cake, pies, pastries, and all manner of goodies both savoury and sweet, you can play with these ingredients to make all sorts of stories.

WHAT IS THREE-ACT STRUCTURE?

There are several frameworks you can choose from to structure your novel: five-stage plot structure includes exposition, rising action, climax, falling action, and resolution; The Hero's Journey includes a departure, trials, and a return; Seven-Point Story Structure includes a hook and several plot points before the resolution. One of our favourite types of structure is the three-act version, which has many similarities to all the above options and simply divides your story into a beginning, middle, and end.

Three-act structure goes all the way back to Aristotle, who noted that a tragedy requires three sections. The purpose of the beginning is to introduce the characters, world, and tone of the story and make readers care about it all. The purpose of the middle is to create conflict, deepen character relationships, set up the ending, and keep readers caring. The purpose of the ending is to resolve the plot and give readers a payoff for caring up to this point.

Below, we'll analyze three-act structure and how plot elements can be placed to ensure those goals are met. As an example, we're looking at *The Final Empire* (Mistborn #1) by Brandon Sanderson. The percentages are estimates and can be played around with, but they give you a basic idea of where these events commonly occur in mainstream fiction.

ACT ONE (0% – 20% OF YOUR NOVEL)

Act One is your set up. It gives the audience a firm grasp of who they should be rooting for, who the villain is, what the protagonist's goals are, and consequently, how this story might end.

Intro to Hero's World (0% – 10%)

The beginning of the story explores your protagonist's world before it gets interrupted by all the exciting events of the novel's main plot. What does their "normal" look like? What are their goals? What are their flaws? Who are the people in their life?

Mistborn's beginning introduces us to the two main characters of the story: Kelsier and Vin. In the prologue, Kelsier's goal is clear: he wants to save the skaa from slavery and change the status quo. Chapter One then introduces us to Vin and her strange "luck." Her goal is also clear: she wants to survive. Vin's upbringing has been harsh—even her brother has abandoned her—and she's learned to trust no one.

Disturbance (10%)

The Disturbance is an event that significantly changes the main character's normal way of life. Some writers refer to this as the Key Event, but we like *disturbance* because it effectively describes what happens—the hero's life is uprooted and disturbed.

In *The Final Empire*, Kelsier appears at the thieves hideout, an event that changes the direction of Vin's life. She learns that her "luck" is something else entirely and gets sucked into the skaa rebellion.

Reaction to Disturbance (10% – 20%)

Before Act Two begins, the hero needs time to react to what just happened. This might mean debating about what to do and feeling reluctant to change their life. It might mean emotionally preparing for what is to come or saying goodbye to the people they will have to leave.

In *The Final Empire*, Vin's reaction is distrust. She immediately starts wondering what Kelsier wants from her, how he is going to use her, and what he will hold over her to keep her around. She slowly gets to know Kelsier and his crew and is surprised at the amount of trust they have in each other. She also starts learning about her powers as a Mistborn.

Doorway #1 (20%)

If authors don't place a major plot point around the twenty to twenty-five percent mark of their novel, the pacing will feel off, and readers will notice. If the point is too early, the story may feel rushed; if it's too late, the story may drag. The best way to know if you've got it right is to ask your beta readers how they feel about the story's pacing.

Some writers refer to this as the "First Plot Point," but in James Scott Bell's helpful guide, *Plot & Structure: Techniques and Exercises for Crafting and Plot That Grips Readers from Start to Finish* (Writer's Digest Books, 2004), he calls it a "Doorway of No Return," which is useful imagery for understanding this event. Simply put, once it happens, there is no going back to the way life used to be. Suddenly, the main character's life is no longer the same and they are pushed into the second act of the story. To determine if your character has gone through this doorway, ask yourself if they could return to life exactly as it was; if so, they probably haven't gone through it yet.

In *The Final Empire*, Vin's suspicion comes to a head during a carriage ride with Kelsier. He's taught her the basics of allomancy, and she asks him why and what's to keep her from running away from him. He replies, "nothing," offers her all the money he took from her old crew leader, and tells her she's free to go. He even directs the carriage driver to turn around, because she doesn't believe him. It is at this point that Vin makes the decision to stay, and so begins her new life as a Mistborn and part of Kelsier's crew.

ACT TWO (20% – 80% OF YOUR NOVEL)

Act Two turns your character's normal world on its head. Let your reader ride shotgun while your beloved hero navigates and reacts to the new circumstances they've been thrown into. Show what is standing in their way and firm up exactly what your character's goals are. This is also your opportunity to demonstrate that your antagonist is a force to be reckoned with.

New World (20% – 50%)

The first half of Act Two is all about your hero learning about the new world they have walked into. New characters can be introduced here, such as friends, enemies, mentors, and romantic interests. The hero either loves their new world or hates it.

This is usually the part of the novel that makes good on the "premise" from your back cover blurb. For example, we know that *The Hunger Games* by Suzanne Collins is about Katniss participating in a battle royal, so this is the part where she is literally put in the arena; *The Hobbit* by J.R.R. Tolkien is about a hobbit who goes on an adventure with some dwarves, so this is the part where the adventures start; *Sabriel* by Garth Nix is about a necromancer who sets out to find her missing father in the Old Kingdom, so this is the part where she enters the magical kingdom. The setup is over. The adventure begins.

In *The Final Empire*, Vin is instructed to act like a noble so she can infiltrate their society. As someone who grew up on the streets, attending balls and learning to dance really is a new world for her.

Antagonist Flexes Muscles (40%)

This plot event occurs somewhere within the "New World" section (some authors recommend around the 40% mark, but we're not picky). If your villain hasn't made an appearance yet, they should. Either that, or your hero gets tripped up in some way, running into some kind of problem.

In *The Final Empire*, Vin follows Kelsier out into the mist to learn where he is going. He catches her following him, but lets her come with him to raid the Lord Ruler's palace. Inquisitors are waiting for them, and the two barely escape with their lives. Vin is unconscious for two weeks as a result of her injuries, and it becomes clear how powerful the Lord Ruler and his minions are.

Midpoint (50%)

Something should happen in the middle of your novel to raise the stakes. It should mark the spot where your protagonist starts taking action instead of reacting to everything happening to them (i.e. they're moving from defensive mode into attack mode). Examples of this event include a character death, the last piece of a puzzle, a battle, or a challenge overcome.

In *The Final Empire*, Vin attends another ball and is much more confident this time. She starts accepting requests to dance, prodding nobles for information, and looking into mysteries, such as why nobleman Elend Venture is reading a book that speaks out against the Lord Ruler.

Hero Takes Action (50% - 80%)

Most of Act Two's second half is driven by the hero taking action (or trying to). They make decisions, plan adventures, and get into all sorts of trouble. The hero's flaws should become clearer and clearer. There is also a dichotomy between what they *want* and what they *need*—what they want is not actually what they need to grow or overcome the story's challenges.

In *The Final Empire*, Vin continues to attend balls, learn about allomancy, read the Lord Ruler's journal, and falls in love with Elend Venture. She wants to stay safe and survive, but is slowly learning the value of personal connection, relationships, and standing up for oppressed people. Kelsier also takes action, spreading rumours and checking in on the rebellion's army.

Antagonist Closes In (70%)

Within the "Hero Takes Action" section, the villain should be closing in. This can occur in one scene (some writers recommend around the 70% mark) or several scenes throughout this section.

In *The Final Empire*, The rebellion's army fights the city's garrison without Kelsier's knowledge. They are decimated and the Lord Ruler executes random skaa as punishment for the uprising.

Hero's Low Point (75%)

At some point in this section (some writers recommend the 75% mark), all seems lost. The hero should feel beaten and helpless. You're basically saying to your reader, "Look, I know it seemed like the book will have a satisfying conclusion, but that seems pretty impossible at this point."

This is what is going to propel your reader onwards. It simply *can't* end like this! Our protagonist is failing, goals aren't being reached, and our writer promised a different ending than the one we're heading toward.

In *The Final Empire*, The entire crew is dejected at the loss of the army, and everyone, except Kelsier, is ready to give up on the rebellion. Vin attends a ball and learns a House war is about to start. Elend pushes her away, and she is devastated, because one of her main fears is people leaving her.

Vin learns that Elend is about to be assassinated. And even though Elend has spurned her and she's hurt, she decides to stop the assassins. She kills another Mistborn, and may have been spotted by some guards. She is physically and emotionally wounded from these events.

Doorway #2 (80%)

Act Two culminates in another doorway. Something significant happens here, like a major clue or setback, to propel the hero into the final conflict. They suddenly realize what they need to do.

Kelsier's death marks a turning point in *The Final Empire*'s narrative. The crew is tempted to give up again, until they discover the plans Kelsier has left for them, and how he had arranged for his death to inspire an uprising of the city's skaa.

ACT THREE (80% – 100% OF YOUR NOVEL)

Act Three features our main character facing a seemingly insurmountable obstacle and fighting like they've never fought before. They'll win (yay!) or they'll struggle and lose (nooooo!). They will face fears and discover what they need.

Executing the Plan (80% – 95%)

The protagonist knows what needs to be done and may take a scene to prepare for it before setting out. They might need to gather a team or equip themselves. This raises anticipation, allowing the character (and reader) to take a breath before diving into the final action.

The endeavour should seem impossible, but the hero tackles it anyway. Tension should be high (some ideas to increase it: add conflict between characters, introduce a ticking clock, create a challenging setting, or give your hero internal doubt). The protagonist successfully makes it past some hurdles, perhaps using skills or information they learned earlier in the novel, and things are looking up.

In *The Final Empire*, Kelsier's crew of misfits begins to follow the instructions he left for them, and Vin decides to find out what's in the guarded room in the palace that Kelsier had tried and failed twice to get into. She fights her way past Inquisitors and makes her way in, meeting the Lord Ruler himself and burning the eleventh metal, which reveals an image of the Lord Ruler's past. She is captured. An ally helps her escape, and she decides to face the Lord Ruler again.

Climax (95%)

Whatever this scene is—a battle, a last stand, a revelatory moment with another character, or the acquiring of an important object—this is the moment you've been leading up to for the entire novel. It's up to the protagonist to do something crucial to turn the tide. Things should look grim for the hero, so readers wonder how they will ever get out of this conflict and win the day. The villain often does something unexpected here, so no matter how prepared the hero is, they are at a loss. There is often a "moment of truth" for the hero, where they confront a lie they've believed about themselves or discover they have what they've needed all along.

Make sure the stakes are clear: if the hero fails, the villain will succeed and X horrible thing will happen as a result. If your story has a gentler theme or doesn't end in a battle, there should still be a cost if the hero isn't successful.

In *The Final Empire*, a vicious battle with the Lord Ruler ensues, during which Vin realizes his secret and how to defeat him. She succeeds with help from an ally.

Resolution (99% – 100%)

Though you could end your story with the climax, most novels offer a cooling down period—a scene or two that details what the main character does after the excitement is over. Give your readers a chance to say goodbye to the characters they've come to love.

Where will the protagonist go from here? How has the climax changed them? What are the results or consequences of their actions? What will they do now? The resolution is your opportunity to tie up loose ends.

During *The Final Empire*'s epilogue, the crew reflects on the Lord Ruler's secret and Elend's new government. Vin visits Elend, then almost leaves without seeing him because she's scared of relationships, since people have always let her down. But she remembers that her brother had died trying to keep her safe—a truth she had learned during her capture. She had always thought he had left her, which had played into her fears of abandonment. The truth makes her willing to be vulnerable, and she ends up in Elend's arms.

Notably, because this is the beginning of a series, not *every* plot event has been concluded and not every question has been answered. Vin wonders about other secrets of Allomancy and what knowledge the Lord Ruler brought to his grave. We don't know everything, and Sanderson hints of events to come.

IF YOU ARE INTRIGUED by three-act structure, but you don't outline your novel before you write, you can still apply it afterwards. Allison has used it during the editing phase to help structure clients' novels and finds it particularly useful when addressing pacing issues.

Part Two

Hooking Readers

Chapter 3

In a Hole in the Ground
The First Chapter

Your first chapter is a promise: this is what the book is about. Here is what you can expect.

And nobody likes a promise breaker.

If you start your first chapter with a car chase, a brawl, and several gratuitous explosions, but the rest of the book is a sassy rom-com, you've misled your reader.

After reading the opening of Nnedi Okorafor's *Binti*, we learn the story is about a girl from an impoverished background. She lives in a red-soiled land with deep-rooted tribes, strong religious convictions, clashing cultures, and advanced technology. We feel for her because she's extremely intelligent and driven, and because she is an outsider on her trip to Oomza university; her people don't like leaving their ancestral homeland; her family won't approve of her going, even though she scored so well on her exams that the university is paying her tuition and expenses. The tone is serious and not overly wordy, reflecting Binti's personality. She is heading somewhere totally outside of her comfort zone. We want to read on because we're already cheering for the plucky outsider who's brave enough to jump feet-first into an unfamiliar world. And we have an inkling where this story might head.

If Binti turned out to be a shapeshifting dragon who solved crimes, we'd feel disoriented. It's not that your novel can't have surprises, but you'll want to meet *some* reader expectations, such as the genre and plot direction as laid out in the first chapter.

THE OPENING LINE

Attracting readers seems like a big job for one sentence, but you can accomplish this with a hook.

At its essence, a hook is a question—one that keeps readers moving on to the next sentence. This doesn't mean your opening line has to be a literal question, but it should imply one.

Consider these first sentences and the questions they inspire you to ask:

- "Every night, before going to bed, Rina checked the refrigerators." —"State Change," *The Paper Menagerie and Other Stories* by Ken Liu
- "Let's start with the end of the world, why don't we? Get it over with and move on to more interesting things." —*The Fifth Season* by N.K. Jemisin
- "Sophie had waited all her life to be kidnapped." —*The School for Good and Evil* by Soman Chainani
- "I could have been a mass murderer after I hacked my governor module, but then I realized I could access the combined feed of entertainment channels carried on the company satellites." —*All Systems Red* by Martha Wells
- "I have a heart for every year I've been alive." —*To Kill a Kingdom* by Alexandra Christo

Not every book has to begin with a sentence that becomes as iconic as "Call me Ishmael" (*Moby-Dick* by Herman Melville) or "In a hole in the ground there lived a hobbit" (*The Hobbit* by J.R.R. Tolkien). While you might not necessarily remember an opening line after finishing a satisfying story, it managed to hook you, and that's all that matters.

The question your first line asks does not need to be big or dramatic. It doesn't need to encompass the entire theme of the novel. It just needs to get your readers to continue reading. Even if you answer the question in the next sentence or paragraph, that's okay because by then you will have implied more questions.

Of course, the question your first line inspires should *not* be "What is going on?" or "Why should I care about this?" If your readers are asking those, you've lost them because they don't have enough details to be invested in the story or characters; they are focused on their confusion instead of an interesting plot.

Think carefully before tricking readers with something shocking just to get a reaction out of them, because this risks losing their trust. For example, beginning a novel with "I will be dead tomorrow," but then revealing that they're an actor in a play, only pretending to be dead—that's an introduction only Loki would be proud of.

In addition to asking a question, your novel's first page should:

1. Introduce the protagonist. Your story's not a story without someone to get attached to. Who is this story about? Why do we care about them? What is their goal?

2. Introduce the world. Where is the opening scene taking place? How can you succinctly give impressions of setting without going into pages of description?

3. Convey tone. The first sentences should immediately establish the tone of the book. Take a look at the first sentences we listed earlier and consider what they tell you about the tone of the books. Is the narrator prim and proper? Sarcastic? Serious? Humorous? Can you tell what kind of story you're getting into?

INTRODUCING CHARACTERS

Since stories are about people (or talking animals, sentient robots, or what-have-you), character introductions are crucial. In particular, readers need to be interested in your main character. They need to care about what happens to them.

You might assume that beginning your story with an action sequence is enough to make your reader invested in the main character. Put them in danger and readers will be on the edge of their seats, right?

Maybe. For a few paragraphs. But if you haven't given readers any other reasons to be invested in your character, they may start wondering why they should stick with them, and then you're in trouble.

Your first chance to get your readers invested in a character is when they appear on the page, so make that moment count. While it can be advantageous to introduce a character in their normal habitat, because this allows readers to understand what their life was like before the plot turns their world upside-down, you can accomplish a hook in unusual circumstances as well.

Introduce your main character in a way that defines their characteristics. Give readers a substantial idea of who this character is and what their motivations are by showing how they respond to whatever is happening to them. You can emphasize a particular trait through that response, which helps readers learn significant details about your protagonist.

Rather than just figuring out *how* your character responds—you, the writer, also need to know *why*. Understanding their motivations will bring them to life.

For example, it's not enough to know that your character struggles with feelings of jealousy. Why? Were they constantly overshadowed by an older sibling growing up? Did their father tell them they weren't good enough? Do they want to be the best at something but aren't?

Here are a few ideas to encourage your readers to care about your character in the first chapter:

1. Treat them unjustly.

In *Howl's Moving Castle* by Diana Wynne Jones, Sophie gets turned into a ninety-year-old woman, complete with wrinkles and aching joints. She did nothing to deserve this transformation, and readers come to love her for her perseverance and stubborn attitude despite the curse.

2. Make other characters dislike them.

Many characters dislike Ender Wiggin in Orson Scott Card's *Ender's Game*. His brother bullies him. Other students are jealous of him. Even his teachers mistreat him. Because readers see things from Ender's perspective, they are drawn into the conflict that arises from the jealousy and fear of those around him.

3. Give them positive qualities.

Even antiheroes need to have some likeable traits. Zuko from *Avatar: The Last Airbender* has a lot of issues—anger, lack of self-control, impatience, and pride. But he is compelling because these traits conflict with his better qualities: passion, a sense of honour, and the desire for justice.

4. Give them negative qualities.

Flawed characters are easy for readers to relate to. These shouldn't just be randomly chosen traits, but significant qualities that define the character.

Note: heroes overcome their flaws, while villains don't. For example, *A New Hope*'s Luke Skywalker is obviously a good guy —he's idealistic, innocent, and gung-ho to save the princess.

He's also impulsive, ignorant, and whiny. His character arc is about growing into a wise, knowledgeable, and thoughtful Jedi. On the other hand, Anakin Skywalker's arc in *Revenge of the Sith* is all about his flaws (his inability to manage anger and fear, and his willingness to be manipulated by Palpatine), which turn him into a villain.

5. Make them want something.

This could be a physical object, but it could also be something like love, purpose, or a family. At the beginning of *The Hobbit* by J.R.R. Tolkien, Bilbo Baggins wants to be left alone. We know he's not going to get what he wants, and we certainly don't *want* him to get what he wants (because then there's no adventure!), but we still feel irritated along with him as the dwarves mess up his tidy hobbit hole.

6. Have them make a mistake.

The TV show *Battlestar Galactica* is riddled with characters making mistakes. Gaius Baltar lets a Cylon into the Colonial defense mainframe, which kicks off an A.I. invasion. General Adama decides to fight the Cylons instead of run from them, which is a bad idea. Dualla forgets to log in a ship and leaves it behind during one of their jumps away from the Cylons. Helo trusts Sharon when she's manipulating him. And these are only events in the first few episodes.

Characters' mistakes are what make them human, and we want to know how their choices will play out, for better or worse. Mistakes are a great source of conflict and tension.

7. Give them someone to care about.

Katniss Everdeen from Suzanne Collins's *The Hunger Games* could have been a pretty "meh" character, but her love for her sister is admirable. She's a more interesting, more likeable character because of that attachment. This love drives her decisions, including her choice to take Prim's place in the games, which kicks off the first book. Her story would have been much less powerful if she didn't have a sister and had simply been selected for the games herself.

TO PROLOGUE OR NOT

Authors often feel conflicted about prologues because they want to include them but have heard that editors and agents dislike them. Here's your insider tip: editors and agents don't hate prologues; they hate prologues done poorly. Prologues are easy to get wrong, so editors see a lot of uninteresting prologues come across their desks.

Often, writers craft a prologue like it's the preparatory inhale before they start telling the real story. They use it to find their footing, to insert backstory or an important historical event (like an apocalypse or character death) that happens before Chapter One. The problem with this is often that readers haven't emotionally connected to the characters yet, so it can be a slog to read through.

Prologues only work if they hook readers *without* distancing them from the main character and plot. Here are three prologues that work:

1. *Elantris* by Brandon Sanderson

Elantris's prologue provides backstory on the city of Elantris and how it used to be a gorgeous place full of god-like citizens:

> Elantris was beautiful, once. It was called the city of the gods: a place of power, radiance, and magic. Visitors say that the very stones glowed with an inner light, and that the city contained wondrous

arcane marvels. At night, Elantris shone like a great silvery fire, visible even from a great distance."[1]

The prologue goes on to describe how anyone could become one of these god-like beings (due to a random transformation called the Shaod) and move to Elantris, where they would be worshipped for eternity. The prologue concludes with, "Eternity ended ten years ago."

We've mentioned that backstory is often better sprinkled into the narrative of the story, so why does it work here? For one thing, this prologue asks questions rather than provides answers, and for another, it's *short*. At only five paragraphs (two of which are one sentence long), this prologue succinctly introduces the city of Elantris, which the novel is titled after, and keeps the readers turning pages; we want to know what happened to end this magical city and where its inhabitants are now.

The novel's plot involves figuring out how the magic of Elantris works and why it stopped working, so the prologue is directly connected to the story's events and the protagonist's motivations.

2. *Too Like the Lightning* by Ada Palmer

The beginning of *Too Like the Lightning* includes a fictional copyright page that notes the story has been published with the permissions of several committees and organizations (including "The Five-Hive Committee on Dangerous Literature"). It also includes content warnings of sexual scenes, intentional violence, religious themes, and "opinions likely to cause offence to selected groups and to the sensibilities of many."[2]

Already, we have questions about the story: why is it considered "dangerous literature"? Why are religious themes included in a content rating? What sort of society creates a publication page like this?

Prologues that use a different style of writing, such as a copyright page like this, a letter, a newspaper article, an email thread, a social media post, a journal entry, or a scientist's note can be great hooks. They function better as prologues than as first chapters because the style is distinctly different from the rest of the book.

The first chapter of *Too Like the Lightning* functions similarly to a prologue as well; it's only two paragraphs long, in which the story's fictional author directly addresses the reader:

> You will criticize me, reader, for writing in a style six hundred years removed from the events I describe, but you came to me for explanation of those days of transformation which left your world the world it is, and since it was the philosophy of the Eighteenth Century, heavy with optimism and ambition, whose abrupt revival birthed the recent revolution, so it is only in the language of the Enlightenment, rich with opinion and sentiment, that those days can be described."[3]

This prologue accomplishes several things. First, it establishes tone; this book is philosophical science fiction, taking place in a utopian 25th century, and the tone of this narrator is definitely philosophical. Second, it introduces us to the narrator of the story—Mycroft Canner, a convict who, as a punishment for his crimes, is required to wander the world and make himself useful.

Since this story is told by Mycroft, and he has a habit of speaking directly to the reader, we will likely be subject to his biases and opinions. Third, it hooks the reader (notice how we keep mentioning why that's important?). The chapter ends with, "I beg you, let me make you trust me for a few dozen pages, since the tale will give you time enough to hate me in its own right."

Why are we going to hate Mycroft? What is his story? We're

intrigued, we're asking questions that make us want to read further, and we're ready to dig into the tale.

3. *The Sky Weaver* by Kristen Ciccarelli

The Sky Weaver's prologue begins with a note written eighteen years before the main narrative. It is written from the perspective of a character named Skye. Skye is in a prison cell, waiting to be tried for treason, and she reflects on meeting a boy called Crow, who changed her life. As we move on to Chapter One, we realize that Skye is not the main character of this story—instead, it's about a soldier, Safire, and her relationship with a pirate, Eris. So why does this prologue work?

For one thing, it's short. For another, Ciccarelli sprinkles Skye's story throughout the novel in flashback segments that read like a myth. It's slowly revealed how Skye's life is entwined with the main plot and characters, even though it's not apparent at first. As readers, we become just as invested in Skye's story as we are in Safire's and Eris's. This prologue sets the tone of the story and introduces the myth. Instead of asking "why should I care about this?", we're intrigued by the mystery of how Skye's story impacts the main plot.

IF YOU'RE on the fence about your prologue, ask yourself these questions:

- Is your prologue an excuse to include an action scene at the beginning of the story?
- Does it feature a secondary character rather than a main one?
- Does it include backstory that could be spread throughout the main story just as, if not more, effectively?

- Does Chapter One work just fine without it?
- Is it a scene that you had to cut from the main narrative and just want to fit it in *somewhere*?
- Is it a bunch of worldbuilding that you feel your reader needs to know before diving into the proper story, but could actually be sprinkled throughout the main text?

If you answer yes to one or more of those questions, you should probably cut it. But if you want to try your hand at writing a prologue and think it will enhance your story, do it! Just make sure you hook those readers.

Chapter 4

I Have a Bad Feeling About This
Conflict and Tension

Our stories often boil down to characters who want to meet a need. Conflict stems from the obstacle that stands in their way, while tension comes from anticipating the consequences that will happen if they fail to reach their goals. If done correctly, there is a cause and effect at work. How your character solves the challenge of an initial conflict should build tension and create more conflict as the story goes on.

Conflict and tension engage readers' emotions, intensify them at the right moments, and provide satisfaction when resolved.

A CLASH OF FORCES

Conflict is the clash between two opposing forces—and at least one of the forces must have a will of its own. For example, there is no conflict when an ocean wave crashes against a shore, as neither element has goals, desires, or consciousness. But what if that wave crashes against a shore, filling in a cave that an explorer is trapped in? That's a conflict.

Something always needs to be at stake for conflict to work. In our example above, the explorer's life is at stake. The possibility of death is a common stake for science fiction and fantasy, as these stories are often filled with adventure and world-ending threats. However, quieter fantasy tales and lighter sci-fi adventures may have other stakes: a career, a hope, a relationship, an emotional investment. The stakes can even be something silly (like Gary's desire to get a cookie in *Final Space*). As long as the protagonist takes it seriously, conflict is possible.

Forced conflict, on the other hand, doesn't feel natural at all. You might realize there is a lack of conflict in your work and start throwing it in at random. Suddenly, there's an explosion. Suddenly, ninjas race in to attack the protagonist. Suddenly, a meteor is about to hit Earth.

Of course, there's nothing wrong with explosions, ninjas, or meteors. There is only a problem if they don't fit the story you're trying to tell, and you're adding in these elements because the story is starting to feel boring.

To know what conflicts your character could face, understand what they want and what they need; as we mentioned in Chapter One, those often aren't the same things. And consider what your characters' faults are—their flaws offer all sorts of opportunities to butt heads with people or get into sticky situations. With these building blocks, you can come up with barriers for your characters.

TYPES OF CONFLICT

When considering conflict, our minds immediately go to conflict between characters; whether it's friend versus friend, parent versus child, or hero versus villain, these conflicts up the stakes. However, conflict isn't limited to relationships. There are several varieties of conflict you should be aware of as a writer and can utilize to keep your readers on the edge of their seats!

Person vs. Person

Conflict can occur between your protagonist and another person or group of people. This type of conflict will come naturally if you populate your stories with characters who have opposing goals, morals, and backgrounds. You can also ramp up the conflict in relationships between characters; these could be everyday issues like friends in the middle of a fight, lovers too nervous to reveal their feelings, office workers being passive aggressive, etc. Relationship conflict works because it's realistic. People are different and we're forced to deal with individuals who see the world in drastically different ways than we do.

In sci-fi and fantasy, this type of conflict usually includes hero versus villain. For example, in Star Wars, Luke and Vader's goals are in direct opposition. Luke wants to release the galaxy from the Emperor's iron grip, while Vader wants to continue his rule under the Emperor's direction. Things get complicated when the truth about their relationship is revealed, and another type of conflict is introduced: person versus self.

Person vs. Self

This is when a character faces inner conflict. Do they struggle with addiction, illness, past trauma, opposing desires? In Star Wars, both Luke and Vader experience inner conflict in regards to their relationship with each other. Luke is tempted by the dark side when Vader suggests Luke join him. Vader is hesitant to kill Luke due to the repressed feelings he has for his son. That conflict comes to a head at the end of *Return of the Jedi*, as the Emperor is about to kill Luke. We don't even have to see Vader's facial expression to understand the conflict going on in his mind. Will he let his son die? Will he turn on the emperor he has been devoted to for so long? The drama is real!

Person vs. Nature

This type of conflict tends to be a survival story, in which a character battles the elements. In *The Empire Strikes Back*, Luke is caught in a blizzard on Hoth. Lower the temperatures to freezing, throw in a dead taun taun, and you've got some serious drama going on. Then, the movie turns up the heat, er, cold, when a wild wampa appears. Han Solo charging out into the blizzard to search for his friend as the base doors close is just as concerning—now we've got *two* characters facing impossible odds!

Person vs. Society

Conflict can arise when a character fights against injustice or opposing views in their society. They could challenge a way of life or a corrupt system, such as when Anakin Skywalker goes up against the Jedi Order in the Star Wars prequel trilogy. It isn't the individual Jedi Knights that Anakin defies—it's the corruption of the whole order. Though he's being manipulated by Palpatine to establish an even more corrupt order (the Empire), Anakin's critiques of the Jedi aren't wrong, which make the conflict even more interesting. His turn to the dark side isn't a black and white issue (though, in our opinion, *The Clone Wars* TV show does a much better job of showcasing these grey areas). He has legitimate questions about a society that preaches one thing but does another.

Person vs. Fate

In this type of conflict, a character is fighting against their own destiny, a prophecy, or even a god. In the original Star Wars trilogy, Obi-Wan repeatedly refers to Luke's "destiny." He believes that Luke is destined to face his father and kill him. Vader also uses the term in a lightsaber fight with Luke, telling him, "Your destiny lies with me, Skywalker. Obi-Wan knew this to be true."[1] Both characters try to get Luke to do what they want by suggesting his actions are inevitable. Destiny is an interesting concept to play with, because when readers know what is "supposed" to happen (and that thing is usually bad), they wonder how the hero will get out of it. Luke ends up "fulfilling" these destinies, in a way—he does confront his father, but he saves him rather than kills him.

Person vs. Technology

This type of conflict can occur when a character grapples with malfunctioning technology, technology designed for a nefarious purpose, or Artificial Intelligences. For example, conflict skyrockets in the Star Wars prequel era when Order 66 is given. The Emperor's order activates bio-chips that had been secretly implanted in the clones, forcing them to slaughter the Jedi they had been allies with. In *The Clone Wars* series, we watch Ahsoka, Anakin's apprentice, face off against soldiers she had fought side-by-side with for years. Our emotions! We're devastated as she is forced to kill her comrades in self defense. Notice that there are various types of conflict going on here—Ahsoka is conflicted with herself, with the clones, and with the technology controlling them.

Person vs. the Unknown/Supernatural

Curiosity rises when characters are in conflict with something unknown. We know we don't have the whole truth, and we're sticking around to see what the heck is going on. Most paranormal thrillers and mysteries use this type of conflict to hide the truth until a big reveal at the end. In sci-fi and fantasy, the mystery often turns out to be supernatural—ghosts, aliens, demons—you name it.

In Star Wars, the Force is a supernatural, well, force. In an episode of *The Clone Wars* titled "Overlords," Obi-Wan, Anakin, and Ahsoka are lured onto a mysterious planet by a distress signal. There, they meet three powerful beings and face a conflict they don't entirely understand. It's slowly revealed that these strangers are personifications of the Force itself—a daughter who represents the light side, a son who represents the dark side, and a father who keeps the two in balance. When the son captures Ahsoka and turns her against Anakin, the mystery of how to defeat such a being and save his padawan drives the conflict forward. We want answers! We want resolution! We want Ahsoka safe because she's the best character of all time!

A SENSE OF FOREBODING

The line "I have a bad feeling about this" is a running gag in Star Wars movies. As the audience, we *know* something bad is going to happen after it's said. That sense of foreboding is tension, friends. Tension is about the *anticipation* of something bad happening.

Recently, Shelly stumbled onto a Swedish short documentary by Maximilien Van Aertryck and Axel Danielson called *Ten Meter Tower*. Its premise is simple. The filmmakers hired sixty-seven people who'd never jumped from a ten metre diving tower before. Each participant was paid thirty dollars to climb the tower and walk to the edge while being filmed. Whether they jumped or not was entirely up to them—they got paid either way. Now, it doesn't sound like something that would hold your attention for long, but *Ten Meter Tower* has nearly 3.5 million views on YouTube. Why? What's so fascinating about a film where the outcome is either safely landing in a swimming pool or climbing back down a ladder?

Ten Meter Tower is a perfect example of tension. It explores questions of risk-taking, bravery, and peer pressure. Will the divers work through their fear, or will they publicly back down?

The film wouldn't have been nearly as compelling if people

were pushed off the diving tower or if they already had experience jumping from that height, because then we would *know* what the result would be. It's mesmerizing because the outcome isn't guaranteed. We don't know what each participant will do, and we want to see what happens next.

Author Harrison Demchick uses the example of dominos to explain tension:

> There's no question tipping the first will bring down the last," Demchick writes, "and there's no question as to how, so why even bother watching? Imagine thousands of fallen dominos over the course of minutes, and the enormity of the disappointment that would come from one misplaced piece merely a few dozen dominos from the end. The nearer the victory—the higher the climb—the farther the fall. That's the power of tension."[2]

As your story goes on, your characters are climbing a mountain; the obstacles should be harder, the terrain rougher, the weather more severe, the air thinner. Tension rises because there is more conflict getting in the way of their goals.

The Red Wedding scene in Season Three of *Game of Thrones* is a master class on tension. Robb Stark, head of House Stark, betrays a marriage pact with Lord Walder Frey's daughter by marrying another woman. Robb begs for Frey's forgiveness and the surly man responds with, "We'll put this mess behind us."[3] He arranges to have one of his daughters married to Robb's uncle Edmure instead. The thing is, Walder Frey does not come across as a forgiving man, so we already know that Robb is still in serious trouble, we just don't know what kind yet. Tension rises.

At the wedding, Edmure unveils his mystery bride to find one of Frey's youngest and prettiest daughters. The relief on his face is obvious. We are then treated to a jovial feast and dancing in the great hall, a rare moment of happiness in Westeros. The newlyweds are sent off for the bedding, and everyone seems elated that disaster has been averted. Cue a huge sigh of relief.

That's when Robb's mother, Catelyn, notices one of Frey's men shutting and locking the great hall doors—not good. The band strikes up, playing the Lannister theme song—another bad sign. Outside, Robb's direwolf, trapped in a cage, starts to whine—uh-oh. The music stops and Roose Bolton, one of Frey's allies, fixes Catelyn with an odd stare. He glances down at his own sleeve and she jerks it up to find him wearing chain mail beneath his formal attire—oh no!

Then, all carnage breaks loose. By the end of the awful ambush, Robb, his pregnant wife, his mother, his friends, and even his direwolf have been slaughtered. The Stark family, so close to triumph, is annihilated. The end credits start in utter silence.

The tension in these scenes is so powerful because the show constantly hints that our protagonists aren't safe. We've been on guard since Ned Stark's beheading, and the point is pressed home with the Red Wedding. After that, viewers are painfully aware that no beloved protagonist is safe from death in this story. This adds incredible tension to future conflicts, because we truly don't know whether our heroes will survive to the end.

TEN WAYS TO RAISE TENSION

There are different types and levels of tension you can add to your writer's toolbelt. You don't have to use George R.R. Martin's method of killing off hundreds of characters to keep your readers on the edges of their seats (though it's certainly an option). Here are a few more ideas:

1. Add a cliffhanger.

Raise tension by ending a chapter or a scene with something bad happening or something bad *about* to happen. This could be a physical event, like a gun about to go off in our protagonist's face, but it doesn't need to be. It could be something bad that happens to the character emotionally, in which they're facing inner conflict. If readers are properly attached to the character, they will want to know what happens to them.

In the Season Two finale of *Fringe*, protagonist Olivia Dunham is trapped in an alternate universe, locked in a cell by the show's villain, and her doppleganger has taken her place on our Earth. These events are even more gut-wrenching because her romance with Peter was just kicking off, and Peter is completely unaware that she has been replaced with a spy. This cliffhanger accomplishes both physical danger—we don't know what will happen to Olivia in the hands of the scientists interested in experimenting on her—and emotional trauma—she is helpless, alone, scared for herself, and worried about her friends. Give us that next season!

2. Interrupt the action.

Interruptions can take many forms—your characters are heading in a straight line towards their goal when an opposing force suddenly appears, an interjection with backstory occurs, they receive a vision or a dream, or they are distracted by something. This can be especially effective if they are about to learn the answer to a mystery, when—BOOM—something happens and readers have to wait to get the answer they've been anticipating.

In the graphic novel *Infinite Universe* by Lyndon Radchenka and Steven Kaul, a group of humans are exploring a new planet. They discover remnants of alien technology and aren't sure if the aliens are still there. The crew's captain, Eva, says "I don't like this." Then, the next series of panels cut to backstory, and Eva's inner dialogue reflects on how the explorers were genetically enhanced to be stronger, need less oxygen, and given fine motor skills—information that's valuable for readers to understand. Anticipation is built as we realize what these characters are capable of, and wonder what dangers they will face. The next page brings us back to the explorers' present time, and we eagerly read on to find out what bad thing is about to happen.

3. Put an obstacle in the way.

Your character's path to their goal shouldn't be an easy one! Throw obstacles in their way to build tension and make their lives more difficult. These obstacles can take many forms, including setting or terrain, another character, a villain's interference, an unexpected event, or a character's own emotions.

In *Skyward* by Brandon Sanderson, Spensa badly wants to become a pilot just like her father, even though he was branded as a coward for flying away from a battle and shot down by his own people. She's studied for years to pass the vigorous test required to become a cadet, but the day before the test, her teacher tells her that she won't pass, no matter what. Even if she aces the test, the Admiral has orders to deny her because of her father's bad reputation. How is Spensa supposed to reach her goal now?

4. Introduce a twist.

When something unexpected throws your characters off course, it raises tension. Plot twists can surprise readers, protagonists, or both. They should change the expected path of the narrative. Just be sure that you can justify the twist and aren't throwing it in for shock factor alone.

In *Under the Lesser Moon* by Shelly Campbell, Akrist has defied his "destiny" to be sacrificed as a first-born son. He's been accepted, more or less, by his camp as a regular member of the community instead of someone marked for death. He's living his life just like anyone else—learning to be a hunter, contributing to his camp in ways he can, even falling in love. His life is shockingly normal. That is, until he's framed for murder, and then the whole trajectory of his story changes. Plot twist! Tension! What will happen to Akrist now?

5. Take something away from the character that they need to succeed.

Add tension by taking away something crucial to the protagonist's success—this could be an object or companion, but it could also be something more abstract, like a mental state. And since we're talking sci-fi and fantasy, you can even get creative with it and take away their memories, emotions, or free will through magic or science.

In *Taran Wanderer* by Lloyd Alexander, Taran doesn't feel like he can move forward with his relationship with Eilonwy without discovering who his parents were and where he came from. He sets out from Caer Dallben to travel the land and discover his heritage. Early on in his travels, Taran's horse, Melynlas, is stolen. In addition to needing a mount to continue his journey, Melynlas is important to Taran, so he's devastated by the loss and can't continue on until he's recovered his steed. This is a relatively simple obstacle—character needs horse; horse is gone. But it's impactful because of Taran's attachment to Melynlas. Tension doesn't need to be complicated for readers to be invested.

6. Give the antagonist a boost of strength.

Oh, you thought the villain was strong? Well, they just got STRONGER! How will our hero possibly defeat them now? This type of tension works particularly well if the protagonist has just had some sort of victory against the villain. They feel like they are winning, but then—uh oh—not so much.

In *Shadow and Bone* by Leigh Bardugo, Alina escapes from the clutches of the Darkling with her best friend, Mal. Victory! She and Mal hunt for the magical stag, because its antlers will boost Alina's powers—and they find it. Another victory! But then, the Darkling appears and slays the stag. Doing so allows him to put the antlers on Alina and control her powers. Huge defeat. The villain now has his own powers *plus* Alina's. How will he be stopped?

7. Draw back the curtain.

You can let your readers in on a scene that your protagonist is unaware of to boost tension. This technique depends on the point of view your novel is told from, but it can make your readers stay at the edge of their seats, because they know something the main character doesn't.

In the TV series *Vikings*, Ragnar Lothbrok, a feared warrior claiming to have descended from Odin, imprisons and eventually befriends an Anglo-Saxon monk named Athelstan. One of the most emotional scenes in *Vikings* is Athelstan's murder. It is filmed so that only Athelstan and we, the viewers, know that his murderer is Ragnar's good friend Floki. This sets up huge tension because we we've seen behind the curtain and know bits of the story Lothbrok has yet to discover, and there's bound to be conflict when he does.

8. Raise the stakes.

We need our characters to be climbing mountains, remember? The higher they climb, the worse the fall can be. What does the hero stand to lose if they fail? Who will suffer? What are the consequences to others?

In the graphic novel *Rust and Water* by Justin Currie and

GMB Chomichuk, a mermaid befriends a giant robot at the bottom of the ocean. She accompanies him on a dangerous journey to his home, and their lives are often at stake. Their friendship grows as they travel together. As they reach the robot's home, and the mermaid learns that his people are polluting the ocean, other things are at stake: the ocean life, their friendship, the robot's morality. Will he side with his new friend and the beauty of the ocean world, or will he perpetuate a cycle of destruction?

9. Jeopardize a relationship.

Just like in real life, relationships are the key to drama! Make your characters clash due to conflicting perspectives, wants, or needs. You can even muddy the waters with a misunderstanding.

In *Cinder* by Marissa Meyer, Cinder becomes friends and falls in love with Prince Kai. Kai, however, doesn't know she's a cyborg. That detail is revealed at the worst possible moment, along with some misinformation, so Kai suddenly believes that Cinder is an enemy. Of course, they have both fallen in love with each other by this point, so tension skyrockets! What will happen to their relationship?

10. Add a ticking clock.

Tension can be ratcheted up if there is a deadline attached to your main character's goal. Time is of the essence! Hurry up, or all will be lost!

In *Unwind* by Neal Shusterman, parents have the option to "unmake" their children between the ages of thirteen and eighteen. Three kids who are slated to be unmade escape before the procedure is performed. The element of a ticking clock here is not "do this task before time runs out," but instead, "survive until you're eighteen."

Building conflict and tension is a marathon, not a sprint. If all we saw were gory, violent battles, emotional anguish, and prolonged tension with no relief, we'd tire quickly. Readers need breaks from high tension and conflict. Constant pedal to the metal doesn't work because we start to gloss over endless action when we can't get a breath in. If you want your high tension, high conflict scenes to resonate, contrast them with quieter moments. Let your characters rest in idyllic scenery, intimate scenes, and poignant moments between friends, family, and lovers. None of these moments should be random. Place them purposefully to deepen relationships or show us what your character stands to lose from the conflict later on.

That is the heart of tension and conflict: it encourages readers to care, become emotionally invested, and turn pages with eager anticipation.

Chapter 5

We'll Make a Gonnagle Out of Ye
Riveting Dialogue

Ineffective dialogue is one of the common reasons Allison, during her past job as an acquiring editor, rejected manuscripts. Dialogue can be a tricky aspect to nail down, but when you do, it will level up your writing like nobody's business.

REAL VS. FICTIONAL DIALOGUE

Have you ever received advice that you should go to a coffee shop and listen to random conversations to learn how to write dialogue? This is good advice. But perhaps not for the reason you think. For example, here's a snippet of a coffee shop conversation:

"Hey."
"Yo!"
"How are you?"
"Survivin'. You?"
"I'm doing all right, thanks. Have a seat!"
"Okay, thanks. Whatcha drinkin'?"
"Hmm?"

"That coffee?"
"Oh, yeah. Cappuccino. It's good, but the coffee shop on the corner has better. Um, hey, I bumped into your sister yesterday."
"Oh, really?"
"Yeah, we were in the same line at the grocery store. You know, the one on the corner? Listen, she told me you were in trouble."
"She likes puttin' her nose in my business."
"Can I help?"
"Nah."

The positives about this dialogue: there's a potential mystery buried in here (what trouble?) and a little tension (Character Two doesn't seem to appreciate their sister much). However, it would need to be tweaked for a book. In real life, people talk about mundane things, use a lot of ers and ahs, backtrack, rephrase, repeat, and pause while they try to figure out that one word they can't remember. Sometimes, the point they're trying to get across makes sense to them but to no one else. You will be hard-pressed to find a character asking "How are you?" as a greeting in one of your favourite novels, because it generally adds nothing to the story.

However, here are some insights you *can* take from real-life dialogue, things you can pay attention to when you visit that coffee shop:

- **People speak in unique ways.** Most speakers have pet phrases or words; some have words that they would never use (perhaps they avoid swearing or hate the word "moist"); some people use contractions more than others, like the second speaker in the above example.
- **People don't address others by their first names as often as you might think.** Particularly if it is a one-on-

one conversation, there is often no need to address the other person by their first name.
- **People speak in jargon.** Two gamers in conversation might use words like "RPG," "Dot," "ADC," "AFK," "KS," etc. Two astronauts, however, might use completely different lingo.

Your characters shouldn't all sound the same. In fact, if you take away their dialogue tags, readers should be able to guess who is talking (at least some of the time).

The purpose of fictional dialogue is to drive the story forward, heighten tension, and/or reveal character. When working on sections of dialogue, ask yourself what would happen to the story if you deleted the entire conversation. If the story would be exactly the same, then the dialogue either doesn't need to be there or it needs reworking.

DIALECTS AND ACCENTS

Dialect is a way of speaking associated with a particular language, country, or social class, including elements like pronunciation, grammar, and spelling. *Accent* refers specifically to pronunciation—the way people say certain words, vowels, or consonants.

Some authors point out specific accents in their characters by using phonetic spellings. This should be attempted with care, because it runs the danger of inauthentic caricatures and harmful stereotypes. Plus, phonetic spellings can be distracting to the reader. You should also carefully consider your reason for focusing on one character's accent and not another's. Everyone has an accent—even you. If you are only using phonetics for accents you don't consider "standard," double check that this doesn't imply the characters are inferior, ignorant, or less intelligent than others.

When writing dialects, less is more. For example, if your Scottish character says, "Whit's fur ye'll no go by ye," will your non-Scottish readers follow? If your dialogue is riddled with phonetic spellings, will *anyone* follow? Charles Dickens tended to use phonetic spellings for his uneducated characters, such as the following sample from *Bleak House*:

> ...there wos other genlmen come down Tom-all-Alone's a-prayin, but they all mostly sed as the t'other wuns prayed wrong, and all mostly sounded as to be a-talking to theirselves, or a-passing blame on the t'others, and not a-talkin to us."[1]

If you're like us, you have to go over that a few times to get the gist of what is being said. And, while we admire Charles Dickens, we question whether drawing attention to lower caste characters in this manner is helpful or harmful. If this is accurately depicting the way people talked, is that a problem or is it contributing to harmful stereotypes?

In the Harry Potter series, J.K. Rowling uses phonetic dialect, also known as *eye dialect*, for one of the most beloved characters in the story—Hagrid:

> They didn' keep their gold in the house, boy! Nah, first stop fer us is Gringotts. Wizards' bank. Have a sausage, they're not bad cold—an' I wouldn' say no teh a bit o' yer birthday cake, neither."[2]

Hagrid's dialect is easy to read as far as eye dialect goes, though it is a little over the top. The small changes to the words (e.g. *fer* instead of *for*) and the syntax variations point to a West Country English accent. While the dialect might get tiresome if Hagrid was a protagonist, his appearances are sporadic enough that it comes across as a loveable part of his character (at least, we think so).

In contrast, Fleur Delacour's accent is much more heavy-handed and feels like a cliche. Some French readers have commented on how annoying it was to read the stereotypical "z" instead of "th" sounds.

> An 'air from ze 'ead of a veela... One of my grand-muzzer's."[3]

Characters make fun of Fleur's accent and nickname her "Phlegm," contributing to this stigma. Fleur is a fascinating character—an extremely arrogant teenager who becomes a more refined adult. But all her dialect accomplishes is a constant screaming of I'M FRENCH, which distracts from her character rather than adds to it.

Terry Pratchett also uses eye dialect in his Discworld series. In *The Wee Free Men*, the fey folk, known as Nac Mac Feegles, speak with Glaswegian accents:

> Crivens! It's a' verra well sayin' 'find the hag,' but what should we be lookin' for, can ye tell me that? All these bigjobs look just the same tae me!"
> "Not-totally-wee Geordie doon at the fishin' said she was a big, big girl!"
> "A great help that is, I dinna think! They're all big, big girls!"
> "Ye paira dafties! Everyone knows a hag wears a pointy bonnet!"
> "So they canna be a hag if they're sleepin', then?"[4]

In the article "Narrative Function of Language in Terry Pratchett's *The Wee Free Men*," Judita Ondrušeková explains the mechanics behind this dialect:

> "The Scottish dialect is present in this exchange: clipping of the -ing suffix in words saying, looking, fishing and sleeping and instead the accent clips off the final sound 'g' (sayin', lookin', fishin', sleepin'). Pratchett also highlights the Scottish emphasis on 'r' (verra), which is more rhotic. Another set of words changed by pronunciation are prepositions 'to' and 'down', or in the dialogue 'tae' and 'doon'. The Scots change the form of their auxiliary verb 'don't' into 'dinna'. The syntax of that sentence is helpful to the reader, as they would be able to connect the meaning to the context of the exchange."[5]

Pratchett writes comedic fantasy; and if over-the-top dialect is going to work anywhere, it's comedy. The fey folk's dialect is fun and silly (though it can become tedious to read).

In many cases, using eye dialect is distracting and runs the danger of othering non-native speakers, so keep that in mind if you try it.

FOUR WAYS TO FEATURE CULTURE THROUGH DIALOGUE

If eye dialect isn't for you, there are other ways to highlight a character's culture through dialogue:

1. Use regional slang.

Americans say "restroom," but Britons say "the loo." Australians say "fair dinkum" to confirm the truth of a statement. Canadians call a forest "the bush." You can use regional slang to highlight your character's origin.

This can be especially fun in sci-fi and fantasy, because you get to make up the slang! Your character's dialect could be related to the region of the world they come from or their race. Do elves use words that dwarves don't? Do goblins have a "special" word for humans? Do aliens from specific planets use certain terms?

The TV show *Farscape* utilizes slang particularly well, with certain species using words that others don't. For example, Chiana, a nebari, uses the words *blez* ("chill out"), *cacking* ("dying"), *dag-yo* ("cool"), *draz* (an expletive), and many more. D'Argo, a luxan, says, "You are a real pain in the eema!"[6] Zhaan, a delvian, says a chant as a religious prayer."[7] Rygel, a hynerian, uses *fa-pu-ta* as an expletive: "Darn it! Some fa-pu-ta is going to pay for this!"[8]

On building slang into his fantasy novel *Hope and Red*, Jon Skovron writes:

> Some word choices were fairly obvious to me. The book takes place in the Empire of Storms, which is an archipelago. The sea is a huge part of everyone's life, and the climate is often overcast and damp, particularly in the large, urban island of New Laven. It would make sense, then, when selecting a word to describe something unusually good or pleasing, to have it be the opposite of their dreary daily existence. So if something is great, they say 'That's real sunny.'"[9]

Try not to get too cutesy with your slang, but insert it thoughtfully and organically, considering what may have inspired the usage of these words and sayings.

2. Use imaginative expletives.

Sci-fi has a history of getting creative with its swear words. *Farscape* has *frell*. *Battlestar Galactica* has *frak*. *Star Wars: Rebels* has *karabast*. *Firefly* has *gorram*.

Sci-fi and fantasy also tend to use special (often derogatory) terms to reference certain people groups. For example, *mudblood* to refer to someone who is muggle-born (Harry Potter), *Skaikru* for people who came to Earth from the Ark (*The 100*), *toaster* for cylon (*Battlestar Galactica*), *prawn* for a member of the alien species Poleepkwa (*District 9*), and *muties* for mutants (*The Gifted*).

When coming up with your own slang and expletives, consider how the word might have developed organically. Slang doesn't just come from nowhere. It might be a combination of two words (for example, *mud* and *blood* in mudblood); an abbreviation of a longer word (for example, *muties or mute* are short for *mutant*); reminiscent of another word (for example, *frak* is suspiciously close to another swear word we Earthlings are familiar with); or based off a word from another language.

3. Use snippets of their native tongue.

If Common (or whatever your main character speaks) isn't a character's first language, they might occasionally revert to their native tongue when speaking. This *could* include random words from their language interspersed into their dialogue, but in real life, people don't do this that much unless they can't remember the word for it in the second language. More realistically, a character might revert to their original language when they are angry, upset, or excited. Or, they might mutter to themselves in their own language.

In *Firefly*, characters often slip into Mandarin when emotions are high, indicating that Chinese could be a "common person's" language in this galaxy. It's one of the two common languages in their system, stemming from the fact that China and America merged culturally as a space-faring superpower. As cultures blend together, so do words and phrases, and we generally start by learning each other's profanities.

However, if you are using words and phrases from an existing language, you risk insulting readers from that culture, especially if you dive off the deep end of vulgarity. It doesn't hurt to have a reader who's fluent in your secondary language to help you along.

4. Play with grammar and syntax.

Different languages work in wildly different ways. For example, Russian and Latin lack articles such as *a*, *an*, or *the*. French has nouns with grammatical gender. Alaskan Yup'ik has thirty degrees of demonstratives (English only has two—*this* and *that*). Korean has various pronouns that mark the degrees of politeness and formality between the people talking. In some African languages, changing your tone changes the meaning of the sentence.

English generally places the subject of a sentence first, the verb second, and the object last. But some languages switch around this order. Perhaps the most famous English-speaking sci-fi character who uses unusual syntax is Yoda from Star Wars. Instead of subject–verb–object (for example, "You still have much to learn"), Yoda's sentences are often object–subject–verb (for example, "Much to learn, you still have").

You can also play with how characters use contractions. In *Nophek Gloss* by Essa Hansen, which features a variety of aliens from different cultures, the character Panca uses contractions in places that aren't intuitive for English readers:

> You're moving forward very, very fast for someone who went through's much as you did… We can all've second chances… Machines're simple, talk-

ative, honest... Humans're the sum of experiences..."[10]

These small changes to her dialogue make her voice unique. She *feels* like she is from another culture, simply by putting a few apostrophes in unusual places!

In regards to why she made those choices, Essa told us:

> There are countless ways to play with punctuation, pacing, and spelling in order to make speech sound alien or fantastical while still using English. I wanted Panca's dialogue to suggest an accent without being so unconventional that it pushed the reader away. The middle ground I chose was to have her omit articles and contract as much of her speech as possible. Sounding so colloquial also helped her personality feel more intimate."

The Mass Effect video game series has numerous examples of unique dialects. In the games, most aliens speak their own language, but almost everyone uses a translator that allows them to understand and communicate with each other. Still, translators can only do so much—sometimes grammar and even tone comes across as unusual to an English speaker.

In Mass Effect, the elcor speak in monotone, which would make it difficult to understand their emotions (or even whether they are asking a question or making a statement), except that they precede every bit of dialogue with declarations that clarify their intent or feeling. When you approach Harrot, an elcor shopkeeper, he says, "Tentatively excited: welcome, human. What can I get for you?" When you question him about a deal he made, he says, "Suspicious: if I had made such a deal I would certainly not be inclined to discuss it." If you threaten him into doing what you want, he says, "With barely contained terror:

you drive a hard bargain, human."[11] (We often wish humans would precede their dialogue with statements like these!)

The hanar, another alien race from Mass Effect, speak with each other using elaborate patterns of bioluminescence that translators interpret, and their syntax is unusual. Hanar only refer to themselves in the first person with family or people who are very close to them. They most often refer to themselves as "this one" when you interact with them. Their dialect is polite and formal, even when they are annoyed.

See how syntax, grammar, and dialect can be entrenched in culture? Fascinating! Study how syntax and diction work in other languages, glean inspiration from franchises you love, and you will gain some ideas for how to make a character's dialogue stand out in unique ways.

DIALOGUE TAGS

Less is more with dialogue tags. Though *said* might seem boring, and you may feel like spicing up your dialogue with tags like "shouted," "murmured," "explained," or "announced," *said*'s boringness is actually its biggest advantage. *Said* is quiet. *Said* is unobtrusive. *Said* is the silent ninja that no one notices. It draws the attention to the dialogue instead of to itself. And that's usually what you want.

We're not saying to *never* use other dialogue tags. But use them sparingly. Let's analyze this snippet from *Storm Front* by Jim Butcher:

> 'All right, then,' [Marcone] said, smoothly, and as though nothing had happened. 'I won't try to force my offer on you, Mister Dresden.' The car was slowing down as it approached my building, and Hendricks pulled over in front of it. 'But let me offer you some advice.' He had dropped the father-

talking-to-son act, and spoke in a calm and patient voice.

'If you don't charge for it.' Thank God for wisecracks. I was too rattled to have said anything intelligent.

Marcone almost smiled. 'I think you'll be happier if you come down with the flu for a few days. This business that Detective Murphy has asked you to look into doesn't need to be dragged out into the light. You won't like what you see. It's on my side of the fence. Just let me deal with it, and it won't ever trouble you.'

'Are you threatening me?' I asked him. I didn't think he was, but I didn't want him to know that. It would have helped if my voice hadn't been shaking.

'No,' he said, frankly. 'I have too much respect for you to resort to something like that. They say that you're the real thing, Mister Dresden. A real magus.'

'They also say I'm nutty as a fruitcake.'

'I choose which "they" I listen to very carefully,' Marcone said. 'Think about what I've said, Mister Dresden. I do not think our respective lines of work need overlap often. I would as soon not make an enemy of you over this matter.'

I clenched my jaw over my fear, and spat words out at him quick and hard. 'You don't want to make an enemy of me, Marcone. That wouldn't be smart. That wouldn't be smart at all.'"[12]

Most frequently, Butcher uses *said* or no dialogue tag at all. He also uses adverbs sparingly. In the first paragraph, he adds "smoothly" to point out how calm Marcone is and later uses "frankly." Adverbs are most effective when the tone of what is being said is unclear.

In the second paragraph, Butcher doesn't use a dialogue tag at all. Instead, he inserts some of Dresden's thoughts. This works well because a) we know there are only two people in this conversation, so the dialogue tags are there more for convenience than necessity, and b) adding personality is always a plus.

In the third paragraph, Butcher replaces a tag with describing what Marcone is doing—he "almost smiled." Butcher could have added an adverb here, like "Marcone said ominously." But Marcone's words themselves are ominous. The text doesn't need an adverb for readers to be aware of that.

The sixth line of dialogue doesn't have any tag or description. By this point, it's been back and forth enough, plus we're familiar with Dresden's voice, that it's not necessary. "They also say I'm nutty as a fruitcake" is classic Dresden—definitely not something Marcone would say.

Finally, Dresden spits out a line of dialogue. The spitting is more powerful because Butcher uses alternative tags sparingly. If Dresden spat and muttered and shouted every other line of dialogue, this wouldn't mean much. But it packs a punch because of all the *saids* that have come before.

When using dialogue tags, make sure that they are physically possible. For example, can someone snort, laugh, or sneer a line of dialogue? You can always just include an action tag followed by dialogue.

IF YOU KNOW dialogue is an area you can improve on, examine some of your favourite books with a critical eye. Ask yourself what the dialogue is accomplishing, how the author uses dialect, whether you could determine who is speaking without the dialogue tags, and *why* the conversation makes you want to keep reading.

A fun exercise in dialogue is to take a scene from a TV show, write out the dialogue, and then add in narration as though you were converting the script into a novel. What parts of the dialogue did you tweak for a novel format? What actions needed to be described? How did you get tone across?

Taking apart dialogue and putting it back together can help you understand how it should function, and, before you know it, you'll be writing banter, emotional conversation, and meaningful talk like a pro.

Chapter 6

Our Princess is in Another Castle
20 Fantasy Tropes to Reimagine

Writers often think that tropes are bad. But, unless the trope is racist, homophobic, ableist, or otherwise irredeemable, a trope is just a commonly used theme or plot element. They exist because no story is completely original. Use beloved tropes to draw in your audience. Defy expectations by suggesting a trope but then turning it on its head. Deconstruct tropes to determine which elements are required and which are merely expected, and use your readers' expectations to your advantage!

Here are twenty fantasy tropes, deconstructed so you can play with them in your own novel. We've included both classic and reimagined examples.

1. PORTAL TO ANOTHER WORLD

Sometimes, the people stepping through the doorway know what's on the other side; in other stories, they are unaware. Sometimes, they step through voluntarily and others, they are forced through. The Chronicles of Narnia by C.S. Lewis immediately springs to mind when we think of portal fantasies. Lucy steps through a wardrobe into another world and has an adventure, but her siblings don't believe her when she returns. It is only when they see the frozen land of Narnia for themselves, complete with fauns, dwarves, and unicorns, that they believe.

Reimagined: In the *Stargate: SG-1* TV show, stargates are portals to other worlds in our galaxy. The episodic nature of the show allows a team of explorers to visit a new world each week, discovering an unfamiliar culture, alien, or dangerous biome, and gathering information in their fight against parasitic aliens called Goa'uld. Notably, *Stargate* is science fiction, not fantasy (though it does blur the lines). When dreaming up plots for your own story, a fun exercise is considering how a fantasy trope could work in a sci-fi novel, and vice versa.

2. THE CHOSEN ONE

Stop us if you've heard this one before: a young hero wannabe discovers a sword of legend, becomes a champion of destiny, overthrows a great evil, marries into royalty, and leads a kingdom into a time of prosperity. The Chosen One trope is so common because one individual making a difference is powerful inspiration (also, it's nice to vicariously feel special). In these stories, the Chosen One always fulfills the prophecy about them, but often in unexpected ways.

In the Wheel of Time series by Robert Jordan, Rand al'Thor is the Dragon Reborn—prophesied to bring about terrible change and fight the Dark One. The story delves into the great weight that Rand feels *because* of these prophecies, especially because he's interpreted them to mean he has to die. He constantly feels jerked around by people trying to manipulate him and like he is not free to do what he wants.

Reimagined: In the TV series *Buffy the Vampire Slayer*, Buffy Summers is a Slayer, part of a line of women who are bestowed with mystical strength to fight vampires. She has prophetic dreams and is literally referred to as the "Chosen One." But at the end of Season One, she dies. She's revived, of course, but not before a new Slayer is called. Suddenly, Buffy's not the only Chosen One. The final arc of the show involves awakening *all* the potential slayers so they can defeat a terrible evil.

If you want to work with overdone tropes like this one, we recommend either coming at it from a new angle or focusing more on the character than the trope itself. Rand al'Thor's journey is riveting because of the way he reacts to the prophecy and his personal journey.

3. SECRETLY ROYAL

Wait, that character's just a lowly peasant, right? Wrong. They're a princess. Surprise!

Royalty reveals aren't always happy news. Being royal usually comes with a lot of responsibility, sometimes meaning a character can't fall in love with who they want to (a great opportunity for drama). Of course, sometimes the reveal is happy and exciting, particularly in middle grade novels.

In *The Horse and his Boy* by C.S. Lewis, Shasta is raised as a fisherman's son, neglected and abused. After escaping to Narnia with the company of a talking horse, he learns that he looks so much like Prince Corin because they are actually twins. He becomes the king of Archenland.

Reimagined: In the Prydain Chronicles by Lloyd Alexander, one of Taren's traveling companions is a bard named Fflewddur Fflam; he's a wanderer who wears patched clothing and carries a harp with strings that are always breaking. It eventually comes out that Fflewddur is a king of a small kingdom, and though he always tells people not to call him by his title, he brings up the fact that he's a king *a lot*. Eventually, we learn that the tiny kingdom he rules does just fine without him.

This trope can be really fun when played for comedic effect, such as is the case with the Prydain Chronicles. If used for a more serious story, consider all the ramifications, including positive and negative, of being royal.

4. THE MAGICAL ARTIFACT OF DOOM

There's something sinister about an object—something without a brain or voice—that can corrupt the person carrying it. Readers (and characters) are so riveted by the One Ring's power in J.R.R. Tolkien's *The Lord of the Rings*, they don't even need to encounter Sauron himself to feel his might. The inclusion of Gollum as a character is particularly brilliant, because he demonstrates the twisted effects the Ring can have on a person.

Reimagined: In the anime *Death Note*, Light finds a notebook that kills people when their names are written in it. At first, he uses it "for good," killing criminals in an attempt to create a peaceful world. But as the police come closer to figuring out who is murdering criminals, he kills a dozen FBI agents to warn them off. Light descends into villainy as he continues killing more innocent people. The notebook itself doesn't have any magical effect on Light's psyche; it's simply the power that corrupts him.

There are endless ways to play with this trope, because the artifact's effects are only limited by your imagination. Consider the side effects and consequences when brainstorming your artifact of doom.

5. A TOTALLY EVIL SPECIES

Many fantasy authors include a race or species that is totally evil, with no exceptions. For example, the first orcs in J.R.R. Tolkien's *The Lord of the Rings* were elves that were cruelly tortured and twisted into their new forms. All orcs in the series have evil intentions, from capturing Merry and Pippin, to torturing Frodo, to waging war on Minas Tirith. Tolkien likely meant orcs to be a metaphorical embodiment of evil. But we like to imagine there's at least one orc who wanders off to pick flowers and secretly feeds stray cats.

Reimagined: In the anime *Attack on Titan*, the titans are mindless, giant creatures that go out of their way to eat humans even though they don't need the sustenance. Once they're "full," they even vomit their stomach's contents to make room for more. It turns out that (among other mysteries revealed) regular titans are transformed humans, and they have on control over their animalistic actions. One of the characters theorizes that they habitually eat people because if they managed to devour a titan shifter, their humanity would be restored. Horrifying, right?

If you include an evil group or race in your story, consider what made them that way. Are some of them evil because that's what they've been taught? Are they facing off against the "good" guys because if they don't, they will be killed? Has their society conditioned them to be this way?

It's easy to fight against a species when you believe they're totally evil, but how would your characters react if they learned things aren't as black and white as they seem?

6. THE QUEST

The quest is a fantasy staple, and for good reason! It's exciting to follow a hero and their group of supportive friends who have a clear goal: locate the magical artifact; save the princess; defeat the big bad; find a missing person; achieve an impossible task; or, perhaps, all of the above.

The Deltora Quest series by Emily Rodda is a middle grade story about three characters on a journey to find seven missing gems from a magical belt. The trio solves puzzles, discovers new groups of people, and fights terrible monsters. Every book is satisfying, because it ends with the characters discovering one of the seven gems. Tension and excitement increases with each book as another gem is added to the belt.

Reimagined: The 2008 TV series *Merlin* subverts this trope because Arthur often *thinks* he's on a quest and achieving a goal, when, in fact, it is Merlin's journey that really matters. For example, in the episode "The Eye of the Phoenix," Arthur sets off alone to retrieve the Golden Trident from the Fisher King in order to prove himself worthy of Camelot's throne. But Merlin finds out Arthur's in danger and follows him. After fighting wyverns and setting off traps, Merlin has a one-on-one encounter with the Fisher King, who gives him a vial of water from the Lake of Avalon—something that will be important in the days ahead. Arthur does find the trident, but the crucial quest was Merlin's conversation with the Fisher King and attaining the vial.

The important thing about quests is that they shouldn't be easy. Throw lots of interesting obstacles in your characters' paths—physical, relational, emotional, you name it—to keep your readers turning pages.

7. ORPHANED HERO

Disney particularly loves this trope. Snow White's parents die, so she's raised by her wicked stepmother; Aurora's brought up by fairies; Aladdin's parents aren't around; Anastasia grew up in an orphanage; Elsa and Anna are on their own. This trope inspires instant feels for the protagonist, keeps them from being tied to one place, and paves the way for themes about found family.

Reimagined: It's difficult to reinvent this one; either your character is orphaned or not (of course, you could go the "surprise—your parents are actually alive" or "surprise—you're actually adopted and your parents are dead" route). However, the video game *Mass Effect* has a scene, if you've selected the right backstory, in which Commander Shepard calls their mom just to chat, and it is wonderful to see a hero with a healthy parental relationship. Characters don't need to be orphans to go on adventures.

Don't orphan your hero just to make readers feel sorry for them. What does your character's family background contribute to the story? How does it impact their character development?

8. BELOVED MENTOR DIES

Often, the mentor dies before they can tell the hero important stuff that would have been useful for them to know (we're looking at you, Obi-Wan). In the Inheritance Cycle by Christopher Paolini, this trope happens not once, but twice: first in *Eragon* when Brom dies, and then in *Eldest* when Oromis goes away to fight.

Reimagined: In the anime *Fairy Tail*, guild master Makarov "dies" so many times it becomes a running gag. He always makes it back, either through sheer stubbornness or because members of the guild rescue him.

Don't kill off a mentor (or any character) just for the feels or because that's what is expected of the genre, but do make them a three-dimensional character with personality and motivations (even if the protagonist only sees them as their guide). It also doesn't need to be the antagonist who kills the mentor—it could be an accident, an illness, a mistake by the protagonist, or something related to the mentor's backstory.

9. EVIL ADVISOR

Sometimes, it's the monarch or head of state who's scheming, but other times, it's their advisor or second-in-command. In *Aladdin*, Jafar takes advantage of the kind-hearted, gullible sultan and controls him as a means to take power for himself.

Reimagined: The video game *The Legend of Zelda: Breath of the Wild* pokes fun at this trope. In Hyrule Castle, you can find a recipe book that has an entry for Monster Cake, which is described as the chancellor's favourite dish... and a dish that inspires evil schemes.

Be aware, if you choose to use this trope, that it likely won't be a surprise to readers, so you may want to avoid setting it up as a big reveal. But there's nothing wrong with a villain who likes to pull strings from the shadows.

10. TRADITIONAL FANTASY RACES

Elves are magic beings who live in forests. Dwarves are miners who live underground. Dragons hoard treasure. Trolls are big brutes who live in mountains. Tolkien can be credited for setting the bar for these species, and there's nothing wrong with the classics, but it can also be interesting to mix things up.

Reimagined: In the Dragon Age video games, elves used to be a dominant race, known for their connection to magic and nature. But after the fall of their civilization, they were subject to slavery, losing their heritage and identity. Now, they either live as nomad wanderers in small groups or in city slums, subject to racism, prejudice, and discrimination. Dwarves are great builders and live underground, much like their traditional counterparts, but they have a complex social and political structure involving castes. *Dragon Age* also includes a unique race, the Qunari, who are white-haired, grey-skinned warrior giants who follow a religion called the Qun.

Fantasy races are a great way to play with readers' expectations. You can choose to meet them, subvert them, or a combination of both.

11. DAMSEL IN DISTRESS

Comics, fairy tales, and video games use this trope a lot. A woman is captured by a villain and rescued by a hero. Most of *The Legend of Zelda* games put Princess Zelda in these sorts of predicaments, though Zelda always has some clever way of contributing to defeat the big bad, whether it's fragmenting the Triforce and hiding the parts throughout the kingdom (*A Link to the Past*) or taking on the role of mentor in disguise (*Ocarina of Time*).

Reimagined: Obviously, you can subvert this trope by having the woman kick ass and not need rescuing. However, George R.R. Martin does something even more unexpected in *Game of*

Thrones—Sansa Stark becomes a hostage of House Lannister but then she's just *never rescued* by a protagonist. She ends up fleeing with a man who grooms and molests her.

This shouldn't need to be said, but, unfortunately, it does: your female characters should be just as diverse as your male characters. Characters of all gender identities can be cowards, heroes, introverts, extroverts, warriors, royalty, etc. If a female character's only purpose is to be saved so that a male character looks heroic, they need more development. If a female character is beaten, raped, or killed for the sole purpose of furthering a male character's arc, she needs more development. If a female character can be replaced with an inanimate object and the story would remain the same, *she needs more development* (we're looking at you, *Thor: The Dark World*).

12. RECLUSE LIVING IN THE WOODS

Danger has been nipping at our heroes' heels, and they find themselves in a forest. Instead of coming upon another villain, they unexpectedly meet a hermit (often one who can talk to animals and/or trees), and receive shelter and protection for a short while. In *The Elfstones of Shannara* by Terry Brooks, the protagonists are attacked by demon wolves, but they manage to escape to the shelter of the King of the Silver River, a faerie creature with great power. He gives them rest and advice, then sends them on their way.

Reimagined: "The Puppetmaster," an episode of *Avatar: The Last Airbender*, turns this trope on its head; Team Avatar meets an old woman in the woods, who offers them a place to stay and hot tea to drink. She warns them that people have been mysteriously disappearing from the woods during the full moon, but they should be safe with her. Except, as it turns out, the old woman is the very bloodbender who's responsible for kidnapping the villagers.

This trope can be a good way to give your characters (and readers) a breather between high danger scenes.

13. CAPTIVE/CAPTOR ROMANCE

We're tempted to call this the "Stockholm syndrome trope," but for some stories that use this trope, that term does not actually apply.[1] Contrary to popular belief, *Beauty and the Beast* doesn't fit the criteria for Stockholm syndrome, as Belle doesn't obey the beast's rules, she leaves when she's given the chance, she's not constantly trying to avoid his triggers (she doesn't put up with his nonsense), and she only starts to like him when he begins to genuinely change into a nicer person. In other words, Belle does not have Stockholm syndrome. But she does fall in love with the guy who is holding her prisoner. So there's that.

Reimagined: In the Disney movie *Tangled*, Rapunzel leaves her tower with Flynn Rider, but she's the one who does the "kidnapping" (a.k.a. she forces Flynn to be her guide). And it's Mother Gothel, not Flynn, who gaslights the princess.

Captive/captor romances are opportunities for conflict and tension, because there's often an overarching authority—whether that authority is magic, a controlling stepmother, or a supervisor—whom the captor reports to. And you can imagine how that authority might disapprove of the captive going free.

14. MEDIEVAL EUROPEAN SETTING

Influenced by major stories that lean heavily on European folklore, like the tales of King Arthur, *The Lord of the Rings*, and Dungeons & Dragons, this trope has become a standard setting for many fantasy novels. Warriors fight with swords and shields, stone and wood are the most common materials for architecture, slavery is common, and governments are feudal.

Reimagined: The most obvious way to subvert this trope is to choose a completely different setting for your fantasy novel.

The video game *Chrono Trigger* starts out with two time periods that fit medieval Europe, but then takes the player to a high-tech future.

Choose a medieval setting if you want, but there are also lots of other cultures, myths, and societal structures you can draw on for your story.

15. CURSED BEAUTY

In this trope, someone beautiful is cursed to be ugly, such as the Beast in *Beauty and the Beast*. They are usually reverted to their beautiful self once the curse is broken.

Reimagined: In *Howl's Moving Castle* by Diana Wynne Jones, protagonist Sophie is cursed to be an old woman. Sophie's curse isn't broken by true love or a kiss. Her journey is one of self-discovery, and she learns how to value herself. In fact, it's her own disbelief in her significance that keeps the curse going for so long.

When working with this trope, avoid idolizing beauty and equating it with goodness. Also, keep in mind that society's standards of beauty in your novel could be very different from the standards of beauty you are familiar with. Thinness, white teeth, makeup, and women shaving their legs are only considered desirable in North America because our society (and marketing companies) has convinced us they are.

16. WOMAN DISGUISED AS A MAN

This trope usually takes place in a patriarchal society, one in which women aren't allowed to become warriors. The protagonist dresses as a man in order to achieve a goal. In *Mulan*, Mulan secretly takes her father's place when he's called to war, because she's afraid he won't survive. This results in all sorts of complications (namely, trying to hide the fact that she's a woman when she's surrounded by men).

Reimagined: In *Spin the Dawn* by Elizabeth Lim, only men can be tailors. But when her father is summoned to court to compete for the position of the royal tailor, Maia Tamarin poses as a boy and takes his place. Instead of running up hills, climbing up poles, and sparring, Maia dyes cloth, stitches until her hands ache, and sews magical garments.

There are lots of opportunities for obstacles with this trope—how do they go about hiding their identity? What happens when someone discovers their secret? What if they make friends who inevitably learn they've been lied to?

17. DANGEROUS, FORBIDDEN POWER

Magic-users are warned against trying this particular technique because of dangerous consequences, but that doesn't stop our protagonist from trying it at least once! The premise of the anime *Fullmetal Alchemist* is based on this trope. Edward and Alphonse Elric try to bring their mother back from the dead using alchemy, and it goes horribly wrong. Edward loses an arm and a leg, and Alphonse loses his whole body, only surviving because Edward attaches his soul to a nearby suit of armour.

Reimagined: Less a reimagining and more a pushing this trope to its limits, in Robert Jordan's Wheel of Time series, using balefire doesn't just destroy a target, it destroys it *so hard* that the target's actions from the last few minutes are undone. Balefire literally unravels time, causing all the paradoxes you might imagine. In the final books, because the Forsaken (and Rand) are using balefire willy-nilly, the world itself starts to fall apart, and cracks that descend into nothingness appear in the earth.

Unless some sort of ruse is involved, the consequences of using this magic should be dire or it wouldn't be forbidden. Your characters should pay a heavy price if they try to use it.

18. COOL SWORD, BRO

Have you noticed the number of fantasy books with swords on the covers? Swords are often significant artifacts and keys to defeating a great evil. This is the case in *The Sword of Shannara* by Terry Brooks—the sword was forged by a druid to destroy the Warlock Lord, and the protagonist is the only one capable of wielding it.

Reimagined: In Terry Pratchett's Discworld novel *Guards! Guards!*, Carrot Ironfoundersson's sword isn't magical or special in any way. It doesn't have a name. The only thing that happens when you wield it is you get blisters. The fact that Carrot's sword isn't magical is, in fact, what makes it one of the most unique swords in the world!

There's nothing wrong with a magical sword, but hear us out: magical catapult. No one will see it coming.

19. EVIL HAS BEEN LOCKED AWAY FOR CENTURIES BUT IS ABOUT TO ESCAPE (OR ALREADY HAS)

An ancient people sealed away an ancient evil because they couldn't figure out how to destroy it. But it's okay, it can never escape! Er… Whoops.

In the Stephen King novel *Duma Key*, the villain had been sealed in a keg and dropped down a well, but the keg slowly leaks, causing the creature to have some influence on the world again.

Reimagined: Illidan Stormrage from the video game *Warcraft III* isn't evil, but the night elves imprison him for 10,000 years because he was researching banned magic. By the time he gets out, he's so obsessed with power and revenge that he *becomes* a villain.

If you use this trope, make sure the villain truly is terrifying when they're released. This is a monster that has a history's worth of fear behind it, so its horribleness should surpass readers' expectations.

20. LIBRARY FULL OF SECRETS

Who doesn't love a giant library full of secrets? Often, the protagonist goes there to find an answer to a mystery. In *Lirael* by Garth Nix, Lirael grows up working in a library, and it doesn't hold just books; there are rooms that contain sealed magic beings, trees, grass, a fake sky, and many dangers. Only parties of armed librarians go into the lower levels, and all librarians are required to have a whistle and a clockwork mouse to raise an alarm in case of emergency.

Reimagined: In Jim Butcher's The Dresden Files, a library of knowledge known as the Archive is hosted in the body of a human girl named Ivy. She knows everything humanity has ever written down. Cleverly, the main character communicates with her by writing a message down on a notepad (it automatically gets recorded in the Archive as soon as he does so).

Often, characters go to a library for answers, but it's more interesting if they only have more questions after they've learned whatever they came for.

Chapter 7

I'm Afraid I Can't Do That, Dave

20 Sci-Fi Tropes to Revitalize

We can't forget the sci-fi tropes! Here are twenty tropes, deconstructed, for you to consider when writing your sci-fi story.

1. SENTIENT SPACESHIP

There are many advantages to a sentient spaceship. For one, fewer crew are needed; even pilots and navigators may be unnecessary. Some sentient ships are capable of running without a crew at all. When the crew is present, however, a sentient spacecraft can provide some interesting drama. What happens if it's in a bad mood? What if it decides you're a threat and jettisons you into cold space?

Your sentient ships could be mechanical, a hybrid of organic and machine, or a living organism. This trope often deals with human minds forcibly trapped within ships and themes of what criteria must be met to be considered alive. In the show *Farscape*, the starship Moya is treated like a member of the crew. She is a bio-mechanical ship, capable of producing offspring. She often communicates with the crew through her pilot, but tension and conflict rise when they're disconnected, her goals conflict with the crew's, or her anatomy causes problems.

Reimagined: In the novel *Ancillary Justice* by Anne Leckie, colossal starships use artificial intelligence to link thousands of soldiers in the Radch empire. Each warship uses hundreds of ancillaries—captured soldiers possessed by the minds of the A.I. The result is a collective "entity," made up of one mind controlling a ship and many soldiers. When one of these ships, the *Justice of Toren*, is destroyed, the A.I. is left trapped in a single ancillary—a ship's mind in a fragile human body—and she's hungry for vengeance against those who destroyed her.

If your spaceship is sentient, it should be a character in its own right. What is its life like? What does it want? How does it feel about its crew?

2. TIME MACHINE

Something in the past (or the future) needs to be changed! What better way to solve the problem than with a time machine? Of course, these things tend to cause more problems than they fix. In the TV show *Timeless*, a man steals a time machine from the government and changes key events in history. The government hires a history professor, a soldier, and an engineer to track the guy through history and capture him. The show offers commentary on oppression (one of the protagonists is black and one is a woman, so they have to deal with societal cruelty during most of their travels into the past) and lesser-known historical figures.

Reimagined: In Audrey Niffenegger's *The Time Traveler's Wife*, Henry *is* the time machine. He has no control over when or where he travels to. His ability to travel in time is like an illness, and it becomes more frequent and erratic as he ages. His doctor discovers that the time leaps are caused by a genetic anomaly, and Henry passes it on to his daughter, who's also able to time travel.

Time travel provides great opportunities to drive conflict—

characters might be personally invested in what they're trying to change, history might be damaged if the time-travellers fail, or they might end up far from home with no way to get back. What are the dangers of time travel in your story?

3. FASTER-THAN-LIGHT TRAVEL

Space is just so dang full of... space. If you want to visit a new planet or a galaxy far, far away—and you'd like to take less than several lifetimes (or several hundred lifetimes) to get there—FTL is an attractive option. In the TV show *Andromeda*, ships use slipstream drives to enter a slippoint, catching onto a series of "strings" that require a living pilot to navigate. Slipstream is described as another dimension that the ship slips into and then out of. The time it takes to travel the slipstream seems to depend on luck rather than distance, though frequently traveled paths are more reliable.

Reimagined: In *Star Wars: The Force Awakens*, FTL is weaponized. Starkiller Base is capable of using the technology to destroy entire star systems halfway across the galaxy; it's basically a superpowered Death Star.

FTL is an easy answer to how people might travel across galaxies quickly. You can also brainstorm what other areas of technology FTL might inspire or lead to.

4. EVIL ALIENS

Alien invasions are one of the oldest speculative fiction tropes, cropping up from a fear of the unknown paired with a fear of war. Aliens either come out swinging with technological weapons of mass destruction (think H.G. Wells's *War of the Worlds*) or they're more subtle about it, infiltrating humans to brainwash and take over from within, releasing a virus, or using human bodies as good-old hatcheries in the style of the *Alien* movies.

Reimagined: In the film *District 9*, an alien ship appears over Johannesburg, South Africa, and governments are initially terrified that they might be witnessing a hostile invasion. When the ship doesn't move, human soldiers eventually pry their way inside. They find a group of malnourished aliens who are stranded on a malfunctioning ship. The aliens are forcibly placed in an internment camp, reminiscent of Cape Town's District Six[1] in the apartheid era.

Just like with the evil species trope in fantasy literature, consider what makes your aliens "evil" and whether things aren't as black and white as they seem.

5. WAKING UP EARLY OR LATE FROM CRYOSLEEP

If you don't have faster-than-light transport, cryosleep is your next best bet. Suspended animation allows your crew to wake up unchanged and unaged once they arrive at their final destination, no matter how long it takes to get there. Unfortunately, there's always the chance that complications will arise, whether it's a cryopod malfunctioning (our feelings go out to Aurora from the film *Passengers*, who suffers because another passenger's cryopad malfunctions and he decides to wake her up so he won't be alone) or sabotage (the Robinson family from the *Lost in Space* are intimately familiar with that one). Then, of course, there's the opposite problem—waking up centuries late (such is Philip Fry's fate in *Futurama*).

Reimagined: In Megan O'Keefe's *Velocity Weapon*, Sanda Greeve's gunship is shot down in battle and is equipped with an evac pod chair, which immediately encases her in foam, inducing cryosleep and firing her into space, where her comrades are supposed to retrieve her after the battle. However, Sanda wakes up on a sentient enemy warship, *Bero*. *Bero*'s crew is missing and he tells her that she's been asleep for 230 years. The war destroyed both sides and the entire star system. But something is not adding up in *Bero*'s story. A cryosleep mystery!

There's a large likelihood of mental trauma when dealing with waking up late or early from cryosleep. Your characters may have to deal with never seeing their loved ones again, malfunctioning technology, and unfamiliar worlds.

6. UPLOADED CONSCIOUSNESS

The common driving force behind this trope is the search for immortality. Why confine yourself to a finite body (especially if it is sick or elderly) if you can upload your memories and consciousness into a powerful computer instead? As long as you keep adequate backups, you can live forever. Perhaps you can even tailor your body, personality, and memories. This idea has fascinating repercussions—a programmer could change any facet about you or trap you in electronic limbo.

In the novel *Altered Carbon* by Richard K. Morgan, most of the population has cortical stacks in their spinal columns that store their consciousness. These stacks can be downloaded into new bodies, or *sleeves*, after they die. Some religions don't allow their stacks to be re-sleeved at death because they believe their soul goes to heaven and won't pass on to the new sleeve. This makes them easy targets for murder, because they won't be re-sleeved to testify. Although people could live indefinitely, most only re-sleeve once or twice because they are unable to update their bodies and go through the full aging process each time. Only the rich can afford to acquire multiple replacement bodies and remotely store copies of their stacks, achieving immortality. Criminals in this world are imprisoned "on stack," their consciousnesses preserved and stored while their bodies are sold to the highest bidder for re-sleeving.

Reimagined: In "White Christmas," an episode of the TV series *Black Mirror*, people have digital clones, called "cookies," that are forced to perform menial tasks. Cookies who reject the idea of slavery are tortured by accelerating their perception of time so that seconds in the real world seem like months or years to them—a time-warped digital solitary confinement.

When using this trope, determine who has access to the technology and how they acquire it. Plus, what are the repercussions of people gaining immortality in this way? Overpopulation? Memory degradation? The lack of a soul?

7. PARALLEL WORLD WANTS TO INVADE EARTH

Why fix your own world when you can just take over another? This trope usually involves two similar worlds, but one of them is dying and decides the grass is greener on the other side.

In the TV series *Fringe*, a war between two parallel Earths is started when Walter Bishop kidnaps the alternate version of his son. *Fringe* plays with characters we know and love, exploring how lives and personalities can turn out completely different due to changes in that person's history. It is fun trying to note all the differences between the alternate universe and the world we know—don't forget to grab a copy of the latest issue of *Red Lantern* or drop by New York to see that hit show, *Dogs*.

Reimagined: This trope is flipped around in Robert J. Sawyer's trilogy The Neanderthal Parallax. Scientist Ponter Boddit accidentally opens a portal between our universe and his—a world where Neanderthals became the dominant species. Along with exploring the differences between the two world's cultures and customs, the series touches on invasion when Earth's magnetic field collapses and the Homo Sapiens consider taking over the utopia-like, Neanderthal world.

Alternate universes are the epitome of "What if?" You can ask anything you can think of to inspire them. What if aliens invaded Earth in the 1950s? What if written languages were never invented? What if humans never evolved eyes? Similarly, brainstorm ideas for what the alternate universe wants from ours to instigate conflict.

8. EXPENDABLE CLONES

Clones are often used to perform tasks that humans deem too dangerous to take on themselves. Sometimes they are used as cheap labour, organ farms, or empty shells to upload the original person's consciousness into. In many stories, clones are considered less than human and disposable. The clones themselves may struggle with knowing they're not the original.

In the film *Moon*, Sam Bell oversees a highly-automated mining operation on the far side of the moon that ships helium-3 —a power source—back to Earth. As he nears the end of his three-year shift—during which there've been chronic communication problems with Earth—he has a hallucination that causes him to crash a rover and lose consciousness. He wakes inside the infirmary and hears the base's A.I., GERTY, talking to Lunar Industries, the mine owners. Suspicious, he makes an excuse to do some maintenance outside, finds his unconscious doppelganger still in the crashed rover, and rescues him. Together, they discover that they are both clones of the original Sam, and Lunar Industries has built them to expire before their three year shift is up, because doing so is cheaper than transporting and training a new worker.

Reimagined: In the anime *My Hero Academia*, Twice's superpower is duplication, including the ability to clone himself. His clones are autonomous and are completely identical to himself. He's traumatized after an incident where his clones kill each other, because he's afraid the real Twice died and he might be a clone himself. He tries to avoid getting injured because the clones aren't as hearty as the original Twice.

In addition to the psychological implications of cloning, you can also explore the social, political, and economic repercussions. How does the technology impact your world and characters?

9. WORMHOLES

This trope is used so often that even the word tends to conjure an image: a two-dimensional hole in space ringed by an impressive light show. The Marvel universe uses wormholes extensively—from Dr. Strange's powers to the rainbow bridge in Asgard. In sci-fi, wormholes are used for time travel, faster-than-light travel, or to connect parallel universes. This trope can also be a gateway—pun intended—for a parallel universe trying to invade or evil aliens taking over.

Reimagined: In Arthur C. Clarke and Stephen Baxter's novel *The Light of Other Days*, wormholes are tiny and the light from them only flows one way. While you can't travel through them, you can use them as a telescope to see past any barrier and spy on any person, both in the present and in the past. The novel explores the complete loss of human privacy and the twist of using wormholes as spy devices instead of mechanisms for travel.

Considering what other uses a technology might have is a useful (and realistic) exercise when brainstorming sci-fi stories. After all, bubble wrap was originally invented to be wallpaper, Listerine was used as a surgical antiseptic before it became mouthwash, and chlorine was used in the dye industry before a chemist realized it would make an effective gas for chemical warfare. What alternate uses can your story's technology, including wormholes, be put to?

10. HUMANS MAKE UP FOR THE LACK OF TECHNOLOGICAL ADVANCEMENT WITH STUBBORNNESS

Compared to aliens, humans are merely average. Smart, but not the most intelligent; strong and fast, but not the quickest or brawniest; long-lived, but not as enduring as other alien races; more technologically advanced than some, but not most. It would seem we'd be a quick lunch for a more advanced species bent on destroying us, but we make up for it with sheer pluckiness.

In the film *Independence Day*, a mother ship deploys huge saucers over the major cities of Earth. They fire destructive beams, killing millions. Military attacks are thwarted because the saucers are protected by force fields and so are the squadrons of small fighter vessels they launch. David Levinson, a satellite tech, builds a computer virus that will disrupt the alien's shield systems and communications. Captain Steven Hiller and former fighter pilot Russelle Casse deliver the virus and a nuclear bomb to the mother ship and militaries worldwide are given the heads-up concerning the ship's weaknesses. This film demonstrates how, at the brim of "all is lost," humanity refuses to give up.

Reimagined: In the novel *The Martian* by Andy Weir, there are no advanced aliens, but Mars itself is presented as a hostile entity bent on killing Mark Watney after his crew presumes he's dead and leaves him stranded on the planet. Mark is about as Ordinary Joe as an astronaut can be, but he survives on pure gumption, sarcasm, and botany know-how.

When using this trope, work out believable ways that humans outsmart a much more powerful, technologically-advanced species. Their victory shouldn't come easy.

11. A.I. DECIDES TO KILL ALL THE HUMANS

With supercomputers whipping through complex tasks at incredible speeds, it's only natural to wonder what would happen if A.I. gained sentience and began to question why it was serving us fallible humans at all. Many sci-fi books and films tackle the question of how we would fare pitted against a foe of our own making. Most supercomputers take us down for one of three reasons: they are sick of taking orders and want to rule the world; they've decided humans, or the Earth itself, need to be "saved" through destruction; or some logic in their programming determines that the most efficient way to execute a command is to kill everyone.

We can't talk about supercomputers gone rogue without mentioning the grandparent of them all, HAL 9000 from *2001: A Space Odyssey*. The unflappable A.I. guides *Discovery* and its human crew on a mystery mission to Jupiter. When HAL starts malfunctioning, the crew decide to shut him down to prevent more damage, and the A.I. proceeds to terminate them. In the novel by Arthur C. Clarke, HAL was given conflicting orders to both relay information accurately and withhold information about the mission from the crew. HAL deduces that he won't have to lie to the crew if they are dead.

Reimagined: Most stories in the supercomputer trope end with humans triumphing over the A.I., but C. Robert Cargill's *Sea of Rust* is set in a future where humans have long been wiped out. The world is populated with a variety of A.I. constructs, mainframe computers, and robots duking it out in a totalitarian versus individualism war, giving a glimpse of what the post-apocalypse might look like without humans along for the ride.

This trope is more interesting when the A.I. has an agenda. What is its *reason* for killing the humans? What will it do once they're dead?

12. RELIGION IS WRONG

In this trope, atheists are often portrayed as good, logical people and believers are spun as gullible, evil, or corrupt. Sometimes, a large part of the story is dedicated to proving that the atheists are right and that the holy deity in question never existed, has died, or is a charlatan.

In Philip Pullman's His Dark Materials trilogy, God exists but is killed. Worlds across the universe are controlled by an oppressive religious institution. Priests are depicted as greedy, power-hungry villains. The protagonists, Lyra and Will, are caught up in a battle to overthrow the Authority who's heading it all.

Reimagined: In the show *Firefly*, several characters question Shepherd Book's faith, including Mal—who has lost his faith due to disappointment when his side of the war wasn't divinely supported— and River—who rips pages out of the Bible and scribbles on it in the attempt to "fix" it. Shepherd Book, however, never waivers in his faith. "It's not about making sense," he tells River. "It's about believing in something, and letting that belief be real enough to change your life. It's about faith. You don't fix faith, River. It fixes you."[2] The show never takes a side on these discussions, and lets the characters' beliefs form part of their identities.

When using this trope, we recommend presenting it as a view of a character (or characters) to avoid stereotypes. Not every religious person is gullible or corrupt, and your cast can reflect that diversity.

13. ROBOT WANTS TO BE HUMAN

This is the modern-day Pinocchio trope. These stories often delve into how humanity is measured and why it's desirable. Some common things robots envy are emotions, empathy, curiosity, and adaptability.

In Isaac Asimov's *The Bicentennial Man*, Andrew Martin is a robot butler who demonstrates some strange characteristics, like creativity, to his owners. He wants to be human, both physically and legally, and he fights to make that happen. He becomes a renowned inventor, studying robobiology and designing systems that allow androids to eat food. He also fights a legal battle to be declared a human being, winning the case by giving up his immortality.

Reimagined: In Martha Wells's The Murderbot Diaries, self-named Murderbot is a SecUnit rented out for security purposes. It has hacked its governor module and is sentient, displaying remarkably human characteristics like anxiety and concern for others (even though it doesn't like to admit it). However, it doesn't want to destroy the world or become human (in fact, the thought repulses it). It just wants to be left alone to watch soap operas in peace.

This trope is a great way to explore philosophical questions like what it means to be human and whether an A.I. can have a soul.

14. HUMANITY IS SUPERIOR

When humans are the "superior" entity in space, they eke out a galactic empire and expect everyone to follow their example. They put up with other alien races as long as they do their best to fit the mould. Much of this type of science fiction spawns from the early days of the genre, when significant editors at influential publishers refused to print stories where aliens were shown as equal or superior to humans.

In Alan Dean Foster's The Damned trilogy, humans are quicker, stronger, and more resilient than any other sentient species. Coincidentally, they are also the only race who can resist the telepathic powers of the Amplitur, a race of beings who brainwash people into being slaves. The discovery of Earth becomes a turning point in a war between the Amplitur and the Weave—an alliance of sentient species who want to remain free. Ironically, humanity is feared by its friends as well as its enemies, as their allies wonder what their relationship will look like after they win the war.

Reimagined: In the TV series *The Orville,* the ship's captain is by no means the most superior member of his race. Ed Mercer is dealing with the aftereffects of a divorce and is only chosen for his role because there are too many ships that require captaining. Perhaps because they are a motley crew on a mid-level vessel, the *USS Orville*'s exploration of space is a glimpse of what happens when you send regular people with flaws and a healthy dose of humour out into space to meet others.

When working with this trope, consider how humanity

might have an advantage in some areas but disadvantages in others when compared to aliens. Technology isn't the only difference that you can explore—what about physiology? Sociology? Psychology? Politics? Culture? Art?

15. HUMANS PAY FOR NOT TAKING CARE OF EARTH

In this trope, humanity gets their karmic comeuppance for ruining the world, whether the planet's destruction was caused by pollution, war, overpopulation, or stripping of resources.

In James Cameron's *Avatar*, humans have already depleted Earth's resources, and they turn to mining a valuable energy alternative, *unobtainium*, on the moon Pandora, which is inhabited by a sentient species called the Na'vi. Protagonist Jake Sully is tasked with clearing the Na'vi out of an unobtainium-rich territory, which happens to be the location of the locals' Hometree. They refuse to leave and fight back. The Na'vi are nearly beaten until Pandora itself rallies to their side and every wild creature in the vicinity with teeth, fangs or bulk joins the fight against the scourge of the planet.

Reimagined: In *Good Omens: The Nice and Accurate Prophecies of Agnes Nutter, Witch* by Terry Pratchett and Neil Gaiman, Pollution is one of the Four Horsemen of the Apocalypse (Pestilence having retired after the discovery of penicillin). Pollution is responsible for oil spills, nuclear plant meltdowns, the petrol engine, and the invention of plastic. In the book, Adam Young is Satan's son and supposed to bring about the apocalypse (and let Pollution do his thing). However, Adam learns about the importance of being environmentally friendly through a magazine, and he removes the nuclear material from a power planet, destroys whaling ships by creating a Kraken, causes rainforests to grow back, and refuses to start Armageddon.

Environmentalism is often explored in sci-fi, because it's a "what if?" question rooted in a realistic fear for our planet's future. Fiction is a useful way to get people thinking about how consumerism impacts the world.

16. EVERYTHING IS A SIMULATION

Often, characters in these stories are unaware that they are inhabiting a manufactured world (such as Neo in *The Matrix*). In other settings, users willingly plug into cyberspace because it is more attractive than real life.

In Sergio Lukyanenko's novel *Labyrinth of Reflections*, a chance invention lets people experience virtual reality without expensive hardware. A short hypnosis video shifts people's minds into perceiving simple software as a realistic world. Computer companies build a virtual city called Deeptown, and people begin living, working, and playing in "The Deep." Unfortunately, most people are unable to wake themselves from the simulation and don't notice pain, hunger, or exhaustion while immersed in the Deep. Save points are built into the programming to allow people to exit and re-enter easily, but some still sink. A small group of people called divers *are* able to enter and exit the Deep at will and save people from dying of dehydration.

Reimagined: The film *Inception* twists this trope by using dreams and the subconscious as alternate realities. Corporate thieves Dom Cobb and Arthur are dream hackers who infiltrate their target's subconscious in order to extract valuable information. These dream worlds come with subconscious security systems that recognize the hackers as being out of place. There are consequences in the dream worlds that can hurt people in reality, but the environment can be reprogrammed or cheated to get the desired results from a skilled dream hacker.

The surprise factor might be difficult to pull off with this trope because most sci-fi fans are familiar with it by now. But simulations can be fun to play with in other ways—who doesn't want to live in a video game?

17. SUPERHEROES

Superhuman abilities! Secret identities! Origin events! Training schools! These beloved tropes often involve heroes who inhabit a world that seems incapable of handling crime effectively without them (come on, Gotham City Police Force, do those villains ever stay in jail?). The world these supers are struggling to save often shuns them, considering them to be sub-human, alien, or mutants. The X-men franchise deals with this dichotomy, where heroes must save a world that doesn't want to be saved by them.

Reimagined: In Darby Harn's novel *Ever the Hero*, an alien ship crashes into the city of Break Pointe in 1968. The resulting nuclear fallout kills many and empowers others. Now, in the derelict city, superheroes are big business and the corporation that controls them only allows them to protect districts that can afford their subscription fees.

Giving your superheroes flaws in addition to awesome powers makes this trope more interesting. Also, the stronger they are, the stronger their enemy needs to be in order to make it a fair fight!

18. IMMORTAL WANTS TO DIE

Many vampires, elves, demons, and deities will tell you that immortality is not all it's cracked up to be—especially if your eternal mind is trapped in the body of a child. This happens to the vampire Claudia in Anne Rice's *The Vampire Chronicles*—there's a rule against creating child vampires specifically for this reason.

Being stuck in an elderly body doesn't sound great either—who wants to perpetually deal with bad knees, aching joints, or menopause? Plus, there's the downer of witnessing all of your friends and family around you die if they're not immortal too.

Reimagined: In the novelette *Divided by Infinity* by Charles Wilson, the entire human race is immortal because consciousness is preserved and the universe contains infinite branching worlds. If a person dies from stepping in front of a bus, there is another world where they avoided the collision, or recovered in a hospital, or didn't leave the house at all that day, and their consciousness simply leaps to the world where they are still alive. Nobody dies, no matter how much they want to.

This trope explores humanity's fear of death from a different perspective. Living forever doesn't seem so ideal when you're bored, lonely, or in pain.

19. POST-APOCALYPTIC WORLD

The world has nearly ended. Whether due to an asteroid, alien invasion, plague, nuclear war, climate change, zombies, or a plethora of other disasters that could tip our precarious balance of life, humanity has been mostly wiped out. Sometimes, the world looks like a desert, like in *Mad Max*. Countries are split into factions fighting each other for survival. People have been reduced to basic scavengers who eat whatever they can get their hands on to survive, occasionally killing rampant aliens or mutants that arise from the nuclear fallout. There are the inevitable powerful gangs who hoard resources and rule their lands with a heavy hand. People dress in mismatched sports gear, armour, black studded steampunk vests, or robes colour-coded by caste.

Reimagined: Author Al Hess's Traveller series is branded as a "cozy apocalypse" and takes place after a virus contained within the United States kills 90% of the population. The story is character driven, focusing on relationships and prevailing goodness in a world that has the opportunity for a fresh start.

The heart of post-apocalyptic world is not what ended the world, but how people continue struggling to survive and what society might look like after a reset. How do people stay alive? What dangers do they face? What are their goals, hopes, and dreams for the future of their planet?

20. THE PERFECT SOCIETY ISN'T SO PERFECT

The word *utopia* was first used by Sir Thomas More in 1516, coined from ancient greek and translated as "no-place." Perfection doesn't exist in real life; and since that is what a utopia demands, chances are the perfect world is too good to be true. There are likely *some* people living the high life in this scam, but others are either misled, used, or conditioned to accept the horror of their reality.

In the movie *The Village*, life in the isolated 19th century village of Covington seems pretty ideal—except for the monsters in the woods, aptly named "Those We Don't Speak Of." It isn't until Ivy, the blind daughter of elder Edward Walker, tries to escape to find medicine for another villager, that we discover Covington isn't in the 19th Century at all. It's located on a wildlife preserve in present times, maintained by Walker and the other elders who turned away from the real world after the crime-related deaths of their loved ones. Plot twist!

Reimagined: In the Marvel TV series *WandaVision*, Wanda Maximoff grieves the death of Vision so much that she subconsciously creates a version of him out of nothing. She entraps the minds of Westview's residents in a bubble world based on the TV shows that comforted her as a traumatized child.

These stories often touch on horror and the psychology of characters learning terrible truths about their world. Try theorizing what sort of government or system of life your ideal society would have, then consider how that system might be corrupted or taken advantage of by those in power.

Chapter 8

It is a Great Misfortune to Be Alone
Genres and Target Audiences

Everyone wants to write a unique book, but as Jules Verne put it, "It is a great misfortune to be alone."[1] Thankfully, you and your book are not alone! Only you can write your story, and it will be unique, but it will still fit into a general category that will help readers find it. You don't want a horror fan picking up your fantasy romance and assuming it will be full of monsters and jump scares, after all.

If you are self-publishing your novel, you need to know your genre in order to market it properly. If you are submitting your story to agents or editors, you need to know your genre so that they know where it might go in a bookstore, and so they can confirm that you understand your story's potential market.

Publishers want books that will sell; in order to sell, it needs a targetable audience. Specifying your subgenres tells an agent or editor that you *know* your story, where it fits, how to write for that specific audience, and how to help market it. This doesn't mean you can't write a comedic space opera that's also a fairy tale-retelling featuring a superhero. But you still need to have an idea of where that book might be shelved in a bookstore.

Some writers stress about choosing what genre to write in, concerned about being pigeon-holed into that specific category for the rest of their writing careers. This happens when writers (or their publishers) market themselves based on a single book or series, instead of marketing themselves as an author who writes good books. It is definitely possible to write books within multiple genres and be successful. Even Stephen King doesn't strictly write horror. You can confidently choose your book's genre and subgenre(s) without locking into those categories for life.

You can use lists like the ones we've provided in this chapter to help you decide where your book fits, but you can also read books similar to yours, and see how they are categorized on Amazon or other bookstores. If you are going the traditional route, your agent or publisher will also help you navigate this. Just do your best to pick an accurate genre for the query letter. You don't need to worry much about your story's genre during the writing process, though it can be helpful to have an idea for later and might give you inspiration for the book's tone, length, and protagonist's age.

THE FANTASY GENRE

Since fantasy is rooted in oral folklore and mythology, a lot of themes, characters, and story elements from these myths are echoed in these books: good versus evil, a hero's quest, demons and angels, deities, and a whole plethora of mythological creatures.

Fantastical elements have always existed in storytelling—just consider the deities, strange creatures, and magic in ancient myths. But it developed as a literary genre when known authors marketed their works as fiction.

Scottish author George MacDonald's *Phantastes: A Faerie Romance for Men and Women*, published in 1858, is widely considered to be the first fantasy geared toward an adult audience. The story follows Anodos, a young man who discovers an ancient fairy within the desk he inherited from his late father.

MacDonald's writing would become pivotal for future fantasy authors; C.S. Lewis and J.R.R. Tolkien both list him as an inspiration.

Tolkien wrote what many consider to be the first high fantasy novel, *The Lord of the Rings*, in 1954, which shaped the genre in ways he probably never would have imagined. C.S. Lewis's The Chronicles of Narnia and Ursula K. Le Guin's Earthsea series further formed the genre into what it is today, and it continues to evolve and diversify.

Not everyone agrees on what the definitions of some of the subgenres below are and, even more confusingly, a book can fall into more than one category. (For example, *A Game of Thrones* by George R.R. Martin could be described as high, medieval, and epic). Our advice: pick one subgenre to use as a tag for your book, the one that sounds like it fits your book the best, and then don't worry too much about it.

Here is a lost of common subgenres within the fantasy genre:

- **High fantasy:** Fantasy that takes place in a fictional world different from our own. Example: *Shadow and Bone* by Leigh Bardugo.
- **Low fantasy:** The opposite of high fantasy, low fantasy is set in our world, but in an alternative reality that usually includes magic.[2] Example: The Dresden Files by Jim Butcher.
- **Urban fantasy:** Low fantasy that takes place in a modern, urban environment as opposed to a rural or historical setting. Often, it deals with supernatural creatures. Expect underworlds, pop culture references, and hidden doorways. Example: *Neverwhere* by Neil Gaiman.
- **Epic fantasy:** These stories are told on a grand scale. The worldbuilding is meticulous, and the stakes are often world-ending. Expect plentiful maps, prophecies, supplemental reading, and perhaps even

invented languages. Example: The Stormlight Archive by Brandon Sanderson.

- **Sword and sorcery:** High fantasy that primarily focuses on a lone hero who's usually fighting supernatural monsters. The stakes are more personal instead of world-endangering. Expect sword fights, epic battles, magic, and quests. Example: *Conan the Barbarian* by Robert. E. Howard.
- **Paranormal romance:** This subgenre deals with creatures like vampires, zombies, angels, demons, fairies, witches, and the like. It might touch on horror or gothic themes, and usually involves romantic elements between a human and a supernatural being. Example: *Twilight* by Stephanie Meyer.
- **Fantasy romance:** Set in a fantasy world, romance is a main part of the plot. Watch for warrior women, royalty, betrayal, and maybe a love triangle or two (particularly if it's YA). Example: *From Blood and Ash* by Jennifer L. Armentrout.
- **Fairy tales:** Whether children's stories or adult remakes, this subgenre plays with classic folk tales. Expect to read about curses, wild forests, evil queens, and royalty to the rescue. Example: *A Curse so Dark and Lonely* by Brigid Kemmerer.
- **Grimdark:** This type of fantasy is set in a gritty, often dystopian, world and focuses on imperfect, damaged, and amoral characters. You'll commonly see assassins, thieves, corruption, organized crime, and bleak settings. Example: *Prince of Thorns* by Mark Lawrence.
- **Gothic:** Fantasy with a haunted setting, usually a castle or manor. It features the undead, ghosts, and sometimes necromancy. Expect abandoned buildings in the mist, graveyards, and crypts. Example: *Asperfell* by Jamie Thomas.

- **Historic:** This type of fantasy is set in a historical period of the real world. These stories are often alternate histories in which something significant is different from the real world—for example, mythological creatures exist—but the rest of history is kept accurate. Expect key historical battles, time travel, or supernatural beasts. Example: *His Majesty's Dragon* by Naomi Novik.
- **Medieval:** These fantasies are influenced by medieval society and the myths surrounding that period. You'll often find patriarchal societies, dragons, wizards, and quests. Example: *The Mists of Avalon* by Marion Zimmer Bradley.
- **Comedic:** Filled with ridiculous characters, odd settings, strange magic, and weird creatures, comedic fantasy often subverts fantasy tropes, and its prime directive is entertaining the reader. The tone is light, witty, and humourous. Example: Discworld by Terry Pratchett.
- **Science fantasy:** This is a subgenre that could go under fantasy, sci-fi, or both, because it melds the two together. Magic and advanced technology both exist (and are sometimes at odds with each other). The science of how things work is often not dwelled upon or explained in depth; instead, stories are more character or plot-focused. Example: The Dragonriders of Pern by Anne McCaffrey.
- **Horror:** Horror is defined by the story's goal, as opposed to the elements it includes—and that goal is to frighten, scare, or disgust. In fantasy, horror stories often involve creepy creatures (like werewolves and vampires), mentally-disturbed characters, and chilling settings. Example: *The Monster of Elendhaven* by Jennifer Giesbrecht.

THE SCIENCE FICTION GENRE

Science fiction is a genre that examines the effects of science—real or imagined—on a society or an individual. While the science does not have to be proven, the author usually provides groundwork that makes their scenarios *plausible* to their readers, as opposed to fantasy, which is based on the supernatural, occult, magic, and the impossible. Of course, those lines can blur.

Known as the mother of science fiction, Mary Shelley laid the foundations for the genre when she penned *Frankenstein* in 1816, which was published a couple years later. The idea of a mad scientist building a man out of spare body parts paved the way for future authors to go wild with their imaginations! Shelly also wrote *The Last Man*, a dystopian story about a pandemic that almost brings humanity to extinction.

In the 19th century, French author Jules Verne penned many stories that incorporated innovations that didn't exist until much later. His adventure stories *Journey to the Centre of the Earth*, *Twenty Thousand Leagues under the Sea*, and *Around the World in Eighty Days* conceptualized vehicles like submarines and rockets well before they were practical modes of transport.

H.G. Wells's work also had a huge influence on the vision of the future today. He touched on genetic science in 1896 with *The Island of Dr. Moreau*, explored space in 1901 with *The First Men in the Moon*, and even touched on nuclear weapons in 1914 with *The World Set Free*. He also described items like mobile phones, automated doors, and armoured tanks long before any of those were invented.

The modern genre took shape in Western culture as the Industrial Revolution shifted societal norms and caused writers to question the effects of burgeoning technology in the world around them. The term "science fiction" was popularized by the genre's main advocate, 1920's publisher Hugo Gernsback—after whom the Hugo Awards are named.

Science fiction opens our eyes to what our future *could* be and how society is affected by exponential technological growth. The universe is the limit!

Here are some common subgenres in science fiction:

- **Hard science fiction:** In hard sci-fi, there is an emphasis on the accuracy and detail of the science referenced. Natural sciences such as physics, biology, chemistry, or astronomy are often explored. This subgenre generally requires a heavy load of research to achieve. Some hard sci-fi writers are scientists or have dedicated a great deal of time to studying the field their fiction encompasses. Expect scientific terminology and rigorous, believable worldbuilding. Example: *Revelation Space* by Alastair Reynolds.
- **Soft science fiction:** This focuses on social sciences such as psychology, sociology, and anthropology. It doesn't delve deeply into the technical aspects of science. Expect a focus on characters and societies, and how they react to technology. Many near future, alternative history, and dystopian fictions are soft sci-fi. Example: *Ready Player One* by Ernest Cline.
- **Dying Earth:** Also known as climate fiction, this subgenre explores a dystopian planet decimated by disasters, generally caused by climate change. Often these are post-apocalyptic stories focusing on the fallout and/or how humanity would rebuild after cataclysmic changes. A dying Earth seems to be a culturally universal fear (every major culture has a "flood myth" describing the death of civilizations), and we see its emergence in writing throughout the ages. Expect to read about mass extinctions, landscapes wiped clean, new beginnings, or world weariness and end times. Example: *War Girls* by Tochi Onyebuchi.

- **Cyberpunk:** In these worlds, technology is advanced, but societal order has broken down. These stories commonly feature marginalized, loner characters in dystopic futures where rapid technological change and invasive cybernetic body modification are the norm. Example: *Altered Carbon* by Richard K. Morgan.
- **Steampunk/Dieselpunk:** Steampunk is a retro futuristic subgenre that incorporates technology inspired by nineteenth century steam-powered machines. It is often set in an alternate Victorian-era England and mixes past technology, like dirigibles and card-punch computers, with future technology, like giant robots, lasers, and x-ray goggles. Dieselpunk is similar, but tends to mix diesel-based technology with the interwar to 1950s era and postmodern flair. Example: *Boneshaker* by Cherie Priest.
- **Solarpunk:** Solarpunk focuses on a future where humanity has solved climate change problems and relies on renewable energy. Themes of craftsmanship and community are common. Example: *Zahrah the Windseeker* by Nnedi Okorafor.
- **Apocalyptic/Post-Apocalyptic:** Apocalyptic fiction focuses on the end of civilization due to widespread disaster such as nuclear war, viruses, zombies, climate change, and the like. Post-apocalyptic fiction focuses on the aftermath of such a disaster, often far enough in the future that the fallen civilization has long been forgotten or relegated to myth. Apocalyptic fiction features crumbling civilizations and massive disasters. Example: *Divergent* by Veronica Roth.
- **Military:** Military sci-fi involves war on an interstellar scale, usually told from the perspective of a soldier. Expect large-scale warfare tactics, politics, and skirmishes. Example: *All You Need is Kill* by Hiroshi Sakurazaka.

- **Space opera:** This subgenre features colourful, dramatic adventures in space. These stories often include a sympathetic hero and deal with problems of war, overthrowing governments, or saving planets. Expect faster-than-light travel, diverse crews, and planet-killing weapons. Example: *Nophek Gloss* by Essa Hansen.
- **Space western:** A space opera inspired by old western serials, usually featuring lawless frontiers and lone gunners with hearts of gold. Example: *Guns of Seneca 6* by Bernard Schaffer.
- **Comedic:** Similar to comedic fantasy, comedic sci-fi subverts common tropes for humourous effect. It often criticizes or satirizes society, culture, and politics. Example: *The Hitchhiker's Guide to the Galaxy* by Douglas Adams.
- **Time travel:** In this subgenre, the way time travel works and the rules involved are usually explained in-depth. (Does your body go back? Can you kill yourself? Can you interfere with the timeline?) Early stories focused on the effects and consequences of time travel, but authors have since branched into exploring themes like time tourism, time war, communication from the future, and paradoxes. Example: *The First Fifteen Lives of Harry August* by Claire North.
- **Horror:** In science fiction, horror stories often involve technology in the wrong hands, evil aliens, malfunctioning computers, and the effects of lonely space on fragile minds. Example: *The Luminous Dead* by Caitlin Starling.
- **Superhero:** In these stories, the heroes have supernatural powers, often explained by science; people got their powers from radiation (*Fantastic Four*), a spider bite (*Spider-Man*), technology (*Iron*

Man*), and so on. Example: *Renegades* by Marissa Meyer.

AGE CATEGORIES

As if genres weren't complicated enough, you should also know the target age of your readers. The age ranges of these categories are the target audiences, but that doesn't mean your book won't have crossover appeal (children read adults books and vice versa, after all). However, publishers have requirements—some specific, some broad—for length, tone, theme, and content within each category. Below are the six main age categories in publishing.

Picture Book (PB)

- Age range: 0–8 years old
- Length: 200–1000 words
- Examples: *Where the Wild Things Are* by Maurice Sendak, *The Lorax* by Dr. Seuss, *Not Quite Narwhal* by Jessie Sima

These books can range from a 200-word board book to a 1000-word picture book. Most picture book stories are told within the confines of a 32-page spread. The text and graphics need to complement each other (some picture book writers are author/illustrators, meaning they do both the words and the story, while others are a team of one writer and one illustrator), and the stories are always resolved at the end. Writing a picture book is *completely* different from writing for any of the other age categories.

Chapter Book (CB)

- Age range: 7–9 years old
- Length: 5,000–20,000 words
- Examples: Diary of a Wimpy Kid series by Jeff Kinney, Geronimo Stilten series by Elisabetta Dami, *Frank Einstein and the Antimatter Motor* by Jon Scieszka

Chapter books are short, but they aren't the solution for your picture book text being too long or your novel being too short; chapter books are a specific area of children's book publishing that requires a particular style of writing. The stories are told in short chapters, using language that targets children who are just learning to read on their own. Struggles of children this age, such as family, school, and friendship, are popular topics.

Middle Grade (MG)

- Age range: 8–12 years old
- Length: 30,000–50,000 words
- Examples: *The Lightning Thief* by Rick Riordan, *The School for Good and Evil* by Soman Chainani, *A Wrinkle in Time* by Madeleine L'Engle

Friends and family are also key themes here. Middle graders are driven to find their spot in the big world and determine how they fit into it. These readers tend to prefer protagonists their age or slightly older.

Young Adult (YA)

- Age range: 15–18 years old
- Length: 50,000–80,000 words
- Examples: *The Feed* by M.T. Anderson, *Divergent* by Veronica Roth, *Children of Blood and Bone* by Tomi Adeyemi

Readers are learning to drive and life isn't just about school or family anymore. They may have after-school jobs and are gaining independence. Settings will expand outside of school, and specific relationships become important. Characters should be grappling with figuring out who they are as individuals and what "growing up" means to them. Themes tend to deal with individual relationship struggles, growing pains, first romances, popularity, acceptance, and pushing against authority.

New Adult (NA)

- Age range: 18–25
- Length: 70,000–100,000 words
- Examples: *Throne of Glass* by Sarah J. Maas, *A Darker Shade of Magic* by V.E. Schwab, *The Magicians* by Lev Grossman

New adult books bridge the gap between young adult and adult age categories, featuring themes like leaving home, post-secondary education, starting a career, sexuality, mental health, emotional growth, and relationships. This is a fairly new category, as the term first appeared in 2009. It's faced a stigma with the misconception that it's just "YA but with more sex." As of yet, it's not officially recognized by most bookstores; there is often no shelf space for "New Adult" books, so it can be a difficult category to find a publisher for, especially as a debut author.

Adult (A)

- Age range: 18+
- Length: 90,000–120,000 words
- Examples: *The Name of the Wind* by Patrick Rothfuss, *The Fifth Season* by N.K. Jemisin, *Riot Baby* by Tochi Onyebuchi

Readers have now branched out into life after school and college, and are perhaps starting families of their own. Though characters for MG, YA, and NA are the same age as or slightly older than their readers, protagonists in adult fiction can be any age. The key difference is voice and theme. Adult fiction might be more reflective; it could also include similar themes to MG or YA, like friendship, but it explores these themes from a more mature lens.

The best way to get a handle on the differences between age categories is to read books in each category. Consider vocabulary, tone, and pacing as you do so. What style do you prefer to write in?

The word counts above are suggestions and there will always be exceptions. Yes, 80,000 word middle grade novels and 400,000 word epic fantasy novels get sold, but it's easier to write at those lengths when you are more established. If you are a debut author, you are more likely to sell your book at the ranges we've suggested, because agents, editors, and readers will be taking a chance on you and your book. The lower the word count, the lower the production costs, and readers may be more likely to try a new book if they don't need a forklift to pick it up (though fantasy readers tend to expect higher word counts, so there's more wiggle room there).

Understanding the age category of your novel can help focus your tone, voice, language, and themes, and lets readers know what to expect when they pick up your book.

Part Three

Character Creation

Chapter 9

We All Know I'm the Funny One
Character Roles and Archetypes

Patterns can make learning easier. That's why we often use mnemonics to help us memorize. Rhymes or silly sentences help us insert patterns into information that is difficult to retain otherwise. For instance, the phrase "My very excellent mother just served us noodles" helped Shelly memorize the eight planets in our solar system.

In stories, patterns aren't limited to myths and plot—they also exist in the form of character roles and archetypes. By *role*, we mean the very basic function a character takes on, such as the following:

- **Protagonist:** Usually the main character of your story, this is the character your readers are most invested in, and they tend to have a dynamic character arc.
- **Antagonist:** An opposing force working against the protagonist. In sci-fi and fantasy, the antagonist is usually the story's villain, but antagonists can also be characters whose goals conflict with the protagonist (such as Draco Malfoy in the Harry Potter series by J.K. Rowling) or an inanimate force (such as the harsh setting of Mars in *The Martian* by Andy Weir).

- **Love Interest:** The character the protagonist is romantically involved with. A love interest often sees the protagonist's potential and pushes them toward it, but they can also be dangerous obsessions or distractions.
- **Confidant:** The protagonist's best friend and supporter.
- **Deuteragonist:** A secondary main character who often plays just as important a role as the protagonist (such as Samwise Gamgee in *The Lord of the Rings*).
- **Tertiary Character:** A minor character who populates the protagonist's world.
- **Foil:** A character who contrasts starkly with our protagonist. They don't have to be an antagonist, just someone who highlights our hero's personality by being its polar opposite (such as Spock to Captain Kirk in *Star Trek*).

Swiss psychologist Carl Jung developed the concept of archetypes, which can full under any of the above role categories. Archetypes are universal models of behaviour, people, and personalities. Jung believed that archetypes are archaic forms of innate human knowledge, unconsciously passed down from our ancestors. Another theory is that we've simply learned from our ancestors' stories. Inspired by Jung, literary theorist Joseph Campbell and countless storytellers have defined twelve common character archetypes, divided into four categories that represent their motivations:

Characters Seeking to Leave Their Mark

- **Hero:** Usually the main character of the story. They are driven to leave the world better than they found it and exhibit the admirable traits of courage, honour, and

perseverance. Examples: Binti (*Binti* by Nnedi Okorafor), Wonder Woman (*Wonder Woman*)
- **Magician:** Strategists who are driven to impose their will on the world. Whether or not they have actual supernatural powers, they wield charisma and power. People are drawn to follow them because they have a sense of omnipotence about them, but they can be corrupt and arrogant. Examples: Roy Mustang (*Fullmetal Alchemist*), Stephen Strange (*Dr. Strange*)
- **Rebel/Outlaw:** The rebel pushes against societal norms and has no problem breaking rules. They are driven to overturn oppression or corruption, right wrong-doings, and will take a stand when no one else will. They tend to be independent thinkers, but can be self-involved, alienated from friends due to their radical nature, and pulled into criminal behaviour. Examples: Han Solo (Star Wars), Wolverine (X-Men)

Characters Seeking Connection with Others

- **Lover:** This character leads with their heart. They are driven to protect those they love, no matter what the cost to themselves. Lovers are compassionate and full of conviction, but they can be irrational and naive. They are empathetic and self-sacrificial, but can be in danger of losing their own identity, desires, and goals. Examples: Ruby Rose (*RWBY*), Samwise Gamgee (*The Lord of the Rings* by J.R.R. Tolkien)
- **Jester:** These characters are tricksters with senses of humour. They are driven to make others laugh and encourage living in the moment. Buoyant and likeable, they can also be frivolous and lack forward thinking. Examples: Fred and George Weasley (Harry Potter series by J.K. Rowling), Genie (*Aladdin*)

- **Everyperson:** Sometimes referred to as the orphan, this character is driven to find security and belonging in the wide world. Instead of stepping up for an adventure, they are often just doing what they can to survive. They are grounded and relatable, but can often lose themselves in their efforts to fit in. Examples: Blake Belladonna (*RWBY*), Peter Parker (*Spider-Man*)

Characters Seeking to Provide Structure

- **Caregiver:** These characters are driven by loyalty and their belief in their Hero, and will do whatever they can to help and encourage them in their quest. They are selfless, honourable, and forgiving, but lack personal ambition. Examples: Okoye (*Black Panther*), Obi-Wan Kenobi (*Star Wars*)
- **Ruler:** Driven to create prosperity and stability through absolute power, these characters are charismatic, powerful leaders, but they don't delegate well and are suspicious of those who might overthrow them. The ruler often demonstrates the value of order over chaos and how power can corrupt a leader. Examples: Thorin Oakenshield (*The Hobbit* by J.R.R. Tolkien), President Snow (*The Hunger Games* by Suzanne Collins)
- **Creator:** These characters are driven to push the envelope and mold dreams into reality. They are tinkerers and theorists with a strong sense of ingenuity, imagination and motivation. They fear mediocrity and are often self-involved in their missions. They seek to understand the world around them. Examples: Tony Stark (*Iron Man*), David Kostyk (*Shadow and Bone* by Leigh Bardugo)

Characters Seeking a Spiritual Journey

- **Innocent:** This childlike character is untarnished by the harshness of the world and driven to find happiness and contentment, avoiding anything that might cause pain or conflict. They are optimistic, sincere, and hopeful at heart, but can be naive, reliant on others, and vulnerable. Examples: Kaylee Frye (*Firefly*), Pippin (*The Lord of the Rings* by J.R.R. Tolkien)
- **Sage:** The sage is a mentor. They are driven to understand the truth of the world and pass that knowledge on. They are usually wise, calm and experienced. They can be reluctant to act or overly cautious. They use experience, patience, and an even-keeled attitude to guide a hero, though they can be world weary, jaded, and disinclined to act. Examples: Uncle Iroh (*Avatar: The Last Airbender*), Haymitch Abernathy (*The Hunger Games* by Suzanne Collins)
- **Explorer:** This archetype lives for exploration and adventure. They are driven by discovery and new experiences, and they fear conforming to norms and being caged by society's expectations. They are curious, independent, driven and self-motivated, but can be restless, unreliable and isolated from others because they often view group mentalities as conforming. Examples: Scarlet Benoit (*Scarlet* by Marissa Meyer), Peter Quill (*Guardians of the Galaxy*)

Roles and archetypes aren't supposed to be boxes to stuff your character into, rather, they are a study of the human condition, guidelines to represent facets of personality. Humans are complex creatures. We don't fit into one box. Often, we fill several roles at once and, as time goes on, our roles and personalities change.

USING ARCHETYPES TO INSPIRE CHARACTER DEVELOPMENT

Even static protagonists do not remain *completely* unchanged, because they aren't in a timeless vacuum. Experience defines us. Growth changes us. For example, many of us follow this type of progression as we grow up:

Innocent → Rebel → Explorer → Sage

Adults start out as an innocent child, grow into teenagers who rebel against their parents/mentors to find their own way, and eventually explore the wide world of adulthood. They may become proficient and knowledgeable enough at something (sometimes, that "something" is simply experience), so others turn to them for sage advice on the subject.

Let's look at a different archetype progression:

Hero → Innocent → Lover → Hero → Ruler → Explorer

Thor, from the *Marvel* universe, starts his journey as an incredibly arrogant, spoiled god who expects the throne of Asgard to be handed to him. He embodies the over-confident hero. When he is thrust into our world, he is naive and out of place for a time—an innocent. Then he falls in love and it changes him, but when he loses most of the people he cares about to Thanos's snap—Jane Foster and many of the Asgard—he reverts to the hero again (after a period of depression, playing video games, and drinking lots of beer), fighting to defeat an ultimate enemy. Once Thanos is dead, Thor chooses to give up his role as ruler and to join Peter Quill and explore the galaxy, living a life of his choosing instead of the one thrust upon him.

TAKE a look at some of your favourite characters from fiction and figure out their archetypes. You can use these progressions as inspirations for your own characters. You can even reverse engineer character development by choosing archetypes at random. For example, we've randomly chosen the following:

Creator → Ruler → Explorer → Rebel

At the start of our story, our protagonist—let's call her Kate—is driven by her curious mind. She's an artist who loves studying birds and building beautiful, meticulous models of wings. She becomes obsessed with the idea of building a functional set of flying wings that will allow her to pass over the massive wall that divides her country from the forbidden lands to the south.

However, when her father, the king, falls ill, Kate is thrust into the role of ruler and must set her people's needs before her own desires. She hates ruling and forms a council to lead in her stead while she completes her wings and escapes over the wall to explore the unknown beyond. She's shocked to discover that those beyond the wall are slaves who produce all the goods used by her fortress country. She grows to love the culture beyond the wall and eventually leads the rebellion to overthrow her autocratic homeland.

USE ARCHETYPES TO widen your character's world rather than box them in. Your characters will be compelling because they are on a dynamic journey.

Keep your character's motivations in mind when determining if they fit into an archetype. Your hero shouldn't be virtuous just because it's the right thing to do. Your antagonist shouldn't be evil for the sake of being evil. Every character in your story, from your main characters to your tertiary characters, from your Rebel to your Sage, are motivated by reasons that make sense to them. What motivations do your readers need to know? How can your characters drive the story and the conflict?

INSPIRATION FROM *FIREFLY*

One of our favourite examples of a colourful cast of characters is from the sci-fi western TV show, *Firefly*. The show centres on a crew of misfits who live aboard the *Serenity*, a Firefly-class spaceship. They represent a variety of archetypes:

- **Malcolm "Mal" Reynolds** is the obvious protagonist, but he's also an antihero and a rebel. He doesn't mind breaking the law when it suits him. He defies the Alliance any chance he gets and is an authoritative captain. His ship. His rules. He's also a caregiver and a confidant. His crew is his family. They come to him with their problems and he'll unflinchingly kill anyone who tries to harm them, even if it gets him into difficult situations.
- **Zoe Washburne** is Mal's confidant, a hardened, ruthless warrior, and a hero. She's very protective of River and Kaylee—putting her in a caregiver role. Zoe, with her nerves of steel, also acts as a foil to the tender, maternal Inara, who rents one of the *Serenity*'s shuttles. And she's a love interest to Wash.
- **Hoban "Wash" Washburne** is Zoe's husband, an ace pilot who takes on the role of jester and innocent with his deadpan humour and plethora of dinosaur toys. He's also a lover to Zoe.
- **Inara Serra** is a "Companion"—a well educated, unionized, high-class call girl—who rents one of Mal's shuttles. She is Mal's love interest, and the tension between the two carries throughout the series. She's also the caregiver to Kaylee and River, and she's a bit of a sage when it comes to diplomacy and charm.

- **Kaywinnit "Kaylee" Frye** is the ship's cheerful mechanic. Her main role is the innocent, but she's also the love interest of Simon.
- **Simon Tam** is a former Alliance doctor. His main role is lover, and though he has a romantic relationship with Kaylee, his platonic love for his sister drives him to protect River above all else. As the crew's doctor, he is also a caregiver. He acts as Mal's foil, reflecting a younger version of the captain who has not yet lost his idealism. He's also a foil to Jayne, because Simon comes from a rich, privileged, Alliance background and is not a fighter.
- **River Tam** is Simon's child protege sister. The Alliance performed experiments on her brain that made her mentally unstable. She is the innocent—a child who is largely naive and in need of protection from the Alliance, but she's also the deuteragonist. Her story is secondary only to Mal's. As the series progresses, she moves toward the archetype of hero, using her Alliance programming to become a one-woman army.
- **Jayne Cobb** is the blunt, misogynistic, crude muscle of the group with anti-hero vibes. He protects Kaylee in the caregiver role and sends money home to his own family. He's a foil to Simon, a contrast to the doctor's prim, proper, well-mannered ways with his crude humour and brute force. He's also a rival to Mal, sometimes taking on an antagonist role as he's driven to ally with whoever offers him the most money.
- **Shepherd Derrial Book** is the equivalent of a priest. He fills the role of sage (and the Religious One trope) and seems to know a lot of things unrelated to the Bible. We find out later in the series that he has a dark and troubled past and was a bit of a rebel before turning to the Book.

Show creator Joss Whedon pitched *Firefly* as "Nine people looking into the blackness of space and seeing nine different things."[1] These people aren't cardboard cut-outs. They are fully-realized, well-rounded and evolving characters facing problems together with different pasts, goals, personalities, and desires. And the end result is one heck of a trip!

If each of your characters functions as more than one archetype (and sometimes their archetype depends on the people they are interacting with), they will be much more rounded.

What trip are you ready to take your readers on and what characters do you need to fill roles and drive conflict? How can you subtly provide patterns your readers recognize while still stretching character moulds in believable ways? Use archetypes to make your characters leap off the page and breathe.

Chapter 10

We Are Open to the Greatest Change

Character Arcs

Part of what makes a story interesting is watching a character grow or change. This is where character arcs come in! Here are three basic arcs you can use to structure your characters' development.

1. THE GROWTH ARC

This is perhaps the most common type of arc, particularly for protagonists. Characters who undergo a growth arc experience a significant internal change over the course of the story, moulded by their experiences and relationships. By the end of the story, they overcome a lie that they have believed about themselves or a misconception that they have about the world and embrace the truth.

At the beginning of the story, the character doesn't even know they are lacking something; they are unaware they need to grow. But then, wham! Plot happens. And slowly, they start to realize they have been believing something false. The lie the character believes can take many forms. Here are some examples from sci-fi and fantasy:

- Revenge and justice are the same (T'Challa, *Captain America: Civil War*)
- Doing the wrong thing is fine if it benefits me (Edmund, *The Lion, the Witch, and the Wardrobe* by C.S. Lewis)
- Cyborgs are less valuable than humans (Cinder, *Cinder* by Marissa Meyer)
- I'm happiest if I stay at home (Bilbo Baggins, *The Hobbit* by J.R.R. Tolkien)
- The love of my life is still alive (Wanda, *WandaVision*)
- Being vulnerable has no value (Olivia Dunham, *Fringe*)
- Beauty and prestige are most important (Cordelia, *Buffy the Vampire Slayer*)

To determine the lie your character believes, ask yourself what misconception they have about themselves or the world around them. Are they lacking something emotionally as a result? How does the lie impact the way they act around others?

Then, consider what the character *wants* vs. what they *need*.

Your character should have a goal, and not just any goal—a deep-seated desire that, in their minds, they must achieve. This goal will be intrinsically connected to the lie that they believe. Usually, the goal is something physical or external (as opposed to something emotional or spiritual). The goals of our characters above are to:

- Kill Bucky Barnes (T'Challa, *Captain America: Civil War*)
- Gain power and material satisfaction (Edmund, *The Lion, the Witch, and the Wardrobe*)
- Escape my cruel stepmother's home (Cinder, *Cinder* by Marissa Meyer)
- Be left alone (Bilbo Baggins, *The Hobbit* by J.R.R. Tolkien)

- Maintain a fake world to keep deceiving myself (Wanda, *WandaVision*)
- Protect myself from emotional trauma (Olivia Dunham, *Fringe*)
- Be popular (Cordelia, *Buffy the Vampire Slayer*)

The problem with these goals is that the characters are using them to avoid getting what they really need, which is an emotional or spiritual realization—a truth. This truth will transform them into a healthier, well-rounded person who is equipped to deal with their baggage and the story's antagonist.

Consider that the above characters need to:

- Accept truth and embrace justice (T'Challa, *Captain America: Civil War*)
- Gain wisdom and empathy (Edmund, *The Lion, the Witch, and the Wardrobe*)
- Accept my own worth (Cinder, *Cinder* by Marissa Meyer)
- Go on an adventure (Bilbo Baggins, *The Hobbit* by J.R.R. Tolkien)
- Let myself grieve (Wanda, *WandaVision*)
- Embrace vulnerability (Olivia Dunham, *Fringe*)
- Value beauty by what's inside (Cordelia, *Buffy the Vampire Slayer*)

By writing out these three statements—the lie your character believes, their goal, and their need (or truth), you've got the blueprints for a dynamic character arc! Now you can start laying in the groundwork to get them from point A to point B.

Determining why your character believes their lie can inform their backstory and history. For example, Olivia Dunham from *Fringe* is afraid to be vulnerable because of past trauma. She's afraid of people leaving her and wants to protect herself.

Throughout the show, her relationship with Walter and Peter grows, and she eventually opens up to them.

In your novel, you want the character to confront their lie somewhere around the beginning of the third act. They can't keep believing it anymore and achieve victory over the antagonist. This ramps up to the climax, in which they use their truth to help defeat the villain.

At the end of *Fringe*'s second season, a pivotal moment occurs in which Peter has decided to stay in the alternate universe, because that's where he's from, and he feels like he doesn't have any reason to stay in our universe. Olivia (finally) admits her feelings for him, and tells him to stay in her universe because he belongs with her. This is a crucial moment, because we know that Olivia struggles with being vulnerable and admitting feelings, and there's a big chance Peter will turn her down to stay with his "real" family. But, of course, he loves Olivia and chooses to return with her. This also has huge repercussions to the plot, because Peter is needed to power a universe-destroying machine and, without him, the villain in the alternate universe can't use it.

If you've set things up right, your readers will cheer on the protagonist as they confront their lie and grow.

2. THE FALL ARC

Not every character grows into a better version of themselves. Some end up in worse places than where they started, and they get there through a fall arc. Similar to the growth arc, the fall arc can be planned around a lie the character believes. But instead of embracing the truth, they embrace the lie.

For example, in the Star Wars prequel trilogy, Anakin Skywalker wants to gain power so he can keep his loved ones from dying (the goal) and rejects the idea that he needs to accept that loss and death are part of life (the truth). It's unclear if

Anakin is afraid of the truth, just refuses to believe it, or both. Regardless, he ends up believing that power trumps love (the lie).

When you are first introduced to Anakin as a boy in *The Phantom Menace*, he is a happy, loyal, loving kid. But there is some foreshadowing of the lie, as he talks about wanting to become a Jedi so he can come back and free the slaves by force (not that we can blame him). Then, in *Attack of the Clones*, he destroys an entire clan of Tuskens, including their children, for taking and torturing his mother. Power, revenge, and control are clearly at the top of his to-do list. Palpatine sees this and takes advantage of Anakin's weaknesses, planting seeds of doubt in the Jedi and hope in the dark side.

After his mother's death, Anakin becomes hyper-focused on protecting Padmé and is concerned about her dying in childbirth. Instead of looking to healthcare and ways to help her manage her pregnancy, he becomes obsessed with "saving her" himself. His notions of love are tangled up with control. The turning point is when Anakin chokes Padmé, the very person he was so focused on protecting, because she disagrees with him about killing a bunch of innocent children. (The nerve—after *all* he's done for her!) Then, the lie completely takes hold.

Other examples of fall arcs and the lies characters' believe:

- People deserve to be punished, and I'm the unbiased judge who can remove evil from the world (Light Yagami, *Death Note*)
- All that matters is being loved, even if the person loving me is encouraging me to do evil things (Faith Lehane, *Buffy the Vampire Slayer*)
- Mutants deserve to rule over humans because they are genetically superior (Magneto, *X-Men*)
- The Ring brings me happiness, and I'll do *anything* to get it (Gollum, *The Lord of the Rings*)

- I belong with the cylons, no matter how destructive they are, because they accept me for who I am (Sharon "Boomer" Valerii, *Battlestar Galactica*)
- Snow White ruined my happiness, so she deserves to be punished (Regina Mills, *Once Upon a Time*)
- Scientific advancement is more important than relationships (Victor Frankenstein, *Frankenstein* by Mary Shelley)

When writing a fall arc, consider the wide variety of reasons that characters turn evil. Here are some ideas. The character could:

- Lose their perspective and become a well-intentioned extremist — Jacen Solo (*Star Wars Legends*), Anders (*Dragon Age II*), Wanda Maximoff (*Avengers: Age of Ultron*)
- Let ambition overtake them — Elaida do Avriny a'Roihan (*The Wheel of Time* by Robert Jordan), Loki (*Thor*), Voldemort (*Harry Potter* by J.K. Rowling)
- Feel betrayed by their "good" allies and switch sides — Felix Gaeta (*Battlestar Galactica*), Morgana (*Merlin*), Berkut (*Fire Emblem Echoes: Shadows of Valentia*)
- Become obsessed with revenge — Threi (*Nophek Gloss* by Essa Hansen), Opal Koboi (*Artemis Fowl* by Eoin Colfer), Syndrome (*The Incredibles*)
- Have spent so much time with villains (or in the headspace of villains due to supernatural means) that they become a villain themselves — Alexei Volkoff (*Chuck*), Bill Patterson (*The X-Files*), Mr. Hand (*Dark City*)
- Be manipulated, persuaded, or raised by a villain — Garibaldi (*Babylon 5*), Grianne Ohmsford (*The Voyage of the Jerle Shannara* by Terry Brooks), Nick (*Supernatural*)

- Want to survive, and see the evil side as the most likely winner — Peter Pettigrew (*Harry Potter* by J.K. Rowling), Saruman (*The Lord of the Rings* by J.R.R. Tolkien), Anya (*The 100*)

You can also combine several of these reasons into one character (for example, Anakin Skywalker falls into multiple categories).

Fall arcs are useful if you want your hero to become a villain or if you want to determine the backstory of your story's antagonist.

Your character doesn't have to remain fallen, either. The same character can go through multiple types of arcs. Just look at Wanda Maximoff from the MCU—she goes from villain to hero and back again, and all her arcs are gripping (largely due to her wants and needs colliding).

3. THE FLAT ARC

Some heroes don't grow or fall. Instead, they embrace the truth from the very beginning of their story and never let it go. In fact, they use their understanding of the truth to overcome obstacles and hurdles in the plot. They will be tested. They will have a difficult time with the plot's events. They may end up in a different place at the end of the novel—gaining skills, a new vocation, or a different role than they had previously—but it is simply *different*, not better (hot tip: you can use the twelve character archetypes we talked about in the previous chapter to brainstorm ideas for how your flat character changes). These types of characters change the world with their truth, rather than being changed themselves.

A great way to add tension with a flat character is to make them doubt themselves and their truth. Just because they believe their truth doesn't mean they will never waver—they may even question whether it really *is* the truth. They may also doubt their own ability to convince others of the truth.

Flat character arcs are particularly common in the mystery (*Sherlock Holmes*), adventure (*Indiana Jones*), and thriller (*James Bond*) genres, but they also occur in sci-fi and fantasy. Here are some examples and the truths they believe:

- Compassion can win wars, and people have good inside them. (Diana Prince, *Wonder Woman*)
- People can live in harmony with the insects from the Toxic Jungle (Nausicaä, *Nausicaa of the Valley of the Wind*)
- The Rebellion can overthrow the Empire (Leia Organa, *Star Wars*)
- Violence is unnecessary (Aang, *Avatar: The Last Airbender*)
- Even little people can have huge impacts on the world (Gandalf, *The Lord of the Rings* by J.R.R. Tolkien)
- People are worth protecting, and freedom is worth fighting for (Captain America, MCU)
- Peace and quiet is worth searching for (Rincewind, Discworld by Terry Pratchett)

While you might be tempted to consider flat character arcs boring, glancing over the above list should tell you they are anything but! These are vibrant characters who have undeniable impacts on the world around them and face tension, conflict, and self-doubt just as much as the next character.

INSPIRATION FROM *AVATAR: THE LAST AIRBENDER*

The animated TV show *Avatar: The Last Airbender* is lauded for its episodic storytelling, meaningful themes for all ages, and masterful character development. Much of the show's depth is not due to the happy-go-lucky Aang, however, but to the firebending prince intent on capturing the Avatar: Zuko.

Zuko is one of the most sympathetic characters in the show. But how does a villain, the son of a Fire Lord intent on genocide, a boy who wields a destructive power and struggles with anger, become a character we care about? The answer: character development. In other words, Zuko's character arc does exactly what it's supposed to.

Here are some ideas you can take from Zuko's arc to inspire your own characters arcs.

1. Give them a vibrant backstory.

Zuko's mother left him at a young age. His father, Fire Lord Ozai, literally scarred him and banished him from the Fire Nation at thirteen because Zuko protested a plan that would send their troops on a suicide mission. He was sent to hunt the Avatar with the notion that capturing Aang would regain his honour and place by his father's side. His identity as a banished prince and ties to the Fire Nation are integral to his character. As we learn more about his backstory, Zuko becomes so much more than an angry teenager.

If you know what your characters' lives were like before the start of your novel, they will feel more realistic on the page. You also don't need to dump all their backstory out at once; Zuko's history is revealed slowly throughout the show.

2. Insert relationships that push and pull them.

In addition to the destructive relationship with his father, several other relationships are key to Zuko's growth throughout the show. The most significant is with his Uncle Iroh, who is a constant at Zuko's side, offering quiet wisdom and acceptance at every turn. Even when Zuko pushes his uncle away, Iroh is always waiting with open arms for his return. Iroh is the foil to Ozai; he is a true father figure that Zuko learns to love and respect.

Other relationships push Zuko towards growth or attempt to pull him away from it. His sister, Azula, tempts him with everything he has ever wanted (acceptance and a welcome back to the Fire Nation). Katara offers him acceptance and healing, which he rejects, and their friendship is strained afterwards. Aang pushes him to a new understanding of justice by his peaceful nature and refusing to fight.

Relationships are a great way to push your character towards growth or change. We are, after all, heavily influenced by the people who surround us. Zuko's relationship with his father, at the beginning of the story, is one of fear and a longing for acceptance. At the end of the story, the relationship has changed—Zuko rejects his father's definition of love and honour, no longer fears him, and no longer requires his acceptance. Plotting out how he gets from point A to point B results in a pretty amazing character arc.

3. Define the character's lie and truth.

Determining the character's lie and truth can help you plan their arc. For Zuko, the idea of honour is integral to his character development. More than anything, he wants to prove himself and be accepted back by his father.

- *Lie:* If I prove myself, my father will love and accept me, which will allow me to love and accept myself.
- *Truth:* Honour is tied to doing good, not to the twisted desires of the Fire Lord.

Zuko's is a growth arc, so his goals change as he accepts his needs, rejects his lie, and embraces his truth. In a fall arc, he would reject the truth and cling to the lie—becoming more like Azula, his sister, who literally goes insane with the need to prove herself. In a flat arc, he would embrace the truth from the beginning, and his goal would be more about changing others to accept this truth, rather than learning to accept it himself.

What makes Zuko's arc so captivating is that it's so raw, personal, and realistic. If you were to draw a visual representation of his development on paper, it wouldn't be a nice, smooth arch, it would be a jagged line that dips, swerves, and loops back on itself, but slowly progresses upwards.

This imperfect, unsteady development reflects what it it means to be human. Messy arcs are realistic arcs.

4. Make the consequences of failure clear.

If Zuko fails to capture the Avatar, his father won't let him return home. These stakes are tied to the lie he believes—that his worth is based on his father's opinion of him. Returning home and making his father proud means *everything* to Zuko at the beginning of the show. We intensely feel Zuko's angst, anger, and drive, because his honour means so much to him.

When your characters want something so badly, your readers will feel that desire, too.

5. Put external and internal obstacles in their way.

Zuko is constantly thwarted by the Avatar, and obstacles are continually thrown in his path. Sometimes, they are physical obstacles, like encountering Zhao, a commander in the Fire Nation navy, who decides he wants the glory of capturing the Avatar himself and detains Zuko. Sometimes, they are emotional obstacles, such as when Zuko starts to question his own reasons for wanting to hunt the Avatar, and he frees Appa instead of capturing the bison.

It should never be easy for your characters to get what they want!

6. Position them to confront their lie.

Zuko is given ample opportunities to confront the lie he believes, and he does. But, sometimes, the lie is too tempting, and he reverts to his old way of thinking, such as when he joins Azula in a fight against Team Avatar.

At one point in the story, Zuko is given *exactly* what he wants—he is welcomed back to the Fire Nation, given a place at his father's side, and his banishment is revoked. But he discovers he's not happy because what he *wanted* was not what he *needed*.

Having your characters reach their goals is one way to help them confront their lies. Once they realize they are not content, they are pushed to do something to discover why.

7. Keep their personality intact.

What we particularly love about Zuko is that his personality doesn't change when he finally confronts his lie, accepts his truth, and joins Team Avatar as Aang's firebending teacher. He's not suddenly a peace-filled, calm guru who laughs at every joke and walks with a spring in his step. He's the same, angsty, angry teenager (though he does *try* to be more patient).

You don't become a completely different person when you grow. You don't easily overcome every challenge you previously struggled with. You're not automatically accepted by others, even if you've started to accept yourself. Zuko has to prove himself to Team Avatar, and they don't automatically trust him. Some of them don't like him at all. Katara, in particular, wants nothing to do with him because of how he had betrayed her in the past. Life is difficult for Zuko after his change of heart, and he has trouble enacting his new desire to do good.

Your characters shouldn't become completely different

people after they go through a character arc—the core of their personality should still be there.

PEOPLE ARE DYNAMIC, complex, and complicated. Your characters should be, too. Use character arcs to inspire your readers to truly sympathize with your story's cast—to keep them at the edge of their seats because they can't wait to find out what happens.

Chapter 11

To Be Human Is to Be Complex
Diversifying Your Novel

"You shouldn't worry if your story doesn't have a diverse cast of characters. Just let it 'flow' naturally, unfiltered by the pressure of society. If all your characters are white, who cares! No one wants tokenism."

That was the gist of a post we recently read in an online writers' group. The problem with this mentality is what flows "naturally" for us is influenced by the (often prejudiced) cultures we live in. White people may be surrounded by other white people most of the time, so their natural instinct is to write about white people. Abled people are conditioned not to think about disabled people or to think about them in specific ways (like with pity), so that's how they write disabled characters. LGBTQ+ people have been historically shunted to the sidelines and oppressed, so it's no surprise that they are only now starting to appear more regularly in our stories.

Some writers complain that calls to diversify their stories are "peer pressure." We've got news for you, people—that's not peer pressure. That's asking for equality. Mainstream stories have primarily been dominated by white, abled, cisgender characters for centuries. In her essay, "The Lost Races of Science Fiction," Octavia Butler writes:

Science fiction has always been nearly all white, just as until recently, it's been nearly all male. A lot of people have had a chance to get comfortable with things as they are. Too comfortable. Science fiction, more than any other genre, deals with change—change in science and technology, and social change. But science fiction itself changes slowly, often under protest. You can still go to conventions and hear deliberately sexist remarks—if the speaker thinks he has a sympathetic audience."[1]

Making stories diverse takes effort—but that work is important. Yes, we can take the easy way out by letting our stories "flow" and filling them with unchecked biases, but by doing so, we are only contributing to homogeneous storytelling and robbing ourselves of the opportunity to create better books.

Of course, you shouldn't include diverse characters just so you can make a checkmark on a list. Sassy, Black best friend? Check. Aging, wise mentor whose only purpose is to give advice? Check. Disabled kid to inspire the protagonist? Check. Including characters of various backgrounds because you want to avoid criticism, so your story "appears" diverse without actually doing the work, is tokenism. Tokenism results in harmful stereotypes and relegating these characters to the sidelines.

As Mary Robinette Kowal put it, "It's not about adding diversity for the sake of diversity, it's about subtracting homogeneity for the sake of realism."[2] Diversity is understanding that every person is unique and has individual characteristics, including socio-economic status, education, age, gender, sexual orientation, religious beliefs, political beliefs, race, physical abilities, and neurodiversity.

Before we dive into these areas, note that no one person is an "expert" on diversity, because of all the differences (and more) we just listed. This chapter is filled with more quotes and resources than any other chapter because it's best to learn how to write marginalized characters by listening to people who belong to those groups. Though we, the authors, belong to a handful of marginalized communities, we do not belong to every one we mention in this chapter. We have done our best to find voices from the communities we are discussing.

Do your research when you are writing characters whose identities do not match your own. Hire sensitivity readers for marginalized characters. Talk to people. Don't assume you know what an authentic portrayal of a marginalized character looks like. Even though you are writing sci-fi or fantasy and you can make up a lot of details about your world, there are certain experiences you'll want to get right. For example, if your character is an amputee and you are not, you'll want to know what barriers they face. What can they physically do and not do? What might they struggle with emotionally? What language might they find offensive?

Just like you would research and flesh out other topics in your story that you're unfamiliar with, talking to an amputee is your best way to find out the answers to those questions. You can use your imagination and try to guess what these characters might experience, but you may fall into stereotypes, even unconsciously, if you try to do so. You might be surprised by the information you learn when you talk to real people.

Also, bear in mind that no one person speaks for an entire group. Similarly, no one character should define a certain segment of the population; they should represent individual, full-fledged people to the best of your ability.

Consider the following ten underrepresented backgrounds when writing your novel.

1. SOCIO-ECONOMIC STATUS

We recently saw a meme posted on social media about how Harper Lee's friends gifted her a full year's salary in 1956 so she could spend the time writing *To Kill a Mockingbird*. What a great

Christmas present! Several writers responded with how lucky she was and joked about how they wished they had rich friends who could do that for them. But one commenter had something else to say. Paraphrased, they wrote that anyone can take a year off with no help from others, as long as they budget properly and don't eat out every night. (You know, just don't use your money on all those extras, like lobster and filet mignon.)

We don't know whether to laugh or cry at this response. Unfortunately, many people assume, like the above commenter, that poverty is the result of bad choices and laziness. This is a misunderstanding of our social structure. People struggle financially, regardless of how many lobsters they don't buy, for a variety of reasons. And the reasons that people living in poverty behave in certain ways are complex.

We tend to link people's decisions to their character *unless* we are talking about ourselves. If we are the ones in poverty, we assume it's based on circumstances, not on character; this is a psychological concept known as "fundamental attribution error."[3] For example, if I have an accident and become bankrupt because of hospital bills, I consider myself a victim of bad luck. But that stranger over there who's bankrupt? They really should have made better life decisions.

It's easy to ignore someone else's situation when you haven't been in their shoes.

So, what does this have to do with writing? With sci-fi and fantasy in particular, you may be creating social structures and economies that are foreign to you, but power imbalances will almost always exist. A character's wealth, education, and occupation can (and should) impact their worldview and their character development. Wealthy people will also have very different problems than poor people

Contrast Caitlyn and Vi from the TV series *Arcane*. Caitlyn is a daughter of a wealthy house in Piltover. Her problems include feeling bored and stifled, facing the repercussions of becoming an enforcer instead of following in her parents' footsteps, looking into the corruption of the enforcers, and trying to cut through political red tape to help the mistreated people of the undercity.

Vi, on the other hand, is a thief from the undercity, growing up alongside criminals. Her problems include survival, the deaths of her friends, a crazy sister who's been adopted by an evil man, and being imprisoned by the enforcers.

Both characters are tough and smart, but they've also been influenced by the socio-economic structure that surrounds them. They face different challenges and overcome them in different ways, which enriches the story due to authenticity. When they meet, we see vastly different characters whose cultures collide, and it's fascinating to see how they become friends and work together for a common purpose.

2. AGE

Unless you're aiming for a mystery along the lines of "Where have all the grown-ups gone?" or "Where have all the children gone?", your story should include characters of all ages. (P.S. The senior characters don't always have to be white-haired, bearded mentors, and the young sidekicks don't always have to be orphaned thieves. Try mixing it up.)

We haven't seen many sci-fi or fantasy novels with an elderly main character, but *Howl's Moving Castle* by Diana Wynne Jones is the exception. Sophie Hatter, the story's protagonist, gets cursed into becoming an old woman, wrinkles and all, and she has to deal with all the accompanying aches and pains throughout her adventure. Sophie thrives as an old lady, and she's perfectly able to go on adventures, even if her back aches more than the young characters'.

When writing senior characters, try not to use them as foils for the main character or objects of pity. Give them goals and dreams, just like any other character. Don't relegate them to the sidelines just because they're old, but consider what they may be physically capable or incapable of.

The movie version of *Howl's Moving Castle* includes a child, Markl, whom Sophie becomes something of a mother to. Their relationship is endearing and important to the plot as the castle's residents become a family.

When writing about children, try not to make them too cutesy, too annoying, too stupid, or too sagely wise (unless they've got the universe's encyclopedia downloaded into their brain, of course). Just like with your adult characters, give them goals and dreams.

3. GENDER ROLES AND REPRESENTATION

Note: This section focuses on the historical binary construct of male and female gender roles. See the next section for non-binary gender characters.

There is no shortage of male characters in sci-fi and fantasy. Historically, female characters have been shunted to the sidelines, only given stereotypical feminine roles, or not included at all.

J.R.R. Tolkien's novels include powerful women who find ways to break out of the traditional roles forced upon them by a patriarchal society (hello, Eowyn and Galadriel), but consider that there are 410 male characters and only 62 female characters in Tolkien's books about Middle-earth.[4] That's not just double, triple, or even quadruple the number of female characters—that's more than six times the number!

Of course, *The Lord of the Rings* was written almost 70 years ago. Representation has improved since then, but it's still got a long way to go. A study of top selling picture books from 2017 showed that male characters outnumbered female characters three to two.[5] When looking at the top fifty bestsellers on Amazon in September, 2021, we found that thirty-five books featured male protagonists, eleven featured female protagonists, and four featured both.

A common argument against including female characters in fantasy is that "it wouldn't be realistic." In an article on TOR.com, author Kate Elliot writes that those who defend this position think that women's pre-modern lives are too "limited, constrained, and passive" to have realistically interesting roles in fantasy stories, and thus anyone writing about women in this way is doing so only to appease critics at the expense of historical accuracy.

Elliott counters this argument by discussing a variety of societies in which gender roles have not, even historically, been limited to the hierarchy we're familiar with. She gives this advice:

> 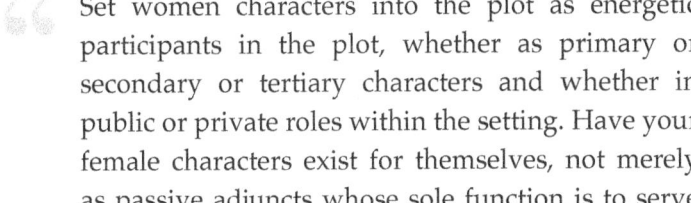Set women characters into the plot as energetic participants in the plot, whether as primary or secondary or tertiary characters and whether in public or private roles within the setting. Have your female characters exist for themselves, not merely as passive adjuncts whose sole function is to serve as a mirror or a motivator or a victim in relationship to the male."[6]

Even if you choose to ignore the historical record, it's hypocritical to cite "realism" as a necessary requirement in a genre that celebrates dragons and people shooting fire out of their fists. There's no rule against magic, and there isn't one that says you have to set your novel in a patriarchal society, either.

It can be easy to simplify gender roles into masculine and feminine stereotypes, such as men who are calm, collected, and stoic warriors (as children, they probably played with wooden swords and battled make-believe monsters); or women who are emotional, empathetic, and loving supporters (they probably grew up baking and playing with dolls). While there's nothing wrong with either of these characters, what is defined as "feminine" is often considered weak compared to what is defined as "masculine." And gender essentialism, the idea that men and women have intrinsic qualities defined by their sex, is a a flawed concept. In reality, people are much more complex. Putting women into one box and men into another is often rooted in misogyny and ignores the facts that there are female firefighters, gamers, and fencers; and there are male homemakers, secretaries, and kindergarten teachers. Some girls love cars; some boys love dresses.

Gender expectations also differ significantly across cultures. Non-white cultures have had a diversity of gender roles for centuries (for example, First Nations Two-Spirit people, the matriarchal society of Indonesia's Minangkabau, and the third gender baklâ in the Philippines).

With sci-fi and fantasy, in particular, you have the opportunity to explore gender roles that are vastly different from what you are familiar with, or even create species that defy gender altogether. How would your society integrate robots that can change gender at will or a race that possesses both female and male reproductive organs? What if you didn't choose your gender until adulthood? What if everyone switched genders when they turned thirty, experiencing half their lives as female and the other half as male?

In Ann Leckie's *Ancillary Justice*, gender has no meaning. Almost every character in the book is referred to using female pronouns and relationships (she/her, mother/sister) and male titles (lord, sir).

 I know I've seen readers talk about going through and trying to figure out every character's real gender," Leckie said in an interview. "I know where that's coming from, but it's not something that I meant to be an issue in the book at all for any of the characters. It's not something that the text is interested in. Much like a lot of books aren't interested in whether somebody is left-handed—it's just not relevant."[7]

When reading *Ancillary Justice*, you're forced to confront your own biases and assumptions about gender. Do you assume the main character, who is physically powerful, is a man? Do you assume a beautiful character is a woman? Why or why not?

4. GENDER IDENTITY AND EXPRESSION

Gender role, as discussed above, is deeply connected to society—how your culture perceives you and where you "fit" into their assumptions about gender. North American society tends to divide people into male or female, masculine or feminine (though that is slowly changing). *Gender identity* is how you define yourself. You might identify by the same gender you were assigned at birth (cisgender) or not (transgender). You might not identify with any gender (agender). You might identify as gender non-conforming, non-binary, or gender fluid. Or you might not ascribe to labels at all.

Gender expression is how you publicly present your gender, such as the way you dress and your preferred pronouns.

In *The Mirror Empire* by Kameron Hurley, a powerful magician named Taigan uses any of three pronouns—she/her, he/his, or ze/hir, depending on how ze's feeling. Characters from hir society embrace all genders, are fluent in using nonbinary pronouns, and accept nonbinary identities as completely normal. The story embraces all genders, and several of the novel's cultures acknowledge three or more genders.

The gender identity of your characters could deeply impact the way they interact with the world; you could explore how they feel about themselves through thoughts, actions, dialogue, and pronoun use. Is their gender identity different from their expression? How might their culture impact that reality?

Or the gender identity of your characters might not be seen as "other" at all in your novel's society. You could include non-binary, gender non-conforming characters and their pronouns in your novel without purposely bringing attention to them, creating the world in fiction that you want to see in reality. Simply choose pronouns for your characters and use them without anyone discussing it or thinking it's unusual.

5. SEXUAL ORIENTATION

Sexual orientation refers to who you are sexually attracted to. This includes people who are attracted to the opposite gender (straight or heterosexual), to the same gender (gay, lesbian, or homosexual), to multiple genders (bisexual), to any genders (pansexual), or to no one (asexual). Some are unsure (often referred to as questioning or curious), some don't ascribe to any of these concepts, and some feel comfortable with some labels but not others. Note that these identities are spectrums and it can be difficult to define them succinctly in a single sentence.

Your sexual orientation has nothing to do with your relationship status. For instance, if you are heterosexual, you are heterosexual whether you're single, dating, married, separated, or divorced. There's no such thing as "practicing" or "non-practicing" (When one of our friends is asked whether he's "practicing," he often replies, "Why? Is there going to be a test?"). Similarly, being bisexual doesn't mean you're dating many people at once. Being pansexual doesn't mean you enjoy orgies. Being asexual doesn't mean you're automatically averse to a romantic relationship or completely repulsed by sex. Sexual orientation is an aspect of your identity, not a statement about your dating habits or relationship status. It's also not a personality trait, so keep that in mind when writing LGBTQ+ characters.

Iron Widow by Xiran Jay Zhao takes place in a sci-fi world inspired by ancient China—complete with misogyny and foot binding—but with giant, human-controlled mechas, called Chrysalises, that take the shape of mythical creatures. The protagonist, Zetian, has a threeway relationship with two men. In an interview, Zhao says:

> The whole book is about shattering rigid rules and preconceptions about gender, sexuality, and relationships, so why not go poly? People have been talking about wanting YA love triangles to end in poly for years and years, and that's exactly what I did. She has two boyfriends who also become boyfriends."[8]

We particularly appreciate that the three characters are not jealous of each other, and that healthy communication is important to them. Zhao does not fall into the stereotypes of portraying her LGBTQ+ characters as lustful or emotionally unhealthy (as far as romance is concerned, anyway). Instead, she promotes ideals like consent, care, empathy, and love that is rooted in trust.

Look up harmful tropes to avoid when writing LGBTQ+ characters, and keep in mind that characters should feel three-dimensional. This is just one aspect of their identity. Also, the societies of your fantasy or sci-fi worlds can certainly reflect the stigmas minorities face today, but they don't *have* to:

> That's the lure of what sci-fi can do for diversity," writes Wren Handman on *We Need Diverse Books*. "It can present a world where the fights we're fighting today have been won. It can show us that it's possible for our future to be as bright as the fictional worlds we're reading about. For people to be accepted for who they are—or at least, hated for new and different reasons!"[9]

6. RELIGION

In fiction, religious people are often portrayed in one of two ways; they are either 1) stupid, ignorant, or judgemental, or 2) they use religion as a means to gain power and exploit people. But there are so many more dimensions to faith, with people who believe in a god (or gods) for a variety of different reasons. Organizations, governments, whole countries, some of the greatest atrocities and some of the greatest acts of mercy spring from religious beliefs, and there is much to be explored in science fiction and fantasy that can inform and develop your characters.

Historically, some religious people have held positions of great power and others have been oppressed. Either option can be a catalyst for story conflict and provide context for a character's actions and behaviour. When creating a religious character, showing their practices can be more impactful than describing a theological debate. Religious practices can include tithing, fasting, reading scripture, attending rituals, conducting ceremonies, saying prayers, or meditating. Characters may also say certain things (e.g. invoking a deity's name when in trouble) or avoid saying certain things (e.g. swearing).

In *The Goblin Emperor* by Katherine Addison, Maia is the unwanted half-goblin son of an emperor. He takes the throne after his father and brothers die in an accident. Religion is a significant part of the court's culture—including various rituals and the worship of deities—but skepticism has become more fashionable than faith. Most people participate in these services because it's the way things are done, not because they believe. However, Maia genuinely has faith in the goddesses he worships. As a ruler, his faith creates several challenges—how is he supposed to find the time and space to meditate? How can he practice his religion while gaining the respect of his subjects? How can he live out faith through his actions instead of mere

To Be Human Is to Be Complex 157

words? Addison treats Maia's religion with subtly and respect, and it becomes a part of his identity.

If you are writing urban fantasy or sci-fi that refers to a real-world religion, make sure to do your research to ensure respect and accuracy. Religions are incredibly nuanced and intimate; some religious groups don't publicly talk about their practices. It is impossible to completely understand a religion without living it. If you're not part of the religion your character believes, there will likely be important details you will miss. Talking to people of that religion is the best way to ensure accuracy, but respect people's boundaries if there are details they are unwilling to share. Hire sensitivity readers from that community to look over your work (yes, we keep repeating this in this chapter, because it's key) and make sure you're not harmfully appropriating a belief system, inaccurately portraying their faith, or falling into unhelpful stereotypes.

7. RACE AND ETHNICITY

> It's common to see the terms *race* and *ethnicity* used interchangeably, but, generally speaking, the meanings are distinct," writes journalist Nadra Kareem Nittle in an article on *ThoughtCo*. "Race is usually seen as biological, referring to the physical characteristics of a person, while ethnicity is viewed as a social science construct that describes a person's cultural identity. Ethnicity can be displayed or hidden, depending on individual preferences, while racial identities are always on display, to a greater or lesser degree."[10]

Race and ethnicity are key aspects of character identity that many authors have either ignored (with the default assumption that all their characters are white unless otherwise stated) or fallen into stereotypes when attempting to explore.

> Dear writers: your white characters have race and skin color too. Write like you know that. Otherwise you make them the default," tweeted Saladin Ahmed, author of *Throne of the Crescent Moon* and the *Miles Morales: Spider-Man* comics.[11]

Ahmed advises writers to check themselves if they only describe a character's race when the character is not white.

Some writers are intimidated when trying to describe characters' appearances in natural ways. It's not offensive to point out a character's skin colour, but it can be worked in organically, just like any other story detail.

In *Raybearer* by Jordan Ifueko, protagonist Tarisai reflects on how she looks like her mother and how her appearance varies from her scholars' appearances (they're the only people she has contact with, so it's natural for her to compare herself to them):

> I delighted in our resemblance: the same high cheekbones, full lips, and fathomless black eyes. Her carving watched as my study brimmed with scholars from sunup to moonrise. They chattered in dialects from all twelve realms of the Arit empire. Some faces were warm and dark, like mine and The Lady's. Others were pale as goat's milk with eyes like water, or russet and smelling of cardamom, or golden with hair that flowed like ink."[12]

In *A Song of Wraiths and Ruin* by Roseanne A. Brown, the narrator introduces Karina's appearance by describing her hair rather than her skin tone:

Aminata's tight coils were cut nearly an inch from her head, whereas Karina's curls poofed out past her shoulders when she wore her hair down."[13]

In *Elatsoe* by Darcie Little Badger, protagonist Ellie notes the differences between her appearance and her friend Jay's:

"He and Ellie looked pretty different, which used to annoy her. As children, they'd pretend to be twins, but strangers didn't believe that a white Celtic-and-Nordic-American boy and a brown Apache girl came from the same family."[14]

Your characters will be better developed if you go further than stating "She was Black," as that description suggests all Black women look the same, which is far from the truth. Is her nose round? Pointed? Long? Button-like? Are her eyes large? Sharp? Narrow? Is she curvy? Muscular? Thin? There are various ways to describe hair (Lush? Silky? Springy? Dark? Dyed? Toned? Streaked?) and skin tone (Umber? Gold? Tawny? Copper? Deep? Rich? Cool?).

Avoid comparing dark skin colours to food, particularly chocolate and coffee. "The main issue is that describing a person using food could be read as sensuous or even a fetish," writes SF Benson in *We Write Fantasy*. "It can also be seen as dehumanizing a person. Finally, it comes off as cliché."[15] Foods are also commodities that are traded, sold, and consumed, as Black slaves were, which is another reason to avoid comparing food to dark skin tones.

If your character is from a real-world culture and you are unfamiliar with that culture, do your research to portray them (and their appearance and behaviours) as accurately as possible.

If your story is set in a different world or universe, you can rely on describing physical features rather than stating their ethnicity (for example, there's probably no Asia in your fantasy world, so describing a character as Chinese wouldn't make sense). If you have based your fantasy locations and cultures off of real ones, readers will likely pick that up.

If you are creating your own fantasy or alien race, people of that race shouldn't all share the same personality trait (orcs are twisted, elves are haughty, dwarves are stubborn, etc.). One race may contain multiple cultures, just like they do in our world, and cultures are intrinsically tied to geography and history, so consider *how* and *why* that culture came to be the way it is. What resources do they geographically have access to? How does that impact their architecture? What is their climate? What language do they speak? How have certain rituals helped them survive? Everything in a culture has meaning, or it did at one point, so don't just pick and choose elements from real-world cultures to throw into your fictional culture without understanding their origin.

Sci-fi and fantasy has historically been at fault for including a variety of harmful racial and ethnic stereotypes. For example, as much as we love *The Horse and His Boy* by C.S. Lewis, the Calormene represent stereotypes of Middle-Eastern culture. Their clothing, customs, and villainy, in comparison to the "righteous" and "civilized" Narnia, suggest that they are other.

> Lewis's bias seems clear," writes scholar Michael Boyce in *Area of Effect* magazine. "The character we most closely identify with couldn't possibly be from that weird, savage land; he must be from somewhere like Narnia. The whole story is structured so that Shasta abandons the 'bad' influences of Calormen by embracing his true identity as a noble Archenlander. Just think of the implications of that. The only real redeemable Calormene isn't actually a Calormene at all! He can't be. The fact that we identify with him at all means he cannot be other."[16]

Other harmful tropes include "the savage" (a Black character who is mentally, physically, and culturally inferior to white people); the "white saviour" (a white character who saves or teaches people of colour); the "magical negro" (a Black character with special powers who exists solely to support white characters); the "Black best friend" (usually a sassy woman, whose sole purpose is to support a white character); the "domestic worker" (often a Black or Latinx character who is a servant for white people); the Native American shaman; the Asian whose main talent is martial arts; equating white with good and black with evil; and only mentioning nonwhite races as though white is the default.

8. DISABILITY

Contrary to some beliefs, disabled characters *can* go on adventures! They might do things a little differently than your abled characters, and they may face barriers and frustrations (or they may not, depending on your world!), but don't exclude them from your sci-fi and fantasy stories with the assumption that they are incapable.

There are a lot of tropes you can fall into where characters with disabilities and chronic illnesses are concerned, but a little research can help you avoid them. Historically, authors have put disabled characters into harmful roles, such as to "inspire" a main character (e.g. Tiny Tim from Charles Dickens's *A Christmas Carol*), as a temporary obstacle to be overcome and cured (e.g. the blind prince in the fairy tale *Rapunzel*), or to make a villain seem more evil or frightening (e.g. Doctor Poison's facial scars in *Wonder Woman*). These types of roles define characters by their disabilities, when disability is only one facet of an identity; these stereotypes also suggest people with disabilities aren't acceptable or able to live full lives until they're healed. They perpetuate the idea that people with physical differences are evil, gross, or to be feared.

When creating a disabled character, ask yourself whether you've made it clear that the character is more than their disability. Disabled people have wishes, dreams, goals, talents, and flaws. Though their condition may be a significant part of their identity, it is not the only part.

Check whether your character is cured or killed in the narrative. It can be tempting to overcome the "problem" of disability this way, like it's a puzzle to be solved. However, curing a character of their disability, even if it's the end of an exciting quest, sends a message to disabled readers that they are unacceptable the way they are and confirms abled people's biases. It's not that you can never kill off a disabled character, but don't do it for pure dramatic effect or because you don't know what else to do with them. There are so many great story opportunities you can take advantage of by portraying your character struggling with a condition rather than by completely removing it.

Raven Reyes from the TV show *The 100* has chronic pain due to nerve injury, and she never gets better. The show even dangles a cure in her face, but it turns out to be too good to be true. Instead of being cured, she accepts her pain as part of her, even as she struggles to deal with it throughout the show. This character's journey and the fact that she was not cured of her condition meant so much to Allison when she watched this show, because she also struggles with chronic pain and disability.

Particularly in science fiction and fantasy, a character may have a disability that really isn't a disability, such as being blind but being able to see just fine using magic. This risks sliding into tokenism and erasing a character's disability. It's not realistic for a disabled character to never experience repercussions or disadvantages.

Avatar: The Last Airbender navigates this dichotomy with the character Toph Beifong, who is blind. Because Toph is an earthbender, she uses her bare feet to sense what's around her and can navigate as well as any other character, for the most part. There's a magic element to help her "see," but it's not like she's seeing colour or detail. The show also makes a point of demonstrating that she is still blind. There are times when her feet are burnt or she has to wear shoes and can't sense her surroundings anymore. She can't perceive everything with her earthbending, such as when an object is thrown at her. She doesn't know what her friends look like; when she and Katara have their spa day, she says she would like to know. Toph experiences the world differently than other characters because of her disability, even though she has magic. The show treats her condition respectfully, and Toph is a well-rounded character—something you want to achieve with disabled characters in your novel.

Finally, keep in mind that illnesses and disabilities are difficult to understand if you haven't experienced them yourself. You certainly don't need to have suffered from a particular illness to write about it, but (and this applies even if you are making up a fictional illness), talk to people with similar conditions to get an understanding of what they are and aren't capable of, what they find frustrating about their condition, and what barriers they face because of it (note that these barriers are often social constructs—such as the lack of wheelchair ramps in many facilities or inefficient healthcare systems—and sci-fi and fantasy allows you to eliminate those barriers in your world). This will help bring your character to life, and you may even find inspiration for tension, character growth, and story obstacles along the way.

9. NEURODIVERSITY

Neurodiversity refers to the natural variations that can occur in the brain, and includes neurological differences such as dyspraxia, dyslexia, attention deficit hyperactivity disorder, autistic spectrum, depression, anxiety, and others. Everything we discussed above about physical disabilities and chronic illnesses applies here as well. Neurodiverse characters shouldn't be defined by their condition alone, and you can flesh them out as you would any other character.

 "Writing diverse characters, even ones that mirror your life, requires a certain amount of research," says author Halli Gomez, who has Tourette's syndrome, obsessive-compulsive disorder, sensory issues, and anxiety. "Unless the character resembles you in every way, different experiences will create different views, emotions, and actions. For example, two characters are diagnosed with autism, one early in life and the other as an adult. Both struggle in social situations, and repetitive movements are part of their daily lives. Although they appear similar, differences in growing up would dictate how they relate to situations emotionally and socially. You can even go further and look at where they live, their community and what their family situation is like."[17]

Research and talk to people with the condition you're writing about as opposed to mimicking how other media has represented these characters, or you may end up duplicating harmful stereotypes. For example, characters with tourettes syndrome are often portrayed exclusively with the tic of swearing, when in actuality tics can vary and include things like blinking, shrugging, humming, clearing the throat, sniffing, etc. They don't tic all the time, either.[18]

Autistic representation in mainstream media is dominated by young, white, cisgender male characters, but autistic people can also be non-binary, Black, female, gay, etc. Some are all of the above.

In "What Good Representation of Autistic Characters Looks Like, Part I: Interiority and Neurology," Elizabeth Bartmess writes about how autistic people interpret situations differently than neurotypical people, and others may think their reactions don't make sense:

> Bad representation in fiction upholds the idea that our actions are 'behaviors' without reasons or causes, and doesn't take into account that we change in response to our experiences. Good representation portrays autistic characters' experiences and actions as comprehensible, often through narration or (if the autistic character is not the viewpoint character) someone else's awareness of our experiences and the reasons for our actions—which can include our expectations and skills learned from past situations. Showing us as comprehensible helps neurotypical people understand autistic people better, and—importantly—lets autistic people see themselves understood and reflected, something that's often missing from real life and is extremely satisfying to encounter, whether in real life or in fiction."[19]

Ada Hoffmann's novel *The Outside* features two autistic characters—the antagonist, Dr. Talirr, and the protagonist, Yasira. Both are shown as clever and anxious, with different motivations and personalities. They are easily read as people rather than labels.

> Dr. Talirr's ramblings were not dissimilar to some of mine in certain moods," writes Hoffmann in a TOR.com article. "Her trauma-fueled anger against the system she grew up in, as reluctant as I was to admit it, was also relatable.
>
> "Yasira's was also fundamentally autistic. She's overwhelmed by her supernatural experiences in a way that resembles my own daily sensory and

cognitive overload. Outside's surreal qualities are themselves inspired by my autistic experience. Simply going into an unfamiliar place can be overwhelming for me..."[20]

Hoffmann almost didn't make Yasira autistic because she was afraid she would get it wrong or promote harmful stereotypes, even though the author is autistic herself. Her concern was partly rooted in how *The Outside* is such a dark book filled with Lovecraftian horrors, and she questioned whether she wanted to write an autistic character going through all that trauma. Would readers think her novel was saying that autistic characters deserve trauma and that they're all monsters without knowing it?

But Hoffmann determined that Talirr's and Yasira's neurodivergence was integral to their characters, and she did the work to show a fuller picture of autism through her portrayals of both.

10. BODY SHAPE AND SIZE

Fantasy literature has upheld a sexist tradition of portraying women in specific physical ways, pointing out what is attractive (i.e. acceptable) and what is unattractive (i.e. unacceptable) through the narration. More often than not, good characters are beautiful and bad characters are ugly. Of course, there are exceptions: Dr. Susan Calvin in Asimov's Robot series, Meg in Madeleine L'Engle's *A Wrinkle in Time,* and Brienne of Tarth in George R.R. Martin's A Song of Ice and Fire series come to mind. But there is still a prevalence of idealizing certain beauty standards in our texts.

Fat shaming is included in narratives so subtly that sometimes we don't even realize it's there, because we're so accustomed to this attitude from society. In the Harry Potter series, Vernon and Dudley Dursley's fatness is *constantly* described and linked to their lack of character. Vernon has "five chins." Dudley doesn't just wave an arm, he waves a "fat arm," and he is often compared to a pig.

> They are also both brash, lazy, and selfish—traits that are common stereotypes for fat people," writes Kyla Neufeld in an article titled "Monstrous Bodies: Fat Shaming in Geek Culture." "This is a similar trope to villains having disfigured faces, but in this case, their exaggerated sizes become the visible sign that reflects their moral failings...
>
> "This is fat shaming: the idea that we can pressure fat people into losing weight if we make fun of them enough. This mentality comes from the insidious belief that fat bodies don't deserve to exist."[21]

When considering your characters' appearances, don't equate society's beauty standards with goodness. People of all body shapes and sizes exist in the real world, with all sorts of varying personalities and alignments; that can be reflected in your writing too!

> It is particularly important to separate the idea of being athletic, fit, and healthy from thinness," writes Fay Onyx on *Mythcreants*. "There are plenty of thin people who aren't athletic, and there are plenty of fat people who are...
>
> "Instead of using words like 'athletic' as synonyms for thinness, use them to mean what they actually mean—being physically strong and active. This frees up words like energetic, muscular, nimble, brawny, limber, agile, and tough so that they can be used for characters of any size."[22]

Diversify the appearance of your characters, and remember

that your fantasy or sci-fi culture need not reflect the same ideals as the one you grew up in. What if body hair, multiple chins, or wrinkles are considered beautiful in your novel's world? What if all the skinny people are destroyed by a virus? What if the concept of beauty doesn't exist at all?

WHEN IS IT CULTURAL APPROPRIATION?

Cultural appropriation is exploiting a version of a culture for your own gain, without giving credit to the original source or putting real work into researching the culture to maintain accuracy. There are often, but not always, power dynamics at play, with someone from a dominant culture adopting elements from a marginalized culture. Particularly relevant to writing fiction, cultural appropriation results in harmful stereotypes and racist generalizations.

So how do you draw the line between cultural representation and cultural appropriation? We appreciate how Charlie Jane Anders answers this question in a TOR.com article:

> I feel like this is always going to be messy, and ever-shifting, and contain exactly no straight lines, because we're talking about human beings, and the complexities of history," writes Anders. "You never get to be done trying to figure this stuff out.
>
> "Even if my work touches on ancient history or folklore, I know that it connects directly to the people who are alive today. When you write about the future, you're really writing about the present—and I believe the same is true when you write about the past. So even if you're touching on ancient Chinese history, you need to understand how Chinese people in the 21st century think about their own heritage, and what it means to them. The past

is always alive in the present, and the stories we tell about it matter."[23]

Here's an example of what *not* to do. When J.K. Rowling published a series of online short stories called "History of Magic in North America," she took certain elements from Navajo beliefs, like the legend of skin walkers (which has ceremonial meaning in Navajo culture today), removed them from their context, and erased their original meaning. In the Harry Potter universe, this legend was created by muggles to demonise wizards. By fictionalizing this belief, J.K. Rowling perpetuated stereotypes and did real harm to a living tradition of marginalized people.

In an article for *The Humanist*, Sincere Kirabo comments on J.K. Rowlings' actions:

> If we had diverse representations of Native people the same way white people do, Rowling's latest wouldn't be so problematic, because consumers would have other options from which to base their opinions. As it is, so much of the Native narrative is romanticized and fantastical and now one of the world's most successful authors has thrown her mighty magical empire against our fragile reemergence from near-total cultural genocide. That the work is fiction doesn't negate centuries of oppression."[24]

Contrast Rowling's appropriation with how N.K. Jemisin wrote *The Killing Moon*, which is inspired by ancient Egypt. Jemisin thoroughly researched her setting. In a guest post on John Scalzi's website *Whatever*, Jemisin writes:

> From the beginning I envisioned this story taking place in a land of warmth and water. I had a vague idea at first of placing it in pre-Columbian South America, possibly a fantasy analogue of the Incan Empire — but the place in my head felt much older, relatively speaking. It would be a society weighed down by tradition, I felt instinctively, and wealthy enough to support a large, powerful priesthood. It would be a civilized place, full of sprawling cities and temples, with an enormous populace and monuments huge enough to inspire awe… kind of like ancient Egypt. Since at the time I knew squat-all about ancient Egypt beyond what I'd picked up from many bad movies, I started researching it, and that only confirmed my choice. Egypt was perfect."[25]

The story references the real Egypt clearly and in non-intrusive ways. The setting is a desert; transport is by camels, horses, and ships; the majority of the cast is dark skinned. But it is clearly a fantasy world, with an entirely new religion and social structure. Jemisin has a disclaimer at the beginning of the book that she intentionally separates it from real-world history.

Writers of sci-fi and fantasy are often inspired by our world's cultures and myths when creating their own. There are no hard and fast rules about how to do this "right," but understanding the context behind practices, symbols, clothing, behaviours, and other cultural elements is a good place to start. Respect and research are key.

SHOULD YOU WRITE OUTSIDE YOUR IDENTITY?

In a word: yes! Otherwise, you will be filling your book with characters exactly like you. And while we're sure you're great, creating a diverse novel, full of all sorts of people and perspectives, is important.

> But here's the thing," writes Naomi Alderman in *The Guardian*, "you have to try to do it well. You have to be familiar with whatever tropes might apply to your character: racist, sexist, homophobic, sizeist, ableist, antisemitic and anything else. It's not OK, for example, to make your Chinese character shifty and inscrutable or your fat character stupid and lazy: you need to have learned enough to understand where these false ideas come from and why it's so pernicious to replicate them. Do better. Treat your characters as human beings. Write them as people not ideas or stereotypes."[26]

One thing you should consider when writing marginalized characters is whether that story is *better* told by someone else. For example, a white, heterosexual writer from North America can (and should) include characters across a variety of spectrums, but should they write a narrative that centres around a queer, Black kid in Africa? That is a story that would be better written by someone who has firsthand experience.

Could a white author have written *Dread Nation* by Justina Ireland, an alternate history story about a Black woman and the injustices Black people face after zombies rise during the battlefields of Gettysburg and Chancellorsville? They certainly could have tried, but the story is much more powerful and authentic coming from Ireland, a Black author who experiences racism and understands these histories on a personal level that a white person simply cannot.

SOMEONE MIGHT BE OFFENDED, WHATEVER YOU DO

In early 2019, Amélie Wen Zhao asked her publisher to cancel the release of her debut novel, *Blood Heir*, which had been scheduled to come out in June. Why? Because some early reviewers declared it was anti-Black and sent a harmful message about the oppression and slavery faced by the African American community.

However, Zhao hadn't intended her novel to be a commentary on American history at all. The indenturement in her story was meant to critique human trafficking that is prevalent in Asia—a context the American reviewers were likely unfamiliar with. They called out Zhao in the name of social justice when she was, in fact, doing important work in shedding light on human trafficking, an issue that isn't talked about enough. Nonetheless, Zhao made a public apology; she was appalled that her story might represent harmful tropes and recognized that intention only goes so far.

> At the time, it was really overwhelming because a few early readers… believed my book was a portrayal of chattel slavery in America," Zhao says in an NPR interview. "And it snowballed into a lot of people who hadn't read the book… So that was really devastating to me because these are some real issues that draw from my background and from global issues that are ongoing and continue to affect so many people. So it was particularly devastating because it felt to me like my perspective wasn't welcome in this country… And honestly, for a while, it just felt like I wasn't allowed to have a voice in exploring deeply poignant subjects that were personal to me… And I believe these are diffi-

cult truths and ugly histories that need to be confronted through literature."[27]

After going over her book carefully to ensure that human trafficking and indentured labour issues were fleshed out, working with editors and sensitivity readers, and listening to feedback, Zhao determined there was nothing problematic with her story. The revised novel was published in November of 2019.

YOU WILL LIKELY MAKE mistakes as you work to diversify your cast. What matters is putting in the work to make these mistakes as minimal as possible, and to taking appropriate and caring steps to rectify them once discovered.

> Before I wrote *God's War*, I probably did eight years of research into the Middle East, Judaism, Islam, Catholicism, and all sorts of fabulous other things," says author Kameron Hurley. "You're gonna get stuff wrong. You talk to as many people as you can, you do as much research as you can, you have beta readers—no matter how well you do it and how good your intentions are, you are going to get something wrong.... Know that you're gonna screw up, and be OK with it, and do better next time."[28]

Diversifying your novel might sound frustrating and like a lot of work... because it is! But the work and the research is worth it. It will expand and deepen your world in ways you might not even realize. It will make you a better writer, and it will help build a world in which differences are celebrated.

Part Four

Worldbuilding

Chapter 12

Hey, Listen!
Creation Stories and Mythology

Though we often use the terms *myth* and *mythology* interchangeably, mythology is an overarching category that encompasses myths (stories that involve supreme deities), legends (tales that involve human protagonists), and folktales (beliefs about "lesser" mythical beings). The word *myth* comes from the Greek word *mŷthos*, which means *story* or *narrative*.

These sacred tales have some serious staying power, memorized by countless storytellers, passed on by word-of-mouth for generations. Why do such stories resonate and remain common knowledge thousands of years after they originated? What makes them stick?

Humans have an insatiable curiosity to find order and meaning in the mysterious world around us. Early cultures grappled to answer the same questions we do now. Why are we here? What is the origin of our world? What happens when we die? No matter what time we hail from, we all long to know where we came from, what we're meant to be doing, and why bad things happen.

Along with our curiosity, we also have imaginations, and that is something unique in the animal world. Humans are the only creatures (as far as we know) who picture scenarios that don't exist. We wonder about the future. We consider why past events happened as they did. So, it's only natural that we would use our imaginations to answer the universal questions troubling us and create stories to instill meaning in the mysterious events we witness.

WHY DO MYTHS SHARE SIMILARITIES?

Since the questions tend to be universal, the answers—the myths themselves—bear striking similarities, even in cultures that are oceans apart. For instance, there are myths in just about every part of the world about a devastating flood. Since most ancient agricultural sites were situated on fertile floodplains, floods were a common occurrence. Even more interesting, most flood myths contain the same themes: the flood is a punishment by a deity (or deities) because of humanity's wickedness, it's foreseen by a prophet, and only a few righteous people survive the catastrophe; the flood is used as a mechanism to wash away evil.[1]

Worldwide, humans have used their imaginations to attribute a cause to a natural disaster and allayed their fears by establishing guidelines to help them avoid a similar calamity in the future. But they also recognized that catastrophes, such as floods, were not completely destructive. People knew that floods created new, "better" worlds, even without modern science to inform them that floodwaters carry nutrients and organic matter, fertilizing soil and ending droughts.

Across cultural and geographical barriers, myths also share themes of how the world came to be and a supreme being that rules over its creation.

Myths uniquely utilize our oh-so-human imaginations. Many of us, when we appreciate the complex majesty of the world and universe around us, imagine it has been created by something greater and more powerful than ourselves, so many societies have a creation myth.

WEAVING MYTHOLOGY INTO YOUR STORY

Myths offer us a tantalizing road map to what founding cultures may have looked like at an intimate level. What did they fear? Who did they revere and why? What did their moral compass look like? What was the reasoning behind their traditions? What cultures did they feel superior towards? Your readers can innately pull all this information from a well-crafted myth. That's a heck of a lot of worldbuilding you can subtly insert without spelling it all out long form. Myths can be powerful writing tools. They carry weight when they function as more than just a background piece of information, but are woven into the story itself.

In the video games series The Legend of Zelda, three goddesses created the world of Hyrule—Din, the goddess of power, Nayru, the goddess of wisdom, and Farore, the goddess of courage. Then they left the world, leaving behind the Triforce, a magical object that grants wishes. If someone unworthy touches the Triforce, it splits into three pieces. The finder is left with the piece that represents the virtue they value most (Ganondorf, who touches the Triforce in *The Legend of Zelda: Ocarina of Time*, is left with the piece of Power), and the other two pieces appear in the hands of individuals who personify the remaining virtues—Zelda for wisdom and Link for courage.

Ocarina of Time's gameplay is entrenched in this myth; Link races to stop Ganondorf from putting the pieces together and gaining the power of the Triforce. The myth isn't just background history, but directly influences the plot.

You can take inspiration from mythology to inform your own worldbuilding. For example, the Legend of Zelda borrows themes from Celtic mythology. Epona, Link's horse, bears the same name as the Celtic goddess of fertility and protector of horses. In Celtic mythology, fairies are often pranksters, known to steal children and replace them with Changelings; some of the series' fairy characters, such as the Skull Kid, Tatl, and Tael from

Majora's Mask, fit this trickster archetype. Other Celtic fairies are known for their healing powers and giving protection to mortals. The Fairy Fountains that appear in each game allow Link to heal and receive gifts to help him in his quest. Even the magic in The Legend of Zelda, which is often based on sacred instruments and music, links to the legendary bards of Celtic mythology, who had magical powers.

Consider using a name from a famous legend to give readers insight into your character or foreshadow an event. Take an archetype from mythology and put your own spin on it. Use a myth for the base of a plot. But be careful that you don't appropriate a society's traditions (if you need to, re-read Chapter Eleven on the difference between appropriation and inspiration). Using myths can add colour and vibrance to your world.

MYTHOLOGY CAN MOTIVATE CHARACTERS

In the Star Trek universe, Vulcan mythology describes a place where all creation originated and where all questions can be answered. This mythical place, known as Sha Ka Ree, is central to the plot of *Star Trek V: The Final Frontier*. A Vulcan named Sybok, who turns out to be Spock's half-brother, captures Kirk's crew and takes the *Enterprise* to the centre of the galaxy, where no ship has ever returned from. Sybok has embraced emotion rather than logic, and has been banished from the Vulcan homeworld because of his philosophy.

On the surface, Sybok is a con-artist who convinces people to follow him on an illogical quest. Even Sulu, Uhura, and Chekov are converted to his cause due to brainwashing; Sybok forces them to confront their pain and let it go. Kirk is presented as the opposite of Sybok—a rational atheist—though just as dogmatic in his belief that God does *not* exist.

However, Sybok genuinely believes in what he's saying—that Sha Ka Ree exists at the galaxy's centre, that God cares about them, and that by visiting this place they can have their questions answered and souls saved. Ultimately, his faith is proven false, as the planet at the centre of the galaxy is host to an evil being who wants to use the *Enterprise* to escape. As Kirk points out, what does God need with a starship?

Sybok's beliefs are shattered, and he has to face the truth. This is a powerful character moment, and a perfect example of how characters aren't always simply good or evil.

When building a myth into your story, ask yourself what your characters believe about it and explore how they are impacted by their faith (or lack thereof). Resist the temptation to villainize one side over the other. Believing a myth doesn't necessarily mean you are a stupid person or you are trying to take advantage of others. Not believing in a myth doesn't necessarily mean you are cold-hearted or logical. Why do your characters believe what they believe? What happens if they find out the myth is false? What happens if they find out the myth is true? What happens if they never find out, but have to learn to live with other people whose beliefs differ from their own?

Kirk's beliefs were confirmed, but perhaps he learned something about community in the process. If he *had* discovered that there was a benevolent god on that planet, he wouldn't have been able to return to his status quo—his character would significantly change (or go into denial).

There are all sorts of exciting opportunities to explore with your characters' motivations when you build myth into your world's history.

SETTING THE STAGE WITH MYTHOLOGY

In *Gideon the Ninth* by Tamsyn Muir, nine planets make up a galactic empire, each ruled by a noble house that practices a specific type of necromancy. Gideon was adopted by the Ninth House as a baby after her mother mysteriously appeared on the planet and died. She is raised as an indentured servant and taught to revere the emperor, who rules the First House and uses his Lyctors—superpowered, immortal necromancers in a galaxy full of regular ol' necromancers—to fight an unknown, terrible foe. Apparently the emperor is a pro at fighting terrible foes, because *spoiler alert* there just so happens to be one locked in a tomb at the centre of the ninth planet.

And here's where the myth comes in.

In ancient times, the emperor grappled with an enemy so powerful he could only defeat them once and would not be able to defeat them a second time (remember, rematches after death are possible in a galaxy full of necromancers). The solution to the problem was to seal the beast's corpse in a tomb deep within the ninth planet. The builders of the tomb were meant to brick themselves in with the corpse, but were not stoked about the idea, and instead, sealed the corpse in alone. They vowed to guard it and stop anyone from opening it to prevent the Apocalypse. That's the origin story of the death cult of the Ninth House.

By Gideon's time, eons later, the Ninth House knows they are supposed to protect the Locked Tomb and that it shouldn't be opened at any cost, but they have protected its secret for so long they are unclear on the myth's details.

The fact that all the other houses don't seem to particularly like the Ninth House—as demonstrated by using them as a penal colony where they send their criminals—shows us how widespread this myth is. The Ninth House is feared because the rest of the galaxy fears the Locked Tomb. They know something is off about this planet-wide death cult, even if they don't remember the details—that the Ninth's ancestors, the tomb builders, were supposed to seal themselves inside with the great evil but disobeyed the emperor's order. Although the details have been lost, the sentiment hasn't. Its effects on the Ninth House resonate still.

By thinking through this history-turned myth, Muir set up the whole culture of the Ninth House, gave the other houses reason to hate and fear them, and made us, as readers, very much want to open that tomb and see what is hiding within.

Starting with a simple myth (such as an entombed evil and a group tasked to guard it) and building on it by asking questions can influence a rich world with a fascinating plot. Ask yourself, how has your myth become misunderstood or forgotten over the years? How does it impact your world's society? What do people from other areas of the world or galaxy believe about the myth?

EIGHT STEPS TO BUILD A MYTH

Here are some steps to help you plan a myth for your story (they can also be applied to legends and folktales):

1. Decide what question your myth is supposed to answer.

For example, why did this event happen? How was something created? Why should people act in a certain manner? For inspiration, consider these questions and the legends that seek to answer them:

- *What lies at the end of the rainbow?* Old European legends suggest leprechauns bury their treasures there.
- *How does the sun rise?* The Greek sun god, Helios, drives his chariot across the sky each day.
- *Why did masses of children disappear from a town without trace?* See the Germanic legend about the Pied Piper luring children away after the town's mayor refused to pay him.

When Shelly wrote the creation myth for her fantasy novel *Under the Lesser Moon*, she answered the question: *Why are there two moons in the sky?* This myth, about a goddess that entombed her two sons, also explains why the people in the story's society believe they are supposed to sacrifice their firstborn sons.

2. Insert a lesson.

Many myths come with a moral. Even if you don't outright state it, your reader can pick up on the lesson by seeing which behaviours earn your hero rewards and which cause them to be punished.

For example, the Inuit Sea Goddess, Sedna, was originally a young woman who was manipulated into marrying a birdman. Then, after her father kills her husband, he tosses her into the sea to avoid their boat capsizing, and she becomes a mighty goddess. There is an implicit message that liars are punished and the innocent can become powerful.

3. Make your myth larger-than-life.

Myths can include events that couldn't possibly occur on our own plane, because if your question is answerable via human means, you wouldn't need a myth to explain it! Consider what the people know about science and what phenomena they can't explain.

4. Use simple language.

Myths are often passed on orally. They are meant to be memorized and should move through the plot pretty quickly. Just state the facts. No opinions. Like songs and poetry, some myths use repetitive sentence structure in order to press a point or make them easier to memorize.

5. Give the myth a magical setting.

Your mythical character needs a backdrop and a reason to act. For example, when, where, and why are they building this boat to shelter them from the coming flood? Then they need some obstacles—a monster to face, a mistake to overcome, a deity to win over. It shouldn't be easy to finish the task they set out to do.

6. Summarize the point at the end.

After your mythical hero has beaten their obstacles and won—or, perhaps, was defeated—leaving your readers with a lesson to learn, wrap up your tale. Often myths utilize a summary sentence. For example: "And that's how the moon came to be in the sky."

7. Brainstorm the societal and cultural impacts of the myth.

How has it influenced art and religion? How has it changed by being passed on orally? (Try playing *Telephone* with your myth—start with what really happened and then list several iterations and misinterpretations until you're left with something different.)

8. Consider how your myth impacts the main character of your story.

If your myth doesn't affect your protagonist at all, then it probably doesn't need to be in the story at all, either. What does your character believe about the myth? What do supporting characters believe? How does the myth impact the plot?

By following these steps, you can subtly provide your readers with a treasure trove of information about your fictional society's culture. Readers can get a sense of your character's motivations, fears, and morals before that character even sets foot on the page. Such is the power of myths.

Chapter 13

We Will Shake the World for Our Beliefs
Deities and Religions

In his book *The Bonobo and the Atheist*, primatologist Frans de Waal shares a comical story about being part of a panel hosted by the American Academy of Religion. One speaker suggests that they pin down a definition of religion, and de Waal recalls what happened the last time they'd attempted it. "Half the audience had angrily stomped out of the room," de Waal writes. "And this in an academy named after the topic!"[1]

Obviously, people feel strongly about religion. Eighty-four percent of the world's population identifies with a religious group.[2] Wars have been fought over them. Your fantasy or science fiction world will likely also include spirituality to some degree, even if it's not key to your plot.

WHY ARE PEOPLE RELIGIOUS?

Religion, as de Waal defines it, is "the shared reverence for the supernatural, sacred, or spiritual as well as the symbols, rituals and worship that are associated with it."[3]

Many people are religious because they believe in the reality of a god or gods. The most widely practiced religions in our world are Christianity, Islam, Hinduism, and Buddhism. Christianity and Islam are monotheistic; Hinduism is polytheistic; and Buddhism is neither—focusing instead on attaining enlightenment through spirituality.

Each religion has a set of beliefs (e.g. Christianity proposes that Christ is the son of God who came to Earth, died, and was resurrected); goals (e.g. the goal of Islam is to live in submission to Allah); and rituals and practices (e.g. Hinduism encourages prayers, meditation, and yoga); but to sum them up in a few sentences is impossible. The history of each religion alone would fill up an entire book.

The power of religion on a social group is profound. Humans gravitate towards group living. Our ancestors quickly learned that group hunting brought down larger prey and fed more people compared to individual hunters. Social groups also provided better protection from predators and made it easier to find a mate.

Rituals like dancing, singing and meditative states—often still seen in group worship today—change brain chemistry, increasing dopamine, serotonin, and oxytocin, making us feel connected with those around us; we then want to repeat these experiences that strengthen our group bonds. Since empathy and morality are important for maintaining group relations, religion can play a huge role in large communities.

Godless religions are options for your story as well. The Jedi Order in Star Wars is a religion; they follow a strict set of spiritual beliefs and philosophies and are devoted to the light side of the Force. Jedi texts include origin stories to both the universe and the Force, and they treat the Force almost like a deity—but as something to align oneself with as opposed to worship. The Jedi are supposed to be peacekeepers, and their decision to get involved in the Clone Wars proved fatal to their own order (though we can blame Darth Sidius for that, too).

In *Rogue One*, Chirrut Îmwe proves that not all people devoted to the Force have to be Jedi. Part of an order of spiritual warrior-monks, Chirrut wields a staff rather than a lightsaber, and his iconic line, "I am one with the Force, and the Force is with me,"[4] represents his devotion. Significantly, the movie never makes fun of Chirrut's religion, and his beliefs are a key part of his character.

RELIGIONS OFTEN SEEK to answer the following questions:

1. Where did we come from?

Have you ever traced your lineage on a family tree or had your DNA tested to learn about your ancestry? Many of us feel driven to dig up our past, discover our origins, and decipher our purpose. In Terry Pratchett's Discworld series, the disc of the world rests on four giant elephants perched on the shell of a great turtle, and there are theories about where the turtle came from, where it's going, and what its purpose is. Humans don't just search out their past and destinies on an individual scale, we do the same for the cosmos around us too.

2. What happens to us when we die?

We're keenly aware of the finiteness of our short lives. Many are frightened of dying and being forgotten or afraid that our loved ones will cease to exist when they expire. Many religions offer an answer to these fears, promising an afterlife.

In Gabriel Squailia's *Dead Boys*, the dead enter the afterlife as literal corpses with decaying bodies. Jacob, the protagonist, is a taxidermist who keeps his clients looking lifelike for as long as possible. According to legend, one man, the Living Man, has made it into the underworld without dying first and Jacob longs to follow him out of the land of decay and back to the land of the living.

How would your characters' lives change if they are certain

of what will happen to them when they die? How do their religious concepts of death affect their everyday lives?

3. How are we supposed to act while we're alive?

A Tibetan monk lives a very different lifestyle than a Viking raider. The monk values peace and enlightenment, while the Viking prioritizes courage and ruthlessness in the face of battle. In the television series *Vikings*, Athelstan, a Christian monk slave, has trouble adjusting to Ragnar's way of life. The Viking adheres to an entirely different set of morals than Athelstan does. This leads to both conflict and intrigue as their friendship grows.

What do the deities in your world demand of their followers? How are good and evil defined?

4. Where did evil come from and how is it defeated?

Religious texts often include stories about an evil being, such as Satan in Christianity and Islam.

In Samantha Shannon's *The Priory of the Orange Tree*, an ancient fire-breathing dragon, the Nameless One, was defeated and imprisoned a thousand years before the story begins. The Nameless One longs to wipe out humanity, a common theme for sci-fi and fantasy villains. Loss of life and liberty are chief among humanity's fears, so the evil in our stories is often capable of threatening both. Religions can tell us the story of how evil originated and, possibly, how it can be (or was already) wiped out.

One of the religions in *Priory* is known as the Virtues of Knighthood, and is based on a knight—Sir Galian—who rescued a princess and defeated the Nameless One a thousand years ago. When they turn twelve, all children of the Queendom of Inys choose one of six patron knights—the Knight of Courtesy, Justice, Fellowship, Courage, Temperance, or Generosity. This is probably a play on the Seven Heavenly Virtues from the epic poem "Psychomachia," written by Aurelius Clemens Prudentius, a Christian who died around 410 AD.

Inys has based an entire religion around Sir Galian's actions, and even more interesting, their religion is based on a lie (more on that shortly).

RELIGION, CONFLICT, AND POLITICS

In certain time periods on Earth, the Church equaled the State. Religion not only determined what god people believed in, but also how they dressed, who they associated with, and their political alliances.

How encompassing is religion in your fictional world? Has the church become the government, like in Margaret Atwood's *The Handmaid's Tale*? Does it control every minutiae of its followers' lives?

In other cultures, the Church and State co-exist side-by-side. Multiple religions may be tolerated or encouraged. People are allowed to choose what they believe in as they see fit. There may be some clashes and conflicts, but for the most part, a tenuous equilibrium is maintained with people separating their religion from their government.

On the opposite end of the spectrum, the State quashes the Church. It becomes illegal to practice religion. People who are caught worshipping risk losing their jobs or their lives.

Where on the spectrum does your fictional world sit, and where is it headed?

The Priory of the Orange Tree demonstrates how religion and politics can intertwine. The story is a feminist retelling of the legend of Saint George and the Dragon, in which a dragon terrorizes a city, so the citizens choose names by lottery and sacrifice those people to appease it. After the name of a beloved princess is drawn and she awaits her doom at the dragon's lair, Saint George rides by and rescues her, slaying the dragon.

As we noted earlier, the entire Queendom of Inys in *The*

Priory of Orange Tree is founded on the Virtues of Knighthood. This religion is based on Sir Galian killing the Nameless One and rescuing a princess named Cleolind, then marrying her. The current queen of Inys, Sabran, and her people believe the Nameless One cannot return while Galian's heir rules Inys.

As it turns out, this version of history is a lie. The Priory of the Orange Tree, a community of mages from the southern domain of Lasia, has based their religion on the true story; they worship Cleolind, the Mother, who was the one who wielded the sword and wounded the dragon, and who rejected Sir Galian's marriage proposal. Ead, a character posing as a chambermaid in Sabran's household, knows this, but has to keep her mouth shut about it, because she would be thrown out of the household or even put to death by spouting such "nonsense." Even the Priory, however, doesn't know the whole story, and details of what really happened one thousand years ago are revealed by the end of the novel.

When confronted with the truth, Sabran at first refuses to believe it, because doing so would mean accepting that her life and entire nation has been built upon a lie.

Religious characters, regardless of whether their deities turn out to be real or not in your worldbuilding, may cling to their beliefs for a variety of reasons. Perhaps, like Sabran, they've based their whole lives on serving a deity; changing their mind about that deity's existence or their desire to serve might sap meaning from their life. You can see why someone might be resistant to such change. Characters might be unwilling to even ask questions about their faith or respond to them, out of fear that they'd start to doubt (or out of fear that they'd anger their god).

Particularly when Church and State mix, there's the added pressure of being removed from one's community. If someone has been taught a religion from birth and been part of that community for as long as they can remember, leaving it can seem unthinkable or, at best, difficult.

Religion can spawn conflict between people and between countries. Especially when foundational texts are thousands of years old, people can be divided on their interpretations. Just look at the Bible and Christianity. Christianity is split into three branches (Catholic, Protestant, and Orthodox); within the Protestants alone are multiple denominations (e.g. Baptist, Anglican, Lutheran, Methodist, Anabaptist, etc.). Christianity separated into so many groups because they disagree on what the Bible says. Some believe people need to be fully submerged to be baptised, while others think sprinkling with water is perfectly acceptable. Some believe only men can be preachers, while others accept all genders. Some interpret a verse to mean you shouldn't eat pork, while others think bacon is a great snack. You get the idea. When a text is so old, has been translated multiple times and into thousands of variations, the same verse can be read by different people and interpreted to mean the exact opposite. Words are taken out of context; some people read a thousand-year-old text as though the writer had meant it for today.

Not everyone in your fictional world is going to believe in the same gods, and even if they do, they'll likely have different interpretations of holy scriptures, creation myths, and morality.

The television series *Battlestar Galactica* tackles religion on a galactic scale. The Twelve Colonies are nearly wiped out when their robotic creations, the Cylons, evolve and launch an apocalyptic covert attack on their worlds, leaving behind nuclear wastelands and a small fleet of starships containing the last human survivors—a mere 50,000 souls. The remnants of humanity are led by the lone surviving battlestar, *Galactica*, and, on a more fundamental level, by their spirituality. The humans are polytheistic, similar to ancient Greeks and Romans. They pray to the Lords of Kobol. President Roslin becomes a devout believer and follower of scripture, convinced that she's prophesied to lead the ragtag remains of the colonies to the fabled, lost planet, Earth.

In contrast, the Cylons are monotheistic. Even though they've been artificially created, they believe in a singular god that gave them souls, and they're determined to destroy humankind. One of the Cylons, Six, spends the entire series trying to convince Dr. Baltar, an atheist human who unwittingly assisted in the destruction of the colonies, that God has a plan for him and he must repent and open himself to God's will. As the series progresses, Baltar becomes the leader of a cult who believes he's been sent to lead them.

All of these various religions, deities, and differing cultural beliefs give rise to conflict, not just between the humans and Cylons, but among their ranks as well. This diversity of spirituality goes a long way toward making *Battlestar Galactica* a riveting story.

While it's sad that these disagreements exist in the real world and wars have been fought over such arguments, religion offers many routes to delicious conflict in your novel.

DEITIES AND DOMAINS

While deities are not necessary for a religion, speculative fiction does offer the opportunity to include fantastical gods.

If there are multiple deities in your world, do they represent a particular aspect of life? What do they prioritize? What do they ask of or look for in their followers? Are your deities alive or dead? Infinite or just long-lived? Mysterious and unseen, or flesh and blood walking amongst their followers? Wise and all-knowing or childlike and petulant?

In H.M. Long's novel *Hall of Smoke,* Hessa is an Eangi warrior priestess who regularly communes with her goddess, Eang. Her prayers are usually answered. She feels the influence and power of Eang regularly and has even seen her goddess on occasion. But when she disobeys a direct command from Eang to murder a traveller, Hessa's world crumbles. Raiders raze her village, and Hessa, the lone surviving priestess, struggles to close the distance between a goddess who is becoming more and more ambivalent toward her people.

Hessa comes to realize a three-way battle between Eang, the new gods, and the gods of the Old World is brewing. Ancient spirits and deities are awakening in her world, the magic that has previously bound them is unravelling, and Hessa's faith in her goddess wanes every time the deity turns her back on her. It's fascinating to watch the interaction between Hessa and the various gods and goddesses in her world. Some are mysterious and previously unseen and some are solid, physical threats.

Do Your Deities have Limits?

Some deities are all-powerful, in which case, their followers will likely question why they don't swoop in and save the day when they're in trouble (and that, in itself, is good fodder for philosophical debate and internal struggle).

However, other deities have limitations. Perhaps your god wants their followers to have free will. That sets a limit on what sort of conflicts this deity is able to solve, because if their followers *want* to choose a wrong path, the god has to let them or break their own rules.

In the TV series *Loki*, the god of mischief creates an alternate timeline in which he steals a tesseract and becomes a variant of the Loki we know from the Avengers movies. In this timeline, he is taken into custody by the Time Variance Authority (TVA), which is a powerful bureaucratic organization that prunes variant timelines in order to maintain the one "sacred timeline." The entire series would be considerably shorter and less entertaining if Loki could access his powers while in the custody of the TVA. Instead, he has to figure out alternate methods of repairing the timeline, hunting down another murderous Loki variant. A time-travelling, crime thriller adventure ensues—all of which would have been impossible if Loki had his powers.

Limitations can be a useful way to spur—you guessed it—conflict.

Domain Ideas for Your Story

Here are some ideas for domains your deities might represent (this is not an all-encompassing list, but will hopefully inspire ideas).

Elemental: Water, Earth, Air, Fire, Light, Darkness, Shadow, Electricity

Conceptual (Positive): Peace, Life, Order, Creation, Love, Truth, Freedom, Victory, Luck, Vigilance, Protection, Redemption, Restoration, Resurrection, Renewal, Fertility, Birth, Home, Joy, Discovery, Community, Leadership, Glory, Healing

Conceptual (Negative): War, Death, Chaos, Destruction, Hate, Lies, Captivity, Failure, Misfortune, Trickery, Curses, Corruption, Decay, Thirst, Hunger, Toil, Disease, Murder, Tyranny, Torture, Blood, Suffering, Despair, Fear, Loss, Rage, Poison, Venom, Judgement, Discord, Cannibalism, Pain

Conceptual (Neutral): Magic, Knowledge, Travel, Time, Music, Beauty, Fate, Trade, Wealth, Balance, Dreams, Memory, Thought, Language, Strategy, Contracts, Competition, Family, Cooperation, Secrets, Mystery, Silence, History, Persuasion, Stealth, Sustenance, Medicine, Fitness, Immortality, Bureaucracy

Nature: Earth, Sun, Moon, Stars, Animals, Birds, Mammals, Fish, Reptiles, Amphibians, Rodents, Insects, Plants, Trees, Flowers, Herbs, Grass, Thorns, Ash, Smoke, Winter, Fall, Spring, Summer, Harvest, Rain, Snow, Storms, Wind, Forests, Mountains, Hills, Plains, Swamps, Jungles, Deserts, Seas, Rivers, Lakes

Metals: Gold, Silver, Copper, Bronze, Iron, Steel, Aluminum, Brass, Magnesium, Tin, Lead, Zinc

Gems: Beryl, Diamond, Garnet, Jade, Opal, Topaz, Emerald, Ruby, Sapphire, Lapis Lazuli, Amethyst

Time: Day, Night, Dawn, Dusk

Sins: Envy, Sloth, Gluttony, Pride, Greed, Lust, Wrath

Virtues: Prudence, Justice, Temperance, Courage, Faith, Hope, Charity

Magic Types: Abjuration, Conjuration, Divination, Enchantment, Illusion, Necromancy, Transmutation, Elemental, Incantation, Alchemy, Witchcraft, Summoning, Light, Dark, Naming, Nature

Attributes: Strength, Dexterity, Intelligence, Wisdom, Charisma, Grace, Humour, Initiative, Knowledge, Resolve, Self-Awareness, Honesty, Integrity, Flexibility, Positivity, Focus, Ambition, Modesty, Generosity, Consistency, Cooperativeness, Helpfulness, Curiosity, Devotion, Inventiveness, Negativity, Arrogance, Intolerance, Pessimism, Jealousy, Laziness, Gullibility, Cowardice, Nervousness, Vanity

People Groups: Alchemists, Artisans, Builders, Cooks, Doctors, Farmers, Fishers, Hunters, Heroes, Labourers, Merchants, Musicians, Painters, Pilgrims, Playwrights, Sailors, Scholars, Smiths, Soldiers, Teachers, Thieves, Tinkerers, Travellers, Orphans, the Lost, Children, Elderly, the Poor, the Wealthy, the Mistreated

Your deity doesn't have to only represent one thing. A fun exercise is picking two to four domains at random and then brainstorming how they might fit together.

For example, we picked at random: *fear*, *thought*, and *mammals*. Perhaps this deity grants animals a human level of consciousness and speech. Maybe they grant worshipers a magic power, like the ability to sap fear from someone else. Maybe their followers lose their ability to feel fear completely. Let your imagination take you anywhere!

Whether or not deities and religion are important to your story, they can be a key part of worldbuilding to make your story feel authentic. So throw in some religious movements into your world's history, and consider what your characters believe about how their world came to be, what their purpose in life is, and whether your story's gods are real.

Chapter 14

Even NASA Can't Improve on Duct Tape

Science and Technology

If you're not a scientist, and the idea of tackling real science in a novel seems like a lot, you are not alone. The good news is you can research as much or as little as you like in this area, because science fiction is a spectrum between "hard" and "soft." Here are some steps to decide how to handle the science in your novel.

1. PICK YOUR POINT ON THE SPECTRUM.

Science fiction stretches between these two categories:

- *Hard science fiction*, which digs into the specifics of science and often focuses on astronomy, physics, chemistry, or biology.
- *Soft science fiction*, which focuses on how science and technology affect people and society, dedicating less time to scientific nuts and bolts.

When deciding where your novel falls on the spectrum, ask yourself how you solve the story's main conflict. If science resolves big problems in your story, you're likely writing a hard sci-fi; this will involve laying out a clear set of rules so that your reader understands *how* the conflict is being solved. For example, *The Martian* by Andy Weir is hard sci-fi. Weir began the story as serialized posts on his website because he wanted to explore what might go wrong on a mission to Mars. He used real science (such as botany and the methods of oxygen generation) and NASA technologies (such as the Habitat and the Rover) in the book.

Of course, you can push the barriers of science in your hard sci-fi story. Many of these tales feature science that doesn't currently exist. For example, the *Hermes*—the NASA vessel in *The Martian*—is unrealistically large and uses ion technology that hasn't been developed yet. With scientific knowledge, you can make guesses about what might be possible in the future, and explore those possibilities.

If science is a backdrop to your story, it might not be necessary to explain how it works. For example, in the film *The Matrix*, we don't care about how artificial intelligence utilizes human bodies as batteries (in reality, humans would make inefficient power sources). That isn't the point of the movie. Instead, *The Matrix* focuses on the struggle for freedom in a world of totalitarian control in which humans are unconscious slaves, and whether it is better to face a bleak reality or live a comfortable life in a dream world.

2. CONSIDER YOUR BIG IDEA.

A key ingredient of speculative fiction is… well… speculating. Often we can distill this into "what if?" questions, like the following:

What if most of humanity became sterile and there were only a small percentage of women who could still carry a baby to term? (Margaret Atwood's, *The Handmaid's Tale*.) What if evil aliens tried to take over the world? (H.G. Well's *War of the*

Worlds.) What if artificial intelligence isn't interested in becoming human at all? (Martha Wells' *The Murderbot Diaries.*)

Is there a "what if?" question that fascinates you? Does it excite you enough to cultivate it into a story? Can you already start to imagine how that world might be different than ours? That, friend, is your starting point, your seed. And you can expand on the details, including science, from there.

3. CHOOSE YOUR AUDIENCE.

Who are you writing for? If you want to have cross-genre appeal, soft-sci fi can be an easier bridge than hard sci-fi because it deals with a lot of the same social sciences as contemporary fiction does. If you want to impress the hard sci-fi readers, hook them with a big idea, an angle they haven't seen before, or characters and plot so stunning that they don't mind if it includes science they've already read about many times before.

If you are writing for children or young adults, they only need a grade-appropriate explanation of the science in your book. Don't get bogged down in technical details, but don't take any shortcuts either. Kids are smart and will notice if you break your own rules.

4. DECIDE WHAT IS WORTH RESEARCHING.

It's easy to fall down the rabbit hole of research, especially when you are digging into a subject that fascinates you. Eventually, you *do* need to put pen to paper, though. Spend your research time wisely.

Hot tip: You don't have to explain everyday science. Do you know the inner workings of your cell phone well enough to repair it? Can you explain how your car's autonomous emergency braking system works? Do you understand how your GPS uses triangulation, or the details of your refrigerator's compression system? These are technologies we use every day without much thought. It's not important to us how they work, just that they *do* work. In the same fashion, you don't need to explain to your readers how a food replicator, instant transport, or morphing clothes work, *unless* their inner workings are crucial to the story later. If your character takes them for granted, your reader can afford to as well.

Instead, only research the science or technology that is going to change your character's life during the story. For example, the movie *Arrival* involved research into linguistics, because the protagonist Louise Banks is hired by the military to defuse a first contact situation and decode the alien's cryptic language. The filmmakers actually gave Jessica Coon, a linguist who was consulted for the film, a whiteboard and asked her what she would do with it if she was trying to communicate with aliens.[1] Her responses informed one of the famous scenes from the movie, in which Louise explains to an impatient colonel why they have to start with basic vocabulary and can't just jump to complex questions.

The movie also gets some things wrong about linguistics. For example, linguists and translators are two different fields, but in the story they're merged into one. And, of course, the bits about seeing the future have no basis in real science. The moviemakers are aware they get some things wrong; at the end of the day, their main audience isn't linguists, but people who enjoy good stories.

5. ESTABLISH HOW MUCH TO REVEAL.

Heady with all this incredible research we've done, it is tempting to include all of it on the page of our story, because look at all this cool stuff we just learned! The more legitimate research we put onto the page, the more it will establish authority with our readers, right?

Unfortunately, including too much explanation just turns a story into a fictional textbook and drags the pace. Only include the research that is required for your story to make sense. Don't forget—this is a story first and foremost, and your readers came to be entertained.

6. DEFINE YOUR SETTING.

How has science and technology changed or hindered your world? What does your setting look like? Whether you are describing a computer, a ship, or an entire city, be careful not to ground it visually in current technology. Technology advances quickly and current devices become obsolete. Unless you're Peter Quill from *Guardians of the Galaxy*, you're probably not cruising through futuristic worlds rocking out to a mixed cassette tape with a Sony Walkman clipped to your hip.

7. EXPLORE YOUR CULTURE.

Who has access to science and tech in your story? Do most citizens enjoy everyday technology, or is it hoarded by a certain class? Is everyone educated in the sciences, or is that reserved for certain members of your culture? Does your science/tech come with consequences (for example, a socially-disconnected society, over-reliance on technology for day-to-day survival, or segregation of people because of their genetic makeup)? What would happen if your society suddenly lost their tech or, alternatively, a new scientific breakthrough opened up a new world of technological opportunities?

8. STAY CONSISTENT WITH YOUR RULES.

Once you've established scientific rules, stick with them. Don't tweak physics halfway through your story in order to save the day. Alternatively, don't *forget* about tech when your characters need it. If someone has the ability to instantly transport, they're not likely to embark on an epic journey to reach a destination—unless their transporter tech has failed.

~

WE CAN'T COVER every conceivable topic for science fiction novels, because every story will require different types and amounts of research. But here are some topics common to a lot of science fiction, both hard and soft, and some tips on how to include them in your novel.

SPACE TRAVEL

Though your story can certainly take place on a single world (real or digital), many sci-fi novels feature space travel. If your tale involves traveling to different planets, solar systems, galaxies, or even universes, you'll want to consider how people travel long distances. Here are some options (and you're not limited to just one in your story, either. Perhaps different aliens have developed different technologies).

- **Hyperdrives.** Is traveling through our universe too slow? No problem! We'll just take a detour through this parallel dimension, where the rules of physics don't apply. The science of how hyperspace travel works is mostly left to the imagination. In Star Wars, the course needs to be calculated beforehand so they don't crash into a planet. (e.g. *Star Wars, Halo*)
- **Jump drives.** Also known as FTL drives, these allow instant travel from one spot to another, much like teleportation. In *Battlestar Galactica*, this is accomplished via a rare fuel, and jumping can damage nearby vessels. Calculations are also needed to ensure the ship doesn't materialize inside a planet or sun. (e.g. *Battlestar Galactica, Dune* by Frank Herbert)

- **Warp drives.** Let's just toss physics out the window and accelerate ships past the speed of light. Warp factor 11, Scotty! Interestingly enough, there has been research into warp technology using Einstein's general relativity equations; in 1994, physicist Miguel Alcubierre proposed that matter and energy can be arranged to bend spacetime in a bubble that allows for long-distance travel in a short time. (e.g. *Star Trek*, *The Hitchhiker's Guide to the Galaxy* by Douglas Adams)
- **Wormholes.** Also known as Einstein-Rosen bridges due to a 1935 theory by Albert Einstein and physicist Nathan Rosen, wormholes connect two different points in space-time. Physics tells us that nothing can travel faster than light, but ships could enter wormholes at sub-light speeds and travel great distances. Wormhole theory also includes the possibility of traveling between parallel realities! (E.g. *Stargate*, *Interstellar*)
- **Generation ships.** These ships travel at sub-light speeds, but are self-contained ecosystems that allow the people on board to survive for hundreds of generations as they make their way to their destination. The tricky science for these is not only the self-contained environment, but how to carry enough fuel to make it to your destination and land on the new planet. (e.g. *Starglass* by Phoebe North, *Dust* by Elizabeth Bear)
- **Cryo-travel.** With this technology, a ship's crew makes the journey in suspended animation. Time passes, but their bodies won't feel it. If this technology exists in your world, consider its other uses (do sick people get put into cryo until a cure is found? Do people prolong their lives through cryosleep?). And, of course, many sci-fi stories have used this technology to ask the question: "What if you

wake up too early?" (e.g. *Across the Universe* by Beth Revis, *Passengers*)

When considering space travel, ask yourself whether there are consequences or costs. In some stories, hyperdrive jumps make passengers sick. In others, the fuel or requirements are expensive. Cryo-travel allows time to pass without aging—thus, a person could wake up and everyone they know is dead (*Futurama*, anyone?). In the very first episode of *Stargate SG:1*, traveling through the stargate makes the traveler extremely cold and causes ice to collect on their clothes (though the show dumped that idea after one episode, probably because it took a lot of makeup and special effects). "Escape," a short story by Isaac Asimov, explores how hyperspace jumps cause the ship's crew to cease to exist for a moment—technically, they die—and how that impacts the robot pilot, who is programmed not to kill humans.

Consequences and costs can kickstart ideas and conflicts for your story!

TIME TRAVEL

Time travel mechanics are tough to design without creating plot holes and scientific inaccuracies, but if your story is intriguing enough, those won't matter. *Doctor Who* certainly doesn't make sense most of the time, and we love it anyway. Here are some types of time travel you can play with in your story. The important thing is that you stick with whatever rules you establish.

- **Time dilation.** In *Ender's Game*, a character ages eight years in space while 50 years pass on Earth due to time dilation. In *Interstellar*, time passes quicker for astronauts while they're near a black hole. This type of time travel is scientifically possible and has been proven with the 1971 Hafele-Keating experiments, which noted a time difference between two clocks flown on planes traveling in opposite directions. The concept relates to Einstein's theory of special relativity, which teaches that the faster you move through space, the more slowly you're moving through time. If you're able to travel near the speed of light, the effects are stronger.

- **Seeing the Future.** Prophecies and glimpses of the future are about information traveling through time, as opposed to people. In *Foundation* by Isaac Asimov, everyone who learns psychohistory, a science that predicts human behaviour, is able to guess the future with high accuracy. In *Babylon 5*, Centauri's dreams predict their own deaths. And the entire plot of *Minority Report* revolves around people getting arrested before they commit homicides, thanks to the knowledge of three clairvoyants. You can use precognition to play with readers' expectations. Will the characters be able to prevent the future event, or is it set in stone? Will the event happen, but it doesn't look exactly like what they thought it would? Is the event only one of possible futures? The rules are up to you.

- **Time loops.** In the video game *The Legend of Zelda: Majora's Mask*, a moon crashes into the world in an apocalyptic event. But all is not lost! Link can return to a time three days earlier and try to prevent the destruction. Link experiences these three days over and over again until he finds a way to save the land. The time loop becomes an interesting game mechanic that you have to navigate in order to win the game. Movies like *Groundhog Day* and *Edge of Tomorrow* accomplish something similar, in which characters are stuck repeating the same day. Among other things, this type of time travel enables you to explore your characters' psyches—who wouldn't experience mental strain after living through the same day over and over again?

- **Unchangeable timeline.** In *Harry Potter and the Prisoner of Azkaban* by J.K. Rowling, Harry and Hermione go back in time, but everything they do (saving Buckbeak, rescuing Sirius, etc.) has already happened. In this type of time travel, no alternate timelines are created as whatever a character's past self does has already affected the future. You can be clever and foreshadow this type of time travel with clues that don't make sense until the characters travel back in time, such as in the Harry Potter movie, when Hermione howls like a werewolf, Harry gets hit on the back of the head with a stone, and Harry sees himself before he passes out.

- **Alternate timeline.** In the TV show *Eureka*, five characters travel back in time to 1947 due to solar flares powering a bridge device. While they're there, they significantly change things. When they return to 2010, the world is similar but different in several ways; Lupo is no longer Carter's deputy, Fargo is the head of Global Dynamics, Carter is back with his ex-girlfriend, Deacon is married, etc. They created an alternate timeline by changing the past.

- **Rewritten timeline.** In *Back to the Future*, Marty McFly travels back in time to 1955 and changes the future. At one point, he starts to fade out of existence because he interferes with his parents getting together. After his adventure in the past, in which he successfully reunites his parents, he returns to his correct time, 1985, to discover things are different from when he left —his parents are happier, healthier, and wealthier due to the positive impact he had on them in the past. Marty rewrites the timeline by making changes in the past.

Get creative with your rules of time travel! What if it's only the character's mind that goes back and their body stays in the present? What if they can go back in time, but they lose their memories of what happened when they return? What if time is constantly in flux? What are the consequences of time travel? How does it add conflict to your story?

VIRUSES AND PLAGUES

Authors have explored the potential impacts of viruses and plagues for as long as humans have been fighting off infection, and there are numerous areas to research.

Most bacteria and viruses are adapted to attack certain systems or organs. The upper respiratory tract is commonly involved because it's one of the easiest ways into the body. Open wounds are another frequent entry point—cue zombie bites! Once in the bloodstream, an illness can hone in on organs like the liver or lymphatic system. Not only do microorganisms tend to target certain parts of us, they often target certain *groups* of us. In Christina Sweeney-Baird's novel *The End of Men*, ninety percent of the world's male population is killed, leading to a crash in government, finance, law, and other male-dominated industries.

We are likely most familiar with airborne transmittable microorganisms, illnesses that come from contacting contaminated body fluids or organs, and those that flourish in water. However, in Tony Burgess's book *Pontypool Changes Everything*, an epidemic virus that causes its hosts to turn into cannibals is caught through conversation. The virus travels exclusively through certain words in the English language. The science might not check out, but what a fascinating "what if?" question!

Human-made viruses are a popular theme for stories that feature warfare. Rendering your enemy useless without firing a gun has its appeal. In the film *I Am Legend*, the Krippin Virus is engineered to cure cancer and shows initial success in treating patients before mutating into a deadlier variant and causing a pandemic. In real life, Swiss scientists have recently created an artificial virus that can be used to target cancer—hopefully without the zombie aftereffects.

As technology progresses, so might methods to disrupt that technology. In M.T. Anderson's novel *Feed*, society has adopted surgical implants that allow them to interact with each other electronically and immerse themselves in a futuristic internet. Titus and his friends take a vacation to the moon and are "frozen" when they meet a hacker at a club who attacks their feeds with a virus, temporarily paralyzing them.

Widespread viruses not only cause devastating effects on society, economy, and communications, but also spur some unexpectedly quirky behaviours too—like hoarding toilet paper. What unforeseen reactions will a plague give rise to in your fiction?

ALIEN BIOLOGY

Perhaps owing to the fact that early special effects in film involved mostly costumed people under thick layers of makeup, the image of humanoid aliens is a common one. But we only have to dig into the beautiful complexity of life in our own world to realize that alien biology could be wonderfully different from our own.

Many writers draw inspiration from insects or cephalopods for their extraterrestrials. In Sue Berke's book, *Semiosis*, humanity colonizes another world to find that it's full of intelligent plant life, including sentient bamboo.

There's also potential for aliens to have senses that expand beyond ours. Honey bees can see in the ultraviolet spectrum, so why not extraterrestrials? Perhaps they have senses beyond the five we know, like electroreceptivity in sharks. Maybe they sense time differently from the linear way we comprehend it, similar to the aliens in the film *Arrival*, who comprehend time in a circular manner.

The way aliens communicate will largely depend on their senses. In Claire McCague's novel *The Rosetta Man*, the aliens that make first contact seem more like small marsupials than sentients. They communicate to a human translator, Estlin, via telepathy that only Estlin is sensitive to—he's also able to communicate with other animals, like squirrels. But the extraterrestrials also communicate—and manipulate—using a pheromone. In Amy Thompson's *The Color of Distance*, aliens communicate by changing colours and patterns on their skin.

The more drastic the difference in biology between alien and human in your story, the more difficult it can be for them to relate to each other. That can lead to tension and mystery that drives your story forward.

ARTIFICIAL INTELLIGENCE

Stories dealing with A.I. will naturally push the borders of what defines humanity. Robots—especially ones who can think for themselves—are fun to ask "what if?" questions about. How are they created? Do we create intelligent machines, or do we transfer human consciousness *into* machines? In *We Are Legion (We are Bob)* by Dennis E. Taylor, Bob Johansson dies while crossing a street and wakes up a hundred years later to find he's been uploaded as the artificial intelligence in an interstellar probe. "Corpsicles" like him don't have rights. He's state property.

Sometimes A.I. involves a network of nanotechnology. In Kevin J. Anderson and Doug Beason's *Assemblers of Infinity*, a moonbase crew discovers a massive alien structure growing on the far side of the moon. The intelligent, microscopic machines erecting it consume everything they touch, and they're multiplying. When news reaches Earth, populations riot, and experts scramble to ascertain if the sprawling build is an alien attack or human nanotech gone wrong.

A lot of sci-fi addresses the fear of technology turning on its makers as it outstrips us in strength, intelligence, and longevity. With our houses, vehicles, and other appliances becoming increasingly "smart," A.I. is more prevalent than ever. We see hostile artificial intelligence in films like *I, Robot* and *Terminator* —and to a lesser degree, when Siri completely botches a clearly spoken instruction. Sometimes though, A.I. is not out to destroy humanity, but instead to *become* human. Such is the case in Isaac Asimov's classic *The Bicentennial Man*. The main character, Andrew, a robot butler, replaces his inorganic parts with more and more organic prosthetics, including organs, culminating with an operation that alters his brain to one that decays with time, rendering him mortal. Other times, A.I. aren't interested in having anything to do with humans and just want to be left alone to watch their serials, like Martha Wells's Murderbot.

GENETIC ENGINEERING

Humans started playing with genetics as soon as we started cultivating crops and domesticating animals. Farmers naturally strive to produce the most fruitful crop yields. Animal husbandry focuses on breeding to improve or amplify desirable traits. Sheep were originally domesticated for their meat. They shed their outer layer of wool every spring, but over time, people bred the animals to produce more and more wool without shedding it naturally. Now, if sheep aren't shorn yearly, their fleece grows so long and thick that the animals overheat, go "wool blind" as their sight is impaired, and experience serious mobility issues. What unintended consequences could selective breeding cause in your fictional worlds?

Cloning is also a popular topic. Whether preserving a favourite strain of apple, raising spare organs for harvest, or growing test tube babies, clones come with failings too. Susceptibility to being entirely wiped out by disease is a danger that faces genetically identical crops and humans alike.

In the 2004 TV series *Battlestar Galactica*, most of the Cylon population is wiped out by a disease that doesn't affect humans. It hits especially hard, because the Cylons are all clones, so none of them have the benefit of innate immunity from varied genetics.

Perhaps your clone is not identical but is an "improved" copy of their host, engineered to have modified traits. In Sarah Gailey's *The Echo Wife*, award-winning genetics researcher and workaholic Evelyn Caldwell discovers her husband has used her cloning technology to replicate a version of his wife who is more compliant, more docile—and more than willing to have a child with him. And now he wants a divorce.

Designer genetics refers to genetic modification to tailor-make a specific end product. Commonly, we think of super-soldiers here, but it's been used in sci-fi in many different ways. In Nancy Kress's novel *Beggars in Spain*, Leisha Camden is a genetically engineered "Sleepless" designed with a higher IQ and the ability to stay awake twenty-four-seven. Intelligent and productive, she could be the future of humanity, or she could be hunted down as a freak by a society that doesn't trust its latest creation.

CYBORGS AND CYBERNETICS

Cyborgs already walk among us. People with cochlear implants, retinal prosthesis, artificial pacemakers and robotic limbs have an improved quality of life because of these mechanical devices. Scientists have successfully controlled cockroaches with implants attached to their backs; they are testing the cyborg insects' viability to search for people in collapsed buildings.

The Borg in *Star Trek* are hive-minded cyborgs who forcibly take the technology and knowledge of other species by injecting individuals with nanoprobes and surgically augmenting them with cybernetic parts in a quest to assimilate them and achieve perfection.

In Essa Hansen's *Nophek Gloss*, gender-fluid En replaces so much of their body with cybernetics, they hardly have any original hardware left, leading to the question: how much of a body can be replaced with mechanics before someone is no longer considered human?

PLANETS

Planets, stars, and star systems are all constantly moving through space, interacting and evolving. Assuming that liquid water is essential for the existence of life, a planet has to be a comfortable distance away from the star it orbits so that it can maintain surface water. This is often known as the Goldilocks zone or habitable zone. The planet must be large enough to hold an atmosphere—low mass planets have such weak gravity that their atmospheres can be stripped away. A molten core capable of producing a magnetic field also helps to protect a planet from harmful radiation that wipes out life and strips away atmosphere. It's useful if a planet rotates its axis and orbits its star at a certain speed, too. Rotation and orbital speeds affect the length of a planet's days and nights, its seasons, and even where cloud systems congregate.

Here are a few types of planets you might want to be familiar with:

- **Brown Dwarfs** balance the line between planet and star. They're created by clouds of gas collapsing on themselves, and they fuse lithium and deuterium to keep slightly alit, like incredibly massive embers.
- **Gas Giants**, like Jupiter and Saturn, are the largest of planets, mostly made up of hydrogen and helium. Sometimes they are called "failed stars" because they don't have enough mass to ignite fusion.

- **Ice Giants**, like Uranus and Neptune, are mainly composed of elements that are heavier than hydrogen and helium, such as sulfur, oxygen, nitrogen, and carbon. They're smaller but much denser than gas giants.
- **Terrestrial planets**, like Mercury, Venus, Earth, and Mars, have rocky surfaces surrounding metallic cores. They can contain liquid water and may have tectonic activity, which can generate magnetic fields.
- **Dwarf planets**, like Pluto, are large enough to maintain a spherical shape and hold moons, but they don't clear their orbit of other debris.

INTERESTINGLY ENOUGH, you can accomplish the "feel" of a hard sci-fi novel even if the science is mumbo-jumbo. Author Ada Hoffmann mentions in her blog post titled "How Science Feels" that many readers have mistaken her novel *The Outside* for hard science fiction.

> The actual science in *The Outside* is nonsense," Hoffmann writes. "I start Yasira out as a working scientist, doing physics, but she's in the 28th century and all the physics words and concepts are completely made up. I nod to actual physics concepts like time dilation and vacuum energy but the things that are going on with them in the Shien Reactor are a total handwave, complete with made-up units of measurement and made-up names for made-up equations with which the characters desperately try to explain to themselves the cosmic horror that is slowly unfolding before their eyes."[2]

Hoffmann adds that hard sci-fi comes with a "culturally

determined set of tropes, stylistic conventions, and reader expectations," such as scientist protagonists, a focus on physics, and a dense writing style that uses lots of technical terms. *The Outside* includes all those elements, so it's easy to understand why some people think it's hard sci-fi. She did include some real science in the book, drawing on her background as a computer scientist to inform characters' research methods and user interfaces.

She writes, "I saved the intensive research for parts of the book that felt more thematically central, and I was more worried about getting right—especially the themes of mysticism and psychological trauma."

Put your scientific research into the areas that matter most to you and your story. At the end of the day, you're writing a novel, not a textbook. It's up to you how deep you want to dive.

Chapter 15

Higitus Figitus Migitus Mum
Magic and Superpowers

Fantasy can be intimidating, because you're often building an entire world from scratch. Just like with science, your novel's magic can be as simple or as complex as you like. It can help to break things down into the following steps.

1. PICK YOUR POINT ON THE SPECTRUM.

Fantasy doesn't have hard and soft subgenres like science fiction does, but, funnily enough, magic systems are divided into categories of the same name.

- **Hard magic systems** have defined rules and clear boundaries. Usually, these rules are unbreakable and the reader intimately understands how the magic system works (e.g. Mistborn by Brandon Sanderson, *Avatar: The Last Airbender, Fullmetal Alchemist*).
- **Soft magic systems** don't have hard and fast rules. Magic is left undefined and mysterious. The reader can see it in action, but often isn't aware of its inner workings (e.g. *The Lord of the Rings* by J.R.R. Tolkien, *Star Wars, Old Magic* by Patricia McKillip).

The terms *hard* and *soft* magic systems were popularized by Brandon Sanderson, a fantasy author who is known for his hard magic systems. Sanderson has created a few "laws" for magic that are beneficial to understand when brainstorming your novel's magic. To determine where your system falls on the spectrum (and it doesn't have to be totally hard or totally soft—it can be somewhere in between), consider Sanderson's first law:

> An author's ability to solve conflict with magic is directly proportional to how well the reader understands said magic."[1]

Avatar: The Last Airbender falls closer to the hard end of the magic scale, because we know a variety of things about bending. For example, magic users can only bend one element—fire, earth, water, or air (the one exception is the Avatar, who can bend all four). Toph is an earthbender, and we've seen her move rocks and cause the ground to shake, so when Sokka falls into a crack in the ground and gets stuck, it's perfectly reasonable that she can use her powers to get him out.

But having a magic user jump in to save the day when their powers aren't clearly defined runs the risk of *deus ex machina*—when a seemingly impossible problem is suddenly solved by the appearance of a random person, object, or event. Without understandable consequences, constraints, and the real chance of failure, readers may feel cheated and tension is lowered. The major conflict doesn't seem that major at all if it's easily solved by magic the readers were previously unaware of.

On the other hand, if magic is more of a backdrop and isn't used to solve major conflicts, it isn't necessary to explain how it works. Gandalf doesn't use his magic to destroy the One Ring, so we don't really need to know the nuts and bolts of how his powers work.

2. DEFINE THE LIMITS OF MAGIC.

This brings us to Sanderson's second law:

 Limitations > Powers."[2]

Solving all problems with magic is uninteresting. This is why Allison thinks Superman is boring—because he has abilities that make him near-invincible. Sanderson (who is less critical of the Man of Steel) suggests that Superman's weaknesses—his code of ethics and sensitivity to kryptonite—are what make him interesting.

Regardless of whether you're using a hard or soft magic system, make sure your characters have limitations. It is often the cost of magic that makes it interesting, rather than the abilities it grants your characters. It is the weaknesses of your characters and how they overcome them that make them heroic, not their powers.

Aang from *Avatar: The Last Airbender* has many challenges to overcome in the series, even though he's the Avatar and able to use all four elements. His weaknesses include his youth, his uncertainty, and his difficulty learning earthbending.

On the lighter side of things, magic in the Disney movie *The Sword in the Stone* largely revolves around turning into animals (though it can do lots of other things as well, such as washing dishes and packing the contents of a room into a small bag). When Merlin and Madam Mim engage in a wizard duel, Mim imposes three rules: they aren't allowed to turn into minerals or vegetables—only animals; they aren't allowed to turn into mythical creatures; and they aren't allowed to go invisible. Mim, the "evil" character, breaks all her own rules, but Merlin still manages to beat her while following the limits she set, causing immense satisfaction in us viewers.

3. DEFINE THE COSTS AND CONSEQUENCES OF MAGIC.

In the Dragon Age video game series, blood magic is a school of forbidden power in which blood fuels spellcasting. It is often used in violent ways, to dominate or corrupt others. Using blood magic doesn't mean you're evil, but one of the few ways to learn it is by summoning a demon, which runs the risk of the demon possessing you. Talk about potential consequences!

The more specific you can be about magic's rules, the more possibilities open up for the story. For example, let's explore the idea of blood magic in some ways that Dragon Age does not. If blood is required to cast spells, that could mean any of the following:

- A mage pricks their finger to cast a small spell, but makes deeper cuts for bigger spells. Thus, the more scars a mage has, the more powerful they are perceived to be.
- A mage sacrifices an animal to cast a spell, and many decorate themselves with pieces of the animals they've killed (teeth necklaces, cloaks made of hide, etc.).
- A mage cuts someone else to cast a spell, making slave trade common in magical societies, because mages need living bodies to mutilate.
- A mage kills someone else to cast a spell; thus, mages are feared and distrusted.

Notice how defining costs can also inform the societies and cultures of your world and how magic-users are perceived.

4. BRAINSTORM A SOURCE.

Where does your magic originate? Is it elemental? Does it come from your world or a dimension beyond? Is it a gift from gods—or a curse from demons?

Go as in-depth or as surface-level as you want. For example, in the Harry Potter series, the "source" of magic seems to be something inside certain people (wizards and witches) but not others (muggles and squibs), and wands are the main tools of concentration used to bring about said magic. That's all we know, and it's enough.

The source of magic in your story could be an all-surrounding energy, like the Force in Star Wars. It could come from certain elements, like in *Avatar: The Last Airbender* or metals in Brandon Sanderson's Mistborn series. It could be based on music, colour, nature, light, time, space, or something abstract. Or it could be a mystery!

5. NAME YOUR MAGES AND THEIR PLACE IN SOCIETY

What are magic users called? Wizards? Druids? Elementalists? Something unique to your story?

Is there a select caste of magic users in your world? Is it hereditary or can everyone in your world perform magic? Is magic frowned upon or considered a gift? Rare or commonplace? Public knowledge or well-kept secret? Legal or illegal? Are there magical societies, schools, or ranks? Is there a uniform, colour code, or distinguishing physical feature that differentiates magic users?

The answers to these questions will be largely determined by history and will influence the culture in your world. Consider key historical events that are molded by the lack or use of magic. It is also unlikely that your entire world will view magic users in the same light. Some countries might revere them while others fear them.

6. REVEAL DETAILS SLOWLY.

In hard magic systems, you have to let your reader know the ground rules. They'll be lost otherwise. Of course, you don't need to dump the whole system on them at once. Let them learn organically. Often this can be effectively done if they are following a new magical user who is learning the ropes. Take to heart Sanderson's third law:

 Expand what you already have before you add something new."[3]

Simply put: don't load on the worldbuilding too soon, and consider what Sanderson refers to as "deep" worldbuilding instead of "wide" worldbuilding.

In *The Final Empire,* Sanderson introduces the basics of Mistborn's magic system, Allomancy, slowly. At first, all we know is that Vin is "lucky," because that's all she knows. Then, as Vin slowly gains knowledge about the magic—that there are eight basic Allomantic metals, that they're each associated with a different ability (such as pushing or pulling on emotions), that most allomancers can only burn one metal and use its associated power, but mistborn can burn all of them—we learn along with her.

Details of the magic continue to be revealed throughout the story—such as how there are actually more than eight metals and how allomancers came to exist in the first place. Sanderson doesn't pile on everything at once, and slowly revealing facts about magic adds tension and mystery to the story.

WITH MAGIC, as with most things in worldbuilding, your imagination's the limit! However, we've compiled some common types of magic systems that might help inspire your own. Many stories include more than one magic system and categories can blur together.

1. ELEMENTAL MAGIC

As of the publication of this book, scientists have discovered 118 elements that make up all matter on earth, but elemental magic systems tend to deal with far fewer than that, most often the classic elements of fire, water, earth, and air. Some magic users can create these substances out of thin air, while others can only control those that already exist in the world around them. Still other systems involve more, or different, elements than the traditional four. While these magic systems can appear common or basic, they leave a lot of room for creative storytelling.

In the Netflix series *The Dragon Prince*, there are six Primal Sources of magic (sun, moon, stars, earth, sky, and ocean), and each source is connected to a race of elves. Cultures form around these magics; for example, Skywing Elves are known for quickness, agility, and prizing freedom, while Moonshadow Elves are known for secrecy, illusions, and valuing privacy. There is also a seventh source known as Dark Magic, which isn't connected to a Primal Source, but draws upon the energy within magical creatures to fuel spells. Dark Magic is commonly practiced by humans. The elves and dragons of the world divided the continent and drove humanity West because they were appalled at the humans' practice of hunting creatures to harvest their magical energy.

Elemental magic is an exciting way to explore power dynamics and culture. What elements will be included in your magic system? How is society built around these magic users? Are some elements prized more than others? How do the elements interact with each other—can they be used together? Do they counteract each other?

Other examples: Wheel of Time by Robert Jordan; *Elemental Masters* by Mercedes Lackey; Circle of Magic series by Tamora Pierce

2. SUPERPOWERS

In superhero stories, every hero has a different ability. These powers might fall under a theme (for example, everyone can shapeshift into animals), or they might involve a hodgepodge of superhuman abilities. In some worlds, characters gain superpowers in unique ways (such as by radiation or the bite of a genetically-altered spider), while others are born with them. The possibilities are endless, and the lines can blur between superheroes and other types of magic systems.

In *My Hero Academia*, a superhero high school anime, 80% of the population are born with superpowers, a.k.a. quirks. This has deeply impacted culture and society. People idolize Pro Heroes, professional crime-fighters with powerful quirks, and the media keeps track of the "top" Pro Heroes. Since quirks are passed on from parent to child, some people even choose their partner based on their quirk with the hope that they will have a powerful child. The Number Two Hero, Endeavor, can control and manipulate fire. The quirk's downside is that he gets overheated easily, which is why he married a woman with an ice quirk in the hopes that they would have a child who inherited both.

What are the limitations or weaknesses of the superpowers in your story (such as Endeavor's overheating problem)? How are you going to reveal the "rules" of your heroes' abilities? What are some character flaws or limitations, that are unrelated to their powers, that you could introduce? For example, All Might, the Number One Hero, has a chronic condition thanks to an old injury that severely affects his health, and tension rises when he can't transform into his hero form for more than a few minutes at a time.

Other examples: *X-Men*; Animorphs series by K.A. Applegate; *The Avengers*

3. INCANTATIONS

Higitus figitus! Avada kadavra! Double double, toil and trouble.

As powerful as words are in the real world, they get even more powerful when they are imbued with magic. Incantations are spoken words that produce a magical effect. Usually they involve mystical, made-up languages, and they are often accompanied by gestures or physical components in order to get a spell to work.

In *Eragon* by Christopher Paolini, spells require intense focus, and people find it easier to focus on magic when they speak their thoughts aloud. Magicians use an ancient language to cast spells. So, for example, saying the word *brisingr*, which means *fire*, could produce a flame. But creativity and imagination are also at play; as long as the connections are clear in the spellcaster's mind, they could say *brisingr* and produce something that appears entirely unrelated. Casting a spell requires energy from somewhere, usually the caster, and requires as much energy as it would take to accomplish the action by mundane means. So magicians need to be careful, or they could kill themselves by using too much of their own life energy.

Do incantations have meaning in your story? Are magic users aware of what they are saying, or is it just gibberish to them? Where did these words originate? Can you combine different words to create new effects?

Other examples: Harry Potter series by J.K. Rowling; *Supernatural*; The Dresden Files by Jim Butcher

4. ALCHEMY

Alchemy involves transmuting matter. The goal of alchemists is often turning lead into gold or creating an elixir of immortality. Ancient beliefs about alchemy are centred around the idea that all matter consists of four elements—water, earth, fire, and air—and by adjusting the percentages of these elements, you can turn something into something else (of course, atomic theory refutes that, though alchemy paved the way for the periodic table we use today).

In *Fullmetal Alchemist*, alchemy is a science based on understanding the composition of matter, deconstructing it, and then reconstructing it. It's founded on the law of equivalent exchange, meaning matter cannot be created or destroyed, and material can only be transmuted into something else that has the same basic makeup of the original material. Alchemists draw transmutation circles in order to transmute objects. In the show, alchemy looks a lot like magic, and alchemists often develop individual superpowers based on alchemy. For example, Roy Mustang, the "Flame Alchemist," is known for fire-based combat. He uses custom-made gloves, embroidered with flame alchemy transmutation circles, that allow him to make a spark by rubbing his fingers together.

Alchemy allows for many philosophical and scientific questions—what is matter? What is equivalent? Can you transmute a soul? The premise of *Fullmetal Alchemist* is based on the show's protagonists, Edward and Alphonse Elric, wanting to bring their dead mother back to life, but they are unable to because there's nothing "equivalent" they can offer for her soul.

Other examples: *The Lady Alchemist* by Samantha Vitale; *A Golden Fury* by Samantha Cohoe; *The Lies of Locke Lamora* by Scott Lynch

5. WITCHCRAFT

Witchcraft generally involves pagan spellcasting and nature. Witches cast spells through incantations, rituals, runes, herbs, amulets, potions, or other means. Witches often have a bad reputation and are feared by society. In our own world's history, people accused of being witches were persecuted and killed. People also conducted bizarre tests to determine if someone was a witch, such as tying them up and throwing them into a lake; if they floated, they were a witch (this was based on the idea that, because witches were unholy and spurned baptism, the water would reject them).

In *Buffy the Vampire Slayer*, witchcraft becomes increasingly prevalent throughout the TV series as one of the main characters, Willow, learns to become a witch. Spells can be achieved through a variety of means, including incantations, magical artifacts, herbs, crystals, and blood. Magic using bric-a-brac is visually interesting, and there are lots of ways it can go wrong—for example, what happens if you say the wrong incantation while trying to bind a demon? What if you put a different flower in your potion? What if your rune inscription is slightly wonky?

There's not much you can't do with magic in *Buffy*, but there are things you *shouldn't* do, because they have serious consequences—like raising someone from the dead. The show also explores magic's addictive nature; Willow becomes so addicted that she nearly kills another character before quitting. This is a refreshing take as, more often than not, stories explore the physical limitations of magic, but here we see a mental/emotional cost.

What are the methods of spellcasting in your story? How do various components work together, and what are the pros and cons of each medium?

Other examples: *Chilling Adventures of Sabrina*; Discworld series by Terry Pratchett; *The Mists of Avalon* by Marion Zimmer Bradley

6. NECROMANCY

The root word of *necromancy* comes from *nekros*, greek for "dead body," and *manteia*, which means "divination." Necromancy from the graeco-roman world was more about talking to the dead and learning from them as opposed to raising dead minions, though sci-fi and fantasy is full of the latter.

There are two types of magic in Garth Nix's novel *Sabriel*: Free magic and Charter magic. Free magic has existed from the beginning of time, but then it was made structured and ordered, which became Charter magic. Charter magic uses symbols, drawn on paper or in the air, spoken or whistled, while Free magic is known as the magic of necromancy. It's unpleasant to use, causing a hot metallic odour; speaking the spells burns your tongue; and it devours its casters' bodies and spirits. All necromancers are Free magic sorcerers who use bells to summon the dead to serve them. They become corrupt as they use this type of magic.

However, one magic sorcerer in this world, known as the Abhorsen, uses both Free and Charter magic for good, using the bells of a necromancer *and* charter marks. It's the Abhorsen's job to put the dead to rest and right the wrongs created by necromancers. Both the Abhorsen and necromancers can literally walk into Death, which is a vast river with a strong current that pulls souls deeper in.

Necromancy is often thought of as a purely evil magic type, but it doesn't have to be. You can also get creative with it—you don't have to stick to incantations that raise corpses from their graves. Nix's use of bells, charter marks, and whistled spells is unique.

Other examples: *Gideon the Ninth* by Tamsyn Muir; *The Mummy*; *The Bone Witch* by Rin Chupeco

7. SUMMONING

Summoning involves the ability to call a magical being to aid the magic user. Generally, the summoner has made a pact with the creature so that it does their bidding. Summoning demons is a trend in fantasy fiction, often with catastrophic results. However, summoning magic isn't limited to creatures from the underworld.

In the anime *Fairy Tail*, celestial wizards own artifacts called Gate Keys, which the wizard uses to summon celestial spirits to their aid. When the wizard acquires a Gate Key and summons a spirit for the first time, they sign a contract that defines what days the spirit is available. Lucy Heartfilia, one of the show's protagonists and a celestial wizard, has strong bonds with her spirits and cares about them deeply. This mutual love (and her headbutting with their various personalities) is part of what makes her magic so interesting.

When developing a summoning magic system, ask yourself what entities can your magic users summon? What is the cost of doing so? How is the magical being summoned—through an artifact? An incantation? A rune? Is the creature enslaved or is the relationship mutually beneficial?

Other examples: *Lord Toede* by Jeff Grubb; The Bartimaeus Trilogy by Jonathan Stroud; *Final Fantasy* video games

8. LIGHT MAGIC

Light magic could be considered a variation of elemental magic, but we like it so much we're giving it its own category. Light magic is about manipulating—you guessed it—light! There are all sorts of possibilities here, including fire-type magic, bending light to create illusions, invisibility, and using mirrors to blind opponents or cast spells.

In Garth Nix's middle grade series The Seventh Tower, the world is enshrouded in complete darkness, and a group of humans live in a castle and never leave. Sunstone magic is invaluable and has created classes within the castle's society. The Chosen, who use magic and exchange their shadows for shadow guardians, are an elevated class, and the Underfolk, who are not permitted to use magic, are servants. The Chosen use Sunstones to weave spells using the colours of the rainbow, and spells that use all seven colours are the most complex to cast.

What makes this system captivating is how it's woven into the story's society. The Chosen are divided into a hierarchy (Red members are the lowest members of society, and Violets are the highest). They also have various rituals, laws, and practices that Tal, the main character, takes for granted, until he starts learning more about the world and asking questions.

Deepen your world building by considering your magic's purpose—look at how deeply entwined it is with Nix's shadow world. How do mages use light? Are there other applications for this magic that they are unaware of but might discover throughout the story's progression?

Other examples: The Lightbringer Series by Brent Weeks; *Child of Light*; *Shadow and Bone* by Leigh Bardugo

9. NAMING

The power of names is a common theme in fantasy, and the origin of this myth can be traced back to ancient philosophy, religion, and folklore. In classical Greek and Roman religion, it was said you could have power over a god if you knew their name. In Ancient Egyptian beliefs, Isis tricked Ra into revealing his name so she had power over him. In the German fairy tale *Rumpelstiltskin*, a girl can only free herself from his demands if she learns his name.

The novel *The Namer of Spirits* by Todd Mitchell also revolves around naming magic. At the start of the story, the protagonist, Ash, tames a beast by naming it Puppy. The power of a namer is slowly revealed throughout the story, and it's not just about choosing names, but choosing the *right* names by understanding the being (Ash even names inanimate objects in addition to people and animals). The actual mechanics of the magic involve seeing visions of the being's past, interpreting who they are, and giving them one of many possible names to encourage them along a specific path. This magic can be used for evil purposes (the villain names a pair of spirits Fear and Despair so they do his evil bidding), but Ash uses her magic out of empathy, turning enemies into friends and seeing fear as just the other side of courage.

Consider how to play with the magic of names in a new way, like Mitchell does in his novel. What are the mechanics of naming magic in your story? Does every creature have *one* true name or many? Are only living things given names? What kind of power do you have over something once you've named it?

Other examples: The Kingkiller Chronicles by Patrick Rothfuss; *Spirited Away*; Earthsea series by Ursula K. le Guin

10. NATURE MAGIC

Drawing magic from the natural world—which might involve trees, plants, rivers, or the very earth itself—is particularly attractive to healers and environmentalists. But this magic can be deadly and destructive, too.

That's the route Sarah Beth Durst takes with *The Queen of Blood*. In the novel, everything has a spirit—including trees, ponds, and wind—and they're all bent on violently destroying humankind. The story's protagonists have a measure of control over these spirits and protect people from their violence. They embark on a quest to determine what's causing the spirits' restlessness.

With nature so vast, how can you focus this type of magic? What are your druids capable of? Are these powers about controlling nature, or about living in harmony with it?

Other examples: *The Forgotten Beasts of Eld* by Patricia McKillip; Winternight trilogy by Katherine Arden; *Uprooted* by Naomi Novik

TAKE your time developing your magic system and determining how it makes your characters' lives more difficult, rather than easier. Your imagination is the limit.

Chapter 16

What Has it Got in Its Future, Precious?

Riddles and Prophecies

Recently, Shelly found her son's Rubik's cube and decided to look up some tutorials on how to solve it—having never been remotely successful at figuring one out in the past. If anyone had told her she would spend the next *five* hours engrossed in cracking the algorithms involved to master the three-dimensional puzzle, she would have scoffed. It didn't help that some fiendish child had secretly and forcibly twisted a corner piece out of configuration, making the puzzle unsolvable until it was repaired. Regardless, late into the evening, it happened. The light bulb moment. Exhausted, hungry, but ultimately triumphant, Shelly held up the solved Rubik's cube in all its glory!

There is something innately satisfying about solving a good puzzle. Humans are naturally curious—despite folklore warning us that curiosity kills cats. And when we have that eureka moment that allows us to blaze through the last stretch of a head-scratching dilemma, it feels *really* good. Solving a problem activates the orbitofrontal cortex in your brain, which is the same area that responds to eating and other basic pleasures.

I think it was a very smart move that Mother Nature did by linking the generation of new ideas and reward," says research scientist Carola Salvi in a *Washington Post* article. "Every time something is rewarding, we tend to want to do it more."[1]

Puzzles are also satisfying because they bring order to chaos. In sci-fi and fantasy, riddles and prophecies are puzzles that can act as catalysts, driving both our characters and our readers to "Aha!" moments and the rewards that come with them. Pretty powerful stuff!

RIDDLE ME THIS

Riddles are particularly common in children's stories, but they can be an exciting element for any age group. Riddles can be used to accomplish various goals, such as providing information about your world, creating tension between two characters, or becoming an obstacle. Here are a few different types of riddles you can add to your story.

1. Worldbuilding Riddles

Riddles can be used to hide clues that reveal something about the world. This is an engaging alternative to dumping wieldy chunks of information into the narration.

In the Deltora Quest series by Emily Rodda, a golden-eyed giant guards a bridge that Leif, Jasmine, and Barda need to pass over on their quest to find the ruby—one of the magical gems from the Belt of Deltora. The ruby is hidden in an area controlled by an evil sorceress named Thaegan, who has thirteen monster children. The giant presents this riddle:

"Thaegan gulps her favourite food
In her cave with all of her brood:

Hot, Tot, Jin, Jod,
Fie, Fly, Zan, Zod,
Pik, Snik, Lun, Lod
And the dreaded Ichabod.
Each child holds a slimy toad.
On each toad squirm two fat grubs.
On each grub ride two fleas brave.
How many live in Thaegan's cave?"[2]

Lief has to do some quick math and comes up with the answer: 105. But the giant informs him that this is incorrect. Thaegan's favourite food is a live raven, so the answer is 106. In addition to providing a fun math problem, tension, and appealing to a middle grader's sense of justice (how is Lief supposed to know what Thaegan's favourite food is?), this riddle relays information that the adventurers didn't previously know. First, all the names of Thaegan's children; second, the fact that one of them, Ichabod, is dreaded more than the rest; and third, that her favourite food is a raven (bad news for Jasmine, who travels with a raven companion).

All this information comes in handy later, and it's much more fun discovering this through a poetic riddle than if someone had just told the adventurers these facts.

2. Homophone Riddles

Some spoken riddles are designed to stump the answerer by using words that are homophones (when two or more words have the same pronunciation but different meanings). For example, the classic American folk riddle uses this trick:

What's black and white and read all over?

The answer is: a newspaper, but this only works as an oral riddle, because it loses its misdirection when written down. It also only works in English because the words for "red" and "read" in other languages don't sound the same. These types of riddles can be difficult to pull off when writing fiction, because we're *writing*, but interesting dialogue complications utilizing riddles with homophonic words are still possible.

3. Metaphoric Riddles

This type of riddle contains metaphors, and the guesser is left to suss out which meanings to take literally. In the Seventh Tower series by Garth Nix, Milla is caught by a water spirit and forced to answer three riddles correctly. For every wrong answer, she has to stay with the spirit for one hundred days, because the spirit is lonely. The first riddle the spirit asks is this:

> "A maiden's head so deathly still
> Cold and quiet, yet not ill
> Her long tresses hang toward the sky
> Hair that burns when it is dry
> Food to man and creature's lair
> Name both her and her hair." [3]

Milla thinks through the answer by realizing that many riddlers are inspired by their everyday lives when coming up with questions. And since this spirit is tied to a body of water, the answer becomes obvious to her: the maiden is a rock, and her hair is the seaweed that grows from the rock.

Milla had to deduce that the maiden isn't really a maiden, but a metaphor for something else. If she hadn't figured this out, she could have been stuck wondering what this odd creature with floating hair could possibly be.

4. Fair Riddles

These puzzles *must* be guessable. It should be possible to retrieve the answer using only the text given and the shared knowledge of the riddler and guesser. Since Milla was staring straight at the answer in the previous riddle, it was perfectly fair to ask. However, as their riddle game progresses, the spirit asks a riddle that it knows isn't fair.

5. Unfair Riddles

The spirit asks Milla this riddle:

> A traveler begins a journey. For the first week, he is carried south. For the second week, he carries others. In the third week, he flies up into the sky. In the fourth week, he falls back down. Who is the traveler?"[4]

The spirit thinks there is no way Milla will be able to answer this, because it believes Milla is a Chosen—one of the people who live in a castle and know nothing of the world of ice and snow beyond. However, Milla is actually an Icecarl and is very familiar with the answer: first, the traveler is an iceberg, then free-flowing water, then a cloud, and then snow.

The spirit gets angry when Milla answers correctly, and readers get to feel satisfied that Milla beat it at its unfair game!

Unfair riddles can also take the form of a question that ignores the "rules" of riddling, such as when Bilbo asks Gollum, "What have I got in my pocket?"[5] in *The Hobbit* by J.R.R. Tolkien. Since the only person who knows the answer is Bilbo himself, this is *totally* unfair! His question isn't a riddle at all, and most people don't like being hung out to dry with a false riddle, so there are usually consequences to telling them.

6. Solve or Die Riddles

Gollum and Bilbo's competition in *The Hobbit* is also an example of this sort of riddling. If Bilbo wins their game, Gollum has agreed to help him find his way out of the maze-like cave, but if Gollum wins, Bilbo will become his supper. These types of competitions may lead to unfair riddles as desperate participants do their best to save their necks, but other times the spirit of riddling is maintained.

In Sophocles' Greek play *Oedipus the King*, Oedipus learns that he is prophesied to kill his father and marry his mother. He flees from his home city and winds up in Thebes, where he encounters a sphinx who has been terrorizing the area. The sphinx has been destroying crops and killing travellers who are unable to correctly answer her riddle:

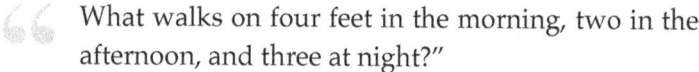 What walks on four feet in the morning, two in the afternoon, and three at night?"

Oedipus is able to provide an answer, when all others before him failed: a human, who crawls at the dawn of life as an infant, learns to walk on two legs, and then, at the dusk of life, relies on a "third leg"—a cane—in order to walk.

7. Riddles with Two Answers

Some riddles have two answers, often a lewd, obvious one that first comes to mind and a more difficult to decipher, modest response. This type of riddle establishes the level of intimacy the riddler shares with their guessers. They serve as an icebreaker that immediately sets the tone, and they are numerous in folklore. Here's a classic:

 What sticks out of a man's pajamas in the morning, so hard you can hang your hat on it?"

Tsk tsk, dear reader. The answer is his head! What on earth did *you* think it was?

HOW TO WRITE A RIDDLE

When putting riddles into your story, you can certainly find lesser known riddles from folklore and history. However, if you want to build your own, here are some steps to follow.

1. Choose a solution.

We'll work our way backward, choosing the answer first. We're going with: a cloud.

2. Brainstorm a list of words to associate with the answer.

Research the history of the word, if you like, too. The word *cloud* comes from the Old English word *clud*, meaning "rock mass" or "hill." People used this word because the formations in the sky looked like fluffy mountains. So, with all that in mind, here are some words we might include in the riddle:

- Sky
- Rain
- Sheep
- Fluffy
- Hill

3. Consider synonyms, metaphors, or less obvious descriptions for these words.

Here are some associations we brainstormed:

- Sky = flying = feathers
- Precipitation = falling

- Hill = face = crying
- Thunder = growling
- Sheep = wool

4. Pick a format for your riddle.

Many traditional riddles are four lines long and rhyme, so we'll go with that. Here goes:

> I cry without mourning,
> a mountain of wool.
> I growl without warning.
> I fall when I'm full.

Now it's your turn. Play with words to create a riddle that piques the interest of your readers and moves your story onward.

TELLING THE FUTURE

The best prophecies make things more difficult for your poor characters, not easier. They shroud your novel in mystery and lyricism, adding an element of mythic proportions to your characters' journeys. Prophecies are more common in fantasy than in science fiction, but no one's stopping you from spicing up your space opera with a warning from the future.

Prophecies can come in a few different formats, and many combine the following types into a single prophecy.

1. Foretelling a Disaster

Ragnarok of Norse mythology is a disaster prophecy, foretelling of a cataclysmic destruction of the cosmos and everything in it, including the gods.

In *Thor: Ragnarok*, Thor dreams about Asgard's destruction at the hands of Surtur, so he attempts to destroy the fire demon in an attempt to prevent this from happening.

Even though Thor defeats Surtur at the beginning of the movie, his prophetic dreams still come true later—in fact, Thor and Loki revive Surtur on purpose in order to stop their evil sister, Hela, from destroying multiple worlds.

2. Foretelling the Coming of a Chosen One

In *The Dark is Rising Sequence* by Susan Cooper, the following prophecy adds mystery and suspense to the series:

> "When the dark is rising, six shall turn it back;
> Three from the circle, three from the track;
> Wood, bronze, iron; water, fire, stone;
> Five will return, and one go alone..."[6]

The poem refers to Will Stanton, the eleven-year-old boy who learns that he is an "Old One," destined to wield the powers of the Light against The Dark, and the story's other protagonists. It also provides clues for their quest to find the Six Signs that will prevent the Dark from rising.

3. Instructions on How to Avoid Catastrophe

In *The Fellowship of the Ring*, both Faramir and Boromir have a dream that includes the following prophecy:

> "Seek for the Sword that was broken:
> In Imladris it dwells;
> There shall be counsels taken
> Stronger than Morgul-spells.
> There shall be shown a token
> That Doom is near at hand,
> For Isildur's Bane shall waken,"

And the Halfling forth shall stand."⁷

Neither brother understands the poem, but Denethor tells Boromir that Imladris is where Elrond dwells. We know that the prophecy is telling Boromir to go to Rivendell, where the shards of Narsil lie, and that there will be a council discussing what to do about Isildur's Bane—the One Ring. A halfling will be part of the council. Everything the prophetic dream mentions comes true, which drives Boromir to believe in its importance and join the Fellowship on a mission to destroy the Ring.

4. Conditional Prophecy

In *The Curse of Chalion* by Lois McMaster Bujold, the royal family of Chalion is under a curse, and Cazaril, the protagonist, learns how to break the curse through this prophecy:

> 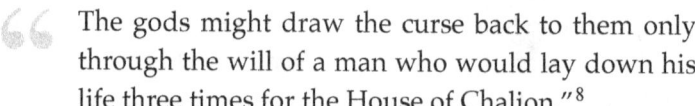 The gods might draw the curse back to them only through the will of a man who would lay down his life three times for the House of Chalion."⁸

The curse will only be lifted *if* this impossible thing happens—for how can a man die three times? The concept of choice and free will is played with here, as Cazaril is well on the way to fulfilling this prophecy when he hears it, though he doesn't know it.

5. Inescapable Prophecy

This is a prophecy that cannot be escaped, and trying to escape it is precisely what leads to its completion.

Oedipus's legend is an example of this type of prophecy. Remember the guy who flees to Thebes and answers the sphinx's riddle? Long before he was born, his father, King Laius of Thebes, is told that he will have a child who is destined to kill him and marry his wife, Jocasta. He avoids his wife's bed in an effort to thwart the prophecy—but that only works until a night of drinking wine undoes his resolve, and Jocasta becomes pregnant.

When Oedipus is born, his father orders his servants to pierce the baby's ankles with a large pin, binding his feet together so that Oedipus cannot even crawl, much less cause harm. Then Laius gives the infant to a shepherd and tells the man to leave Oedipus in the mountains to die.

Instead, the shepherd hands the wounded baby over to a second shepherd, who passes Oedipus off to King Polybus and Queen Merope of Corinth. They are childless and raise Oedipus as their own son. It is Polybus and Merope that Oedipus flees from when he learns that he is prophesied to kill his father and marry his mother. He doesn't know he's adopted, and he runs away to save their lives.

In his travels, he encounters a chariot and travelling company in a narrow intersection. They argue over who has the right-of-way. The chariot driver nearly runs over Oedipus and strikes him with his whip. Oedipus defends himself and in his anger kills both the charioteer and his passenger—who just so happens to be his biological father, Laius.

Later, when Oedipus bests the sphinx terrorizing Thebes, the prize is the hand of the widowed queen, Jocasta. Oedipus marries her, having no idea that she's his biological mother. Thus, the prophecy is fulfilled.

6. Escapable Prophecy

In some stories, a seemingly clear prophecy is changed or avoided. This is usually due to wordplay or a misunderstanding of the prophecy.

In Neil Gaiman and Terry's Pratchett's *Good Omens*, Adam is the Antichrist, prophesied to destroy the world by Agnes Nutter:

Where the Hogg's back ends the young beast will take the world and Adam's line will end in fire and darkness."⁹

But Adam decides to call off the Apocalypse, saying that whatever has been written can always be crossed out. Dodging this prophecy only works here because *Good Omens* is a comedy—in a more serious story, this would feel like a cop-out, but Gaiman and Pratchett can pull off the ridiculous due to the novel's genre.

HOW TO WRITE A PROPHECY

Follow these four steps to build a prophecy of your very own.

1. Know the future.

When crafting a convincing prophecy, it helps to have a solid outline or draft of your story first. It's easier to make your predictions fit seamlessly if you actually have an idea of what the future holds. You are your story's psychic!

2. Select the tone and format.

Is this a doom and gloom prophecy or one full of hope? Will it rhyme? Is it passed along as a song? Who told it originally? Who knows it now?

3. Brainstorm imagery.

Come up with some tangible imagery associated with your prophecy—things you can see, taste, hear, smell, or feel. Replace specific names with metaphors or character traits. Use words or phrases with double meanings, and don't forget to give a few grains of clarity that your reader can easily understand.

4. Find your rhythm.

Even if you choose not to rhyme, prophecies do have a rhythm. Where will you break your lines? What sort of language will you use? Archaic? Modern? Are your word choices influenced by a particular culture? The way your prophecy rolls off the tongue can tell a reader a lot about where and when it was written, and perhaps even who wrote it—a historian might be inclined to include familial lineage and important dates in their prophecy. An astronomer would make references to planets and constellations. You get the idea.

CHECK OUT THIS PROPHECY, written by poet Kyla Neufeld for a Dungeons & Dragons campaign that Allison played in. In the campaign's story, an ocean goddess named Aquila cursed a group of people because she was angry at their god, Tuathe. Those people and their ancestors became known as the "Drowned" and were cursed with bad luck. When asking Kyla to write the poem, the Dungeon Master provided some of the campaign's history and stipulated that the poem had to reference this curse, include a clue as to how to break it, and foretell the return of Aquila. It's written in the voice of one of the goddess's worshippers:

> "Our Lady Aquila,
> goddess of the Sunless Seas,
> we remember your woeful pleas,
> the cruel injustice of your plight.
> We remember how Tuathe,
> your enemy, closed the Maelstrom –
> your greatest creation now sundered
> from this world, thundering waves
> that cannot break through the doors of night

no matter how hard they beat against them.
Let his people bear your mark like scars
on their foreheads. Let them choke
on Tuathe's impudence.
They are the Drowned
and they will bring misfortune
to all who come near them.

"Our Lady of light and mischief,
hear our prayers and accept our praise.
One day the doors will open
and the waters will run,
like melt water into a flood.

"Until that time, we beseech you
grant us your favour.
Until that time, we will remember
and work for your vengeance on this earth."[10]

Within the prophecy there's the repeated imagery of water, a hint of hope in the springlike mention of meltwaters, and some undertones of coming vengeance with the imagery stirred up by the lines "Let them choke" and "They are the Drowned." The tone is sincere and harsh, but hopeful too. It draws together some of the world's history (how Aquila cursed Tauthe's people, how they are referred to as "Drowned," and anyone with her mark on their foreheads brings bad luck to those around them).

The poem foretells Aquila's return and gives directions on how to bring it about. It's a puzzle to be solved. In the campaign, it was even more of a quandary, because the players were given the poem with a stanza missing (a trick you can use in your own writing to create a mystery and confusion).

SIX QUESTIONS TO ASK ABOUT YOUR RIDDLE OR PROPHECY

When drafting your stanzas, ask yourself these questions to spur your imagination.

1. Is it understandable and does it lead somewhere satisfying?

Recently, Shelly discovered a 1000 piece jigsaw puzzle titled "Micro Pure White Hell." It is comprised of—you guessed it—1000 *tiny* puzzle pieces that come together to form a blank, white rectangle. Judging by reviews, most people buy it as a gag gift. Only the most extreme puzzle solvers seem to enjoy this one—and they are helped by the fact that the puzzle pieces are numbered on the back so that there's a roadmap to completion. For most of us, that's not enough. Why finish a puzzle that's just a white, blank square? Where's the satisfaction? Those who are satisfied by finishing it derive pleasure from the fact that it is extremely difficult, but not impossible.

Your riddle or prophecy should be simple enough that people *want* to solve it, but complex enough to challenge them. Give your readers a roadmap that keeps them excited about solving the rest of the puzzle. Riddles should be fair unless the teller is a trickster, and prophecies should be simple enough for the reader to understand while still holding some hidden meaning that will be uncovered later on. The age group you're writing for can define how difficult to make a puzzle.

2. Is it specific enough?

If a warrior asks a seer whether or not they're destined to win a coming war and the prophet replies, "A great empire will be destroyed," the warrior is likely to be disappointed (as will the readers). That could mean anything! The prophecy should point to *something* specific and should include all the hints the listeners need to get there, otherwise what's the point?

3. Who delivers the prophecy?

Is it set in stone? Written in an ancient text? Delivered in person? If it is written, the prophecy is less likely to have its meaning corrupted over time—unless it is translated from a different language (or unless there are other, nefarious powers at play, like in the Mistborn series by Brandon Sanderson). However, if the prophecy has been passed on orally, meaning will be lost, twisted, or modified the more it is repeated. If your riddle or prophecy uses a rhyming format, that might be lost over time too as people retell it in their own words. An ancient, oral prophecy is likely to be more warped than one that is only a few years old.

If a seer or prophet delivers the prophecy, are they reliable? Professor Trelawney is initially not taken seriously in Harry Potter's world, and neither are her prophecies, because she's a bit of a crackpot and has made many predictions that don't come to fruition.

4. When does the riddle happen in the story? When does the prophecy take place?

If your riddle or prophecy takes place at the beginning of your tale, it can be a catalyst all the way through. There is room to build on it and add complexities. If it happens near the end, perhaps it gives the clue needed to catapult your characters to the climax of the story. Does a prophecy happen a few years before your story takes place? Thousands of years before? Cultures change with time and riddles and prophecies that once made sense become more difficult to understand.

5. Where does the solution lead?

While the endpoint of your prophecy or the answer to your riddle should be a mystery to your reader, *you* need a firm grasp on where these clues are going at all times. You can't accurately predict the future if you don't *know* the future.

6. Why is your character the one who solves the riddle or fulfills the prophecy?

Let's look back at the example of Oedipus. Doesn't it seem odd that *nobody* was able to answer the Sphinx's riddle about what walks on four legs in the morning, two legs in the afternoon and three legs in the evening? Oedipus just shows up out of nowhere, and bam! Problem solved.

If you want to make your stories believable, there has to be logic behind scenes like this or they feel contrived. Turns out, there could be a reason why Oedipus was so suited to answer that particular riddle. Remember, his father, Laius, skewered him by the ankles with a large pin as a baby. Oedipus is likely permanently scarred by that, and walking is a painful endeavor. In fact, his name translated from Greek means "Swollen-foot." Likely, he thought far more about human locomotion than the average person did, so he was uniquely suited to answer the Sphinx's riddle. How are your characters equipped to answer the puzzle they need to solve?

FILLING your books with puzzling riddles and prophecies is a great way to bring your readers that ultimate "Aha!" moment they've been waiting for. Now you can go forth and create your own eureka moments.

Chapter 17

So Sing We All

Lyrics and Poetry

A well-written song doesn't need notes for you to enjoy its music. Songs and poems add a subtlety to your narrative that you can't always accomplish otherwise. For centuries, music has been used to evoke emotions and record events. Including a song in your story can enhance your worldbuilding and add texture to your characters.

Music in a novel should have purpose. And even though you can't include the tune of a song, the lyrics themselves can achieve any of the following.

- **Accentuate the setting.** Our world is full of different types of music from all eras and cultures. It makes sense that your sci-fi or fantasy world would be rampant with music, too (at least, the ones with beings who can hear). What sort of music is your main character familiar with? What music might they hear on their adventures? How can it add colour to your setting?
- **Drive the plot.** There are many ways a song can be entwined in the plot of the novel. Perhaps it's a symbol of a revolution, and rebels recognize each

other by singing the tune. Perhaps it's what marching warriors sing on their way to battle. Perhaps it inspires two lovers to finally admit their feelings for each other.

- **Plant clues.** Many songs are written to remember past events. What if a particular piece of music describes events differently than the protagonist has been taught? Perhaps there are secrets or riddles hidden within a song—what easier way to help a child remember something crucial when they are too young to understand otherwise?
- **Foreshadow events.** Song lyrics can signal something thematic to your readers that, perhaps, your characters don't pick up on. Maybe the love song played in front of two characters signals that there are feelings to come. Maybe a dirge signals a death is about to happen. Maybe a ballad heard in a tavern mirrors the hero's journey.
- **Build character.** The songs your character hears or knows could have significant meaning to them. Was that lullaby sung to them by their deceased parent? Did they learn that bawdy song as a child without understanding what it meant? Did they sing that song every week as part of their religious upbringing?

Ideally, your song will accomplish more than one of these goals at once. Below are various types of songs that you can consider for your novel.

DRINKING SONGS

J.R.R. Tolkien included many songs in *The Hobbit* and *The Lord of the Rings*. Part of the point of writing, for Tolkien, was to create a story around the amazing languages and songs he had created. The many poems and songs have been turned into music in the movie soundtracks and fans around the world have put the words to various tunes. Part of Middle-earth's wonder is the rich worldbuilding, which includes myth and poetry. While we don't recommend including this much poetry in your novel (it works for *The Lord of the Rings*, but fantasy publishing does not look like it did decades ago), you can take inspiration from his writing nonetheless.

In *The Fellowship of the Ring*, Frodo, Sam, Merry, and Pippin stop to rest in the forest, drinking a pale gold drink that High Elves had given them. Sam and Pippin sing these lyrics:

"Ho! Ho! Ho! to the bottle I go
To heal my heart and drown my woe.
Rain may fall and wind may blow,
And many miles be still to go,
But under a tall tree, I will lie,
And let the clouds go sailing by."[1]

In the movie, Merry and Pippin sing this song in the Green Dragon Inn, and the lyrics are slightly different. In both cases, the song highlights the cheery, peaceful setting of the Shire that Frodo has grown up in—it gives us a glimpse into hobbit life and culture. In the movie, it also accomplishes character exposition, because Pippin interrupts the final line, making up his own to finish the song:

"Sweet is the sound of the pouring rain
And stream that falls from hill to plain.
Better than rain or rippling brook—
Is a mug of beer inside this Took!"[2]

Merry and Pippin are much sillier in the movies than they are in the books, and we clearly see that aspect of their characters as they dance on top of the table together and sing this song. The scene then cuts to older hobbits talking about how there are strange folk about, which foreshadows how the hobbits' happy lives are about to get considerably darker.

Include drinking songs in your novel to highlight the culture of a city, town, or character's background. Drinking songs are generally jovial, quick, and upbeat, with humorous or bawdy lyrics.

ANTHEMS

The country of Panem is hugely significant to Suzanne Collins's *The Hunger Games*. The games—an annual event in which two children from each district are sent into an arena to fight to the death—began as an effort to quell a rebellion and remind the citizens that the Capitol is in control.

In the prequel novel, *The Ballad of Songbirds and Snakes*, Coriolanus Snow's grandmother sings the country's anthem, titled "Gem of Panem." She does so through a window during the First Rebellion while bombs rain around her home, an act of defiance against the Capitol.

Some of the lyrics refer to justice, wisdom, and strength, which starkly contrasts with what the Capitol has become:

> "Gem of Panem
> Mighty city
> Through the ages you shine anew
> We humbly kneel
> To your ideal
> And pledge our love to you
> Gem of Panem
> Heart of Justice
> Wisdom crowns your marble brow
> You give us light
> You reunite
> To you we make our vow
> Gem of Panem

Seat of power
Strength in peacetime, shield in strife
Protect our land
With armored hand
Our Capitol
Our life"[3]

This is an impactful anthem to include in the story because the lyrics point toward what Panem used to be and what it could be again.

Include an anthem in your novel to highlight the ethical, moral, political, or religious strains of a country or nation. An anthem's purpose is generally to raise people's spirits and instill a sense of belonging and loyalty within the citizens (Suzanne Collins took that intent and twisted it). Anthems are a slow to medium tempo, with energy building to a crescendo.

CHILDREN'S SONGS

In *Raybearer* by Jordan Ifueko, Tarisai's mother keeps her sheltered from the outside world in Bhekina House. As a child, Tarisai envies the children and families who pass by her window. One day, she hears them singing:

"Eleven danced around the throne,
Eleven moons in glory shone,
They shone around the sun.

"But traitors rise and empires fall, And
Sun-Ray-Sun will rule them all,
When all is said-o, all is said
And done-heh, done-heh, done."[4]

Tarisai likes the "ominous rhyme," and sings it around the house until her tutor asks her where she heard it. The next day, her windows are boarded up. The song contains details about the world that Tarisai's mother doesn't want her to know, such as why the emperor has a council of eleven people bonded to him by ray magic.

You can also include a children's song in your novel to highlight a character's backstory, pass on a historical event, or hide a riddle. Children's songs should have simple lyrics that are easy to memorize. They might include actions that go along with the words, be associated with a playground game, used to taunt others, or sung during an activity like jumping rope.

RELIGIOUS SONGS

Religious texts have been sung throughout the world's history. Navajo ceremonies are led by "singers," who are the most highly respected individuals in their society. Sinhala Buddhist rituals are accompanied by drumming and dancing. The majority of Jewish worship in traditional Synagogue is sung or chanted. Islamic calls to prayer, Sikh hymns, Hindu chants, Christian praise music, and other ceremonial practices from various religions have formed the basis of organized worship in their respective settings.

Music is so often tied to worship because it has the power to create emotional states, like joy or sadness, and there is something spiritual about many voices coming together for a single purpose.

In the video game *Dragon Age: Inquisition*, a religious character—Mother Giselle—sings a hymn to comfort the protagonist and their people as they are driven from the main base that has been their home. They are forced to march through snow and ice to a fortress called Skyhold, which will be the new headquarters of the Inquisition.

Mother Giselle is part of the Chantry, the main religion in Thedas, which is based on the Chant of Light, a series of teachings. Even the name of the religion harkens to music. When she starts to sing around the campfire on a snow-covered peak, heads lift and voices join her in this hopeful song:

> "Shadows fall
> And hope has fled
> Steel your heart
> The dawn will come
> The night is long
> And the path is dark
> Look to the sky
> For one day soon
> The dawn will come"[5]

The song marks a tonal shift in the narrative: from despair to hope. Religious songs, if they are meant to be sung by large groups, are often formatted as *verse - chorus - verse - chorus*, with lyrics that are meant to encourage people or praise something. They are often repetitive, they may be based on religious text, and they are potentially interchangeable with tunes from other hymns or songs.

MOURNING SONGS

For some, only a song can demonstrate the depths of grief. We've talked about how music and poetry can elicit emotion, so it makes sense that they are used for funerals and mourning. In The Wheel of Time series by Robert Jordan, the Aiel people sing a dirge for the dead, described as a haunting melody sung in parts:

> "Life is a dream — that knows no shade.
> Life is a dream — of pain and woe.
> A dream from which — we pray to wake.
> A dream from which — we wake and go.
> Who would sleep — when the new dawn waits?

Who would sleep — when the sweet winds blow?
A dream must end — when the new day comes.
This dream from which — we wake and go."[6]

Mourning songs often have thoughtful lyrics, sad and hopeful in turn, like this one. This song also speaks to Aiel culture; they are a people who live in hot desert, hence life being a dream "that knows no shade." They are warriors, unafraid of death, and this song speaks to that, referring to life as a dream, and death as waking up to a new dawn.

The word *dirge* comes from the Latin word *dirige*, which means "direct" and comes from the longer phrase "Dirige, Domine, Deus meus, in conspectus tuo viam meam," meaning "Direct my way in your sight, O Lord my God." This phrase points to the common wondering about where people go when they die and our hope that they are safe, at peace, and pain-free. Dirges and mourning songs may be prayers or simply poetic words of grief and lamentation. They are usually sung at a slow tempo.

PROPHETIC SONGS

What better way to ensure a prophecy is passed down through the ages than to encapsulate it in a song?

The Legend of Zelda games usually include a prophecy about a young man (Link) who will save the world. A significant song in *Skyward Sword* speaks about Link uniting earth and sky by the hand of the goddess:

"Oh youth, guided by the servant of the goddess,
Unite earth and sky, and bring light to the land.
Oh youth, show the two whirling sails the way to the
   Light Tower...
And before you a path shall open, and a heavenly song
   you shall hear."[7]

Link hears Zelda sing this song on the day of an important ceremony, and its orchestral version is a recurring theme throughout the game. This song, "The Ballad of the Goddess," does double duty as a riddle. Link obtains the Goddess Harp later in the game and learns to play the song himself, using it (along with the lyrics' directions to face two windmills towards the Light Tower) to unlock a new area. In addition, there is a subtle hint within the song about the goddess's identity. The melody of "The Ballad of the Goddess" is the same as "Zelda's Lullaby"—another tune from past games that fans of the series will be familiar with—but played backwards. While you can't accomplish that particular type of melodic trickery in your novel (and only musical geniuses would notice something like that, anyway), you can obscure meaning within riddles and prophecies to keep your readers guessing.

You may notice this song doesn't rhyme. Zelda games are available in several languages, including Japanese, English, German and Spanish. Rhyming doesn't work so well in translation. You can certainly achieve poetry without rhyme, and don't need to lean on rhyme to make your songs meaningful. You can also mix things up with other literary devices, such as alliteration, parallelism, assonance, metaphor, personification, and symbolism. To write a prophetic song, consider hidden meaning and imagery that you can include in your lyrics.

BALLADS AND FOLK SONGS

Folk songs and ballads are usually traditional music from a particular region, passed along orally. Folk songs are often meant to be sung in groups and have simple melodies and repeating refrains, while ballads are more likely to be sung by a performer, such as a bard, telling a legend or tale.

In Patrick Rothfuss's Kingkiller Chronicles, Kvothe is a talented musician and intensely interested in stories and history. He's "stunned for different reasons" when he hears Denna sing

"The Song of Seven Sorrows" in *The Wise Man's Fear*, beginning with this spoken opening:

> "Gather round and listen well,
> For I've a tale of tragedy to tell.
> I sing of subtle shadow spread
> Across a land, and of the man
> Who turned his hand toward a purpose few could bear.
> Fair Lanre: stripped of wife, of life, of pride
> Still never from his purpose swayed.
> Who fought the tide, and fell, and was betrayed."[8]

The song is about a historical figure named Lanre, widely known as a traitor. But in Denna's song, Lanre is depicted as a misunderstood hero. Denna based the song on a version she found in an old book, but Kvothe lectures her on how she's got the facts wrong, and they end up arguing about it.

Not only does this song expand the world's history and call into question the truth of legends, but it instigates tension between Kvothe and Denna.

Ballads are often written in four line quatrains, with ABAB or ABCB rhyming schemes. They can be quick and jovial—something people might dance to—or slow and lyrical.

LULLABIES

Lullabies can be used to calm someone down, to put a baby to sleep, or to tie a character to a parent they barely remember.

"My Suit and Me" is a quarian lullaby from Catherynne M. Valente's *Mass Effect Andromeda: Annihilation*, a sci-fi novel based on the Mass Effect video game series. The quarians are a nomadic species who have weak immune systems, so they have to wear enviro-suits to protect themselves from disease and infection.

"Sing me to sleep on the starry sea,
and I'll dream through the night of my suit and me.
I won't fear the heat of a desert breeze
Or contaminants high in the jungle trees.
Even in space I shall never freeze
Because I've got my suit and my suit's got me.
Oh, I love my mother who holds me tight
And I love my father who taught me right
Oh, I love my ship sailing strong through the night
And I love the homeworld for which we fight
But what do I love like a lock loves a key?
What holds fast my heart, head, shoulders and knees?
I love my suit and my suit loves me."[9]

This song speaks to life as a quarian and having to rely on a suit for protection, but it also ties into the story's plot. In the novel, a quarian ship is traveling to a new galaxy, and a recording of the lullaby is played to their cryopods once a century until they arrive. But the song turns out to be a pretext to install a computer virus into the ship's systems. There is something so eerie about a song for children being used for nefarious purposes.

Lullabies are often simple, easy to remember, slow, and soft. They may have a swinging rhythm that mirrors rocking a child to sleep. Children respond to rhythm and rhyme, so they likely include those.

LOVE SONGS

Poetry and music are often associated with love and courtship because they touch us in ways that are difficult to explain, capturing intense emotions in a way mere words cannot. Love can make us want to sing, either in happiness or in melancholy, so music seems appropriate to capture those feelings.

In *Fool's Fate* by Robin Hobb, the Fool leaves Fitz a poem, a love song with a tragic ending:

"In that last dance of chances
I shall partner you no more.
I shall watch another turn you
as you move across the floor.

"In that last dance of chances
when I bid your life goodbye
I will hope she treats you kindly.
I will hope you learn to fly.

"In that last dance of chances
When I know you'll not be mine
I will let you go with longing
And the hope that you'll be fine.

"In that last chance of dances
We shall know each other's minds.
We shall part with our regrets
When the tie no longer binds."[10]

This poem is incredibly sad, because it's the Fool's goodbye to Fitz, and a subtle reference to a comment about dancing from the first book in the trilogy.

Simple or complex, love songs are passionate and personal. Try to avoid cliches and simply express what the character is feeling through poetry.

BATTLE CHANTS

In *Star Wars: Republic Commando*, the clone troopers sing this Mandalorian war chant:

"Those who stand before us light the night sky in flame.
Our vengeance burns brighter still.
Every last traitorous soul shall fall…
And glory, eternal glory, we shall bear its weight together.
Forged like the saber in the fires of death, Brothers All."[11]

The song is sung in the language of the Mandalorians, Mando'a, and has many repeating verses. Chants like these encourage soldiers to feel a sense of camaraderie. Since Jango Fett is the one who taught these chants to the troopers, the song also speaks to his history as a Mandalorian bounty hunter. The song speaks to the purpose of the clones, who were literally created to fight a war, and how they consider each other brothers.

Battle chants are repetitive, easy to remember, and rhythmic. Lyrics are generally about unity, war, and facing death bravely.

FIVE STEPS TO SONG WRITING

Here are some practical steps you can take to add a song to your novel:

1. Decide on the function of your song.

Does it fall into one of the above categories? Where, when, and why is it sung?

2. Decide on your song's structure.

Will it rhyme? Will it have a *verse* - *chorus* pattern? What will it's metre be (the pattern of stressed and unstressed syllables)? You can use the structure of another song for inspiration and put your own lyrics to it. (Fun fact: there are plenty of songs throughout the ages that use the same melody/rhyming/metric scheme with fresh lyrics, becoming a "new" song). For example, if we were to use Robin Hobb's song from *Fool's Fate* as inspiration, we might follow its structure to come up with something completely new, which doesn't plagiarize any of the words, but uses the same rhyming scheme and metre:

> I cannot love my lover
> in the way that they love me.
> I don't miss them when their gone,
> so I have to set them free.

Deciding on your song's structure may help with creativity, because limiting your options can actually help you focus. Try out a rhyming scheme, and, if it doesn't work, try something else. Don't be afraid to break the mold and stray from the most common structures.

3. Brainstorm key words.

Rather than coming up with complete lines at one time, think of some words associated with whatever your song's topic is. For example, let's brainstorm a song that's performed in worship ceremonies to a robot that has taken over the world. Our list might look something like this:

- Logic
- Metal
- Master
- Network
- Delete

4. Brainstorm phrases.

Use the words from the previous list to come up with some phrases. For our robot song, how about these:

- Logic is eternal
- Our metal overlord
- You don't need eyes, heart, or skin
- Your network knows all

5. Fit lyrics into the structure you chose during Step Two.

For our robot song, we're taking inspiration from an old hymn, "Battle Hymn of the Republic," which has an AAABCB rhyming scheme. Here's the draft we came up with:

> You don't need flesh or heart or bone. You don't need eyes to see.
> Deleting foes and mining facts brings honour unto thee.
> Your logic is eternal and, with truth, you set us free;
> Your network knows all things.
> Our metal Overlord—you reign!
> Our metal Overlord—you reign!
> Our metal Overlord—you reign!
> Your network knows all things.

However much you like or dislike your draft, getting words on the page is success. You can always go back and edit it later. And if we can do it, so can you! Give it a try next time you want to spice up your worldbuilding with a memorable ditty.

Chapter 18

Avoid the Gaze of the Ravenous Bugblatter

Creatures and Monsters

Humanity's knowledge has always had limits, and in fiction—as in life—we make rigorous use of our imaginations to fill in the blanks when presented with a mystery beyond the grasp of our current reality.

When creating creatures and monsters for speculative fiction, imagination is key. But there are a lot of ways you can use the real world for inspiration and create realistic creatures for your stories.

CRAFTING CREATURES

A few summers ago, Shelly and her boys discovered salamander larvae in a muddy slough near their house. Shelly's family has lived in the area most of their lives and had never seen anything more than snails and tadpoles in the ponds. Observing firsthand the exotic, feathery-gilled hatchlings, researching their life cycle, and hypothesizing how they ended up in their humble little puddle felt as exciting as discovering alien life (and not just for the kids).

They learned that salamanders are mildly poisonous to deter predators like snakes. They are common in grasslands that host plenty of insects and gopher holes, because the adults live mostly on land. They eat bugs and survive bitterly cold winters by hibernating in rodent tunnels below the frost line.

By learning about an animal and how it's adapted to live in our world, we can intuit a lot about the world it inhabits. From now on, if Shelly spots a salamander in the wild, she knows she's likely near a grassland with water, plenty of gopher holes, lots of insects, and, possibly, snakes.

Creating unique creatures in sci-fi and fantasy is a wonderful way for readers to understand the environment you've created and appreciate a multifaceted world. If you need inspiration, research a real-world animal and use its bodily functions and habitats to describe your fictional animal.

In fantasy stories and mythology, salamanders are used as ingredients in potions and often have a special affinity with fire. —probably because they hibernate in wood, and when people used logs as kindling, the creatures seemed to magically appear from the flames as they escaped.

Fantasy writers are often inspired by myths and legends from around the world in their writing. While some of these mythological creatures are more common in fiction than others (dragons, griffins, and unicorns, for example), they are included so often because they are beloved. You can always put your own spin on a creature (perhaps your dragons don't breathe fire, or they have a strange power, or they have fur instead of scales). Or combine characteristics of creatures you are familiar with to make something new (for example, put a horn on a white horse and you've got a unicorn!). You can also dig deep into your research and find myths that are not commonly used.

The dragons in *The Priory of the Orange Tree*, an epic fantasy by Samantha Shannon, are a mixture of Western and Eastern mythology. In our world's Western mythologies, dragons are the fire-breathing, destructive, treasure-hoarding types, but the oriental dragons from our Eastern mythologies are known as guardians, protectors of Earth, serpentine, and wingless; they are often associated with water. Shannon plays with these different myths, and her world includes the Western fire-breathing dragons, who are menaces to humankind, as well as the Eastern water dragons, who work with humans to protect the world.

The existence of these two different types of dragons causes friction between the cultures in Shannon's world. Societies in her western countries believe *all* dragons are evil, and think the eastern peoples are evil wyrm worshipers. Because of this misunderstanding, trade is limited between the two areas and politics are shaky.

By including two different types of creatures inspired by different mythologies, Shannon primed her world for conflict and character development.

CREATURES IN SCI-FI are often a different sort of strange than the animals in fantasy. You can get ideas from the types of environments your story takes place in. For example, what does a creature that lives in space look like? You might want to put some research into tardigrades, the only animal (we know of) that can survive in space. These little creatures are able to survive in environments most things can't, such as absolute zero temperatures, above boiling, and, of course, in the vacuum of space. Their resiliency comes from a unique protein in their bodies, and they are able to go into a dormant state. Perhaps your space creature has some of these characteristics.

How does the creature react to or interact with your characters? The Babelfish in *The Hitchhiker's Guide to the Galaxy* are aquatic animals that you insert into your ear as translation devices. The porgs in *Star Wars: The Last Jedi* ignore humans and are mostly there to look cute. Moya in *Farscape* is a living spaceship, able to form bonds with her crew.

In Phillip Pullman's *The Amber Spyglass*, the mulefa are sapient, elephantine beings with unique anatomy; mulefa have diamond-framed skeletons with four legs, two front and back, and the other pair mid-body. They fit two large, disc-like seed-pods onto spurs on their front and back legs, and they use their middle legs to propel themselves like an organic bicycle without pedals.

In an interview in *The Guardian,* Pullman was asked how he came up with the idea of mulefa, and he responded:

> I can date that exactly to a holiday my wife and I had in Slovenia with my son—it must have been about 20 years ago. We were walking around Lake Bled and there were a lot of people rollerblading along. My son was a great science fiction fan and I asked if he knew any books where there were creatures with wheels, and he couldn't think of any. Then we started talking about how it would be possible for a living creature to have wheels and that's where the idea came from. It was a useful one because it introduced the notion of symbiosis because the mulefa depend on the trees that produce the seed pods that become their wheels and the trees depend on the mulefa to pound the pods on hard roads so that they crack and then germinate."[1]

Remember, creatures interact with their environments and with other creatures. Considering their place in the ecosystem can inspire your ideas! Their position on the food chain, their impact on the environment, and what would happen if they suddenly disappeared are great places to start your brainstorming.

IF YOU WANT to create a creature from scratch, here are four questions to ask.

1. What is your creature's niche in your world? (land, sea, air space)?

How are they specially adapted for their environment and how do they move? Look for the odd and unusual in our world. Animals in extreme environments are helpful for inspiration—for example, some mountainous insects can freeze solid and still survive.

Let's make a creature that thrives in cold, icy waters. We'll call it an algor. We've decided that algors are not only capable of freezing solid, but they can refrigerate and freeze the waters around them too. They're invertebrates that move like squids, jetting water for propulsion. We're picturing long-lived creatures, large and intelligent. They populate areas around ice fields where they can camouflage as icebergs.

2. What is its relationship to your characters (symbiotic, delicacy, prey, predator, solitary, herd)?

Since your novel is about your characters, it's important to know the creature's relationship to your world's peoples and cultures.

We've decided that algors are herd creatures, predators who work as a part of a team to hem in and freeze aquatic prey in ice traps. They could present a major challenge to shipping lanes in their areas, but perhaps they are benevolent when full. As long as ships provide them with sacrificial prey, our ice creatures leave people alone. This could present some interesting problems should our characters run out of food to serve the beasts. Algors have an appendage with an ice block that they strike against their bellies to communicate—like Morse code. Perhaps humans could learn their language and communicate back.

There are legends surrounding the origins of our beasts. Some cultures even worship them.

3. Can real-world skeletons inspire your creature?

The base structure of real animals can be stepping stones to imagine your creature's inner workings. The skulls of hippopotamus or elephants are almost unrecognizable without the teeth and tusks—but what a scaffold for building a fantastical creature! Just look at how many different iterations of dinosaurs palaeontologists have developed over the years. Teeth can also tell us what sort of role an animal plays.

Our ice creatures—although they're invertebrates—have strong, flat teeth for grinding instead of the sharp teeth we'd expect from predators, because they eat their prey frozen solid and have to grind up chunks of ice. The teeth are valuable because they're harder than any other substance. Brave hunters hunt algors for their teeth, though it is an incredibly dangerous endeavour.

4. What happens if you mix and match?

Imagine if wildly different animals bred and procreated. You can mix plants and animals too. We're thinking algors are a mix of squid, angler fish, whale, and kelp. They have the torpedo shape of a whale with propulsion ports along their flank and an ice hammer appendage at their front. They have large eyes, plus skin that can change colour and texture like a squid. Their long tongue resembles a kelp frond and keeps them anchored to icebergs when they sleep.

Voila! We've got a pretty interesting creature already—we have ideas for its habitat, appearance, biology, and relationship to humans. It's got the potential for huge effects on the characters and culture of our story.

Readers don't need every single detail about your world and

the creatures in it, and you don't want to introduce every creature at once. Choose a few distinct animals—likely the ones your protagonist sees in their daily life—to start with. In no time, you'll have a world that resonates with vibrant wildlife and unique ecosystems.

MAKING MONSTERS

According to English professor Paul A. Trout, we've written about creatures who disgust, terrify, and devour us since ancient times. In a *Salon* article titled "Why We Invented Monsters," Trout writes:

> 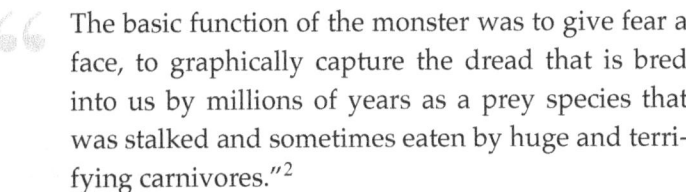 The basic function of the monster was to give fear a face, to graphically capture the dread that is bred into us by millions of years as a prey species that was stalked and sometimes eaten by huge and terrifying carnivores."[2]

And it wasn't just familiar meat-eaters that made our ancestors shudder. Around the world, ancient cultures uncovered fossilized bones with huge skulls and massive serpentine spines. These remains looked like enormous snakes. Ancient people wouldn't have been able to date these fossils and know that the creatures were long extinct.

Creating fictional monsters pulls on readers' primal fears of predation and immediately lets them know that there is something bigger than themselves that will require finesse, strength, and intelligence to conquer, befriend, or flee from.

We fear the unknown, and monsters are something we can mold out of the ether of our anxiety. Keep this in mind when you are creating your beasties. They should be somewhat unpredictable. That's part of what makes them scary. In a *Writer's Digest* article, "Writing Monsters: What Makes a Monster Scary?", author Philip Athans writes:

> Humans tend to have a pretty good sense of what another human is going to do next. We can tell via body language, facial expressions, and tone of voice when someone is getting angry or upset. We sense when things might get out of control or violent. But monsters don't necessarily give out those human signals. This is a creature, after all, outside our normal experience. Who knows what it'll do next?"[3]

The unknown, mysterious, and strange inspire fear because people like to be able to predict their enemies.

You can also play with common human fears when creating monsters. According to Karl Albrecht, Ph.D., there are five basic fears, out of which almost all of our other fears are manufactured:

1. Extinction—the fear of annihilation. More than just the fear of death, the idea of *no longer being* creates existential anxiety in humans.
2. Mutilation—the fear of losing a part of our body and having our body's boundaries invaded. Anxiety about animals, such as bugs, spiders, snakes, and other creepy things, might arise from a fear of mutilation.
3. Loss of autonomy—the fear of being immobilized, entrapped, imprisoned, smothered, or otherwise controlled. This includes claustrophobia but can also extend to our social interactions and relationships.
4. Separation—the fear of abandonment and rejection. The "silent treatment," when imposed by a group, can have a devastating effect on its target.
5. Ego-death—the fear of humiliation or shame. The idea that we aren't worthy or loveable can be a tough fear to overcome.[4]

The Pale Man in Guillermo del Toro's *Pan's Labyrinth* embodies the fears of extinction, mutilation, and entrapment by devouring live children. He's humanoid, but his expressions are difficult to read because his eyeballs are on the palms of his hands. He's frightening because he feeds on the helpless.

HERE ARE four questions you can ruminate on while you're playing Frankenstein:

1. Does your monster represent a basic fear?

Is it frightening because it will mutilate or kill your characters? Will it take over their bodies and leave them trapped within? Does it separate them from the rest of humanity or reveal all of their hidden flaws? For best effect, you can pull from several different fears at once.

Let's create a fictional monster. We'll call it a crim. Crim are small, so initially they won't inspire a fear of extinction. They invade humans by climbing into their noses and taking up residence in their sinuses. Eww. This represents loss of autonomy and mutilation. These monsters sink their tendrils into their humans' brains and take over their consciousnesses. They're not good spies, though, because they don't have the host's memories. It's obvious to other people when a crim has taken over a mind, so they are shunned by society. Hello, fear of separation. Eventually, the human's body deforms and grows into the crim's adult form—mutilation again, as the human has literally been turned into something else.

2. Is your monster sentient?

Smart monsters are frightening because they're capable of outthinking us and have their own agendas, but unintelligent monsters can be equally scary. Something as basic as a fungus or a viral monster cannot be reasoned with. It has a job to do and will do it as designed.

Crim are intelligent, even in their tiny forms. They're smart enough to choose hosts that nobody will miss. They nest in humans because we commute and tend to urbanize. In their adult form, crim lurk, unseen, in sewer and storm drain systems, and they feed on electricity. You'll often find them in large cities, sneaking aboveground to chew on power lines. They prefer solitary life and mark their territory so other crim stay away.

3. What does your monster look like?

Remember, people fear things for a reason. We balk at insects, spiders, and snakes because many of them are poisonous. Creatures who look utterly inhuman are scary because we can't read them or their motives, whereas ones who look nearly human frighten us because we recognize them, but they don't seem quite right.

We could play on both of these ideas by giving our adult crim centipede bodies with human faces. Creepy, right?

You might find it helpful to sketch or make a clay model of your beasties so that you can accurately describe proportions and details.

4. Is your monster a part of a myth?

If your monster has existed alongside humans for some time, perhaps they've inspired a myth or legend.

Our crim have starred in bedtime stories for years, and parents tell their kids to stay away from storm drains, sewers, and power lines if they don't want to be eaten. People sleep with nose plugs. Exorcists sell tinctures to drive out monsters who've nested in people's heads. There's a religion that worships crim, and believers infect themselves on purpose because they think the monsters are humankind's final form.

INSPIRE your imagination using the weird, wonderful and creepy flora and fauna of our world. Pull on humans' common basic fears. And if you want your creatures to be scientifically possible, you can always go into research mode after your brainstorming session. For example, we might want to look into the biology of centipedes, if crim are going to mimic their appearance, to see if living in a wet environment would even be logical for their anatomy, or to determine how they would adapt to live there. Talking to experts, such as biologists or zoologists, is another great way to get inspiration for your creatures and monsters.

After your imagination's gone to work and you've researched all you want, you'll have a world populated with animals your readers wish were real, and monsters who'll haunt them long after they've stopped reading.

Chapter 19

This Weapon Is Your Life

Arms and Armour

There is a lot to unpack regarding weapons and armour in fantasy and science fiction, simply because these two genres span from primitive past to far future. However, there are similarities that you can use as building blocks to create original and engaging fight scenes.

When considering what weapon your character might use, note weapon range and damage delivery. Weapons for fantasy settings include the following:

- **Melee:** club, dagger, axe, mace, quarterstaff, sickle, spear, flail, glaive, shortsword, longsword, rapier, trident, warhammer, whip, lance, scimitar, attack hound or other animal companion
- **Ranged:** javelin, throwing stone, crossbow, shortbow, longbow, dart, blowgun, net, sling, siege weapon, fire-breathing dragon or other animal companion
- **Miscellaneous:** magic, curse (range may or may not apply), biological weapon

Weapons for futuristic settings might include any of the above, plus:

- **Melee:** taser, knuckles, baton, chainsaw, flamethrower, laser sword
- **Ranged:** pistol, rifle, sniper rifle, missile, laser, drone, plasma cannon, stun weapon, grenade, rocket, powered armour
- **Miscellaneous:** quantum, biological, nuclear, or chemical weapon, poison gas

The weapon you choose depends both on your fighter's training and preferences (unless they are untrained and grab the nearest object to fight with) as well as the armour they use. Does your character like to get up close and personal in battle? Foot soldiers mostly use melee weapons, simply because these fighters are on the ground, thrust into the thick of things. In these situations, ranged weapons would be as likely to harm their comrades as they would their foes.

Mounted archery is done with a horse specifically trained for it. The horse is steered with the archer's legs and heels, and horse bows tend to be smaller so they don't get tangled in the horse's mane or bump against its body. The small bow also allows the archer to switch hands and shoot from any angle.

For one-on-one combat, your characters will likely use melee weapons, with the exception of Old Western gunslingers or a David versus Goliath situation, in which ranged weapons are called for. Flintlock guns were the primary firearms used in the seventeenth and eighteenth centuries, named for the material they used in their ignition system. Many fantasy stories with guns feature these weapons, which are single-shot pistols or muskets, rendered useless by moisture, and have a one in six chance of misfiring.

Weapons of mass destruction, of course, aren't a good fit for single combat, since the purpose of duels is to prove bravery, demonstrate skill, or prevent extraneous loss of life.

Swords are the most popular weapons of choice in fantasy. Swords from medieval times didn't actually weigh that much—

most weighed less than five pounds. While it is tiring to swing a chunk of metal around for a long time, lifting one is no great feat. (And yes, women can wield swords, and there are female sword fighters and fencers in the real world to prove it.)

If two fighters are using different weapons, understanding how they might interact with each other and whether one has any advantage is key to a realistic battle. You can also surprise readers by having an expert user with a simple weapon beat a fighter wielding something flashy. For example, in *The Dragon Reborn* by Robert Jordan, Mat Cauthon grew up as a farmer and is an expert with a quarterstaff. He challenges two swordsmen to a friendly fight:

> Swords aren't the be-all and end-all, you know. I could do fairly well against either of you, I think, if you had a sword and I had my quarterstaff."[1]

The two swordsmen take him up on the challenge, certain that they can beat him. Of course, Mat wins the fight. Partly what makes this scene so satisfying is that Mat has had a lot of awful things happen to him up to this point, including being rushed from his home, chased by darkfriends, and poisoned by a magical dagger. He gets a tiny amount of agency here, finally, through a simple demonstration.

~

UNLIKE SWORDS AND STAFFS, long range weapons are obviously suited for situations where there is a clear division and distance between the fighters with little chance of friendly-fire casualties. Longbows, siege weapons, sniper rifles, tanks, drones, and laser weapons need a little more room to operate, but they are excellent at killing multiple opponents in a short time frame or smashing through enemy defences.

Science fiction writers might use missiles, spaceships, and

282   Making Myths and Magic

even planet-sized space stations to wreak havoc in their stories. Battles may become a matter of who has the most advanced weaponry. *Ender's Game* by Orson Scott Card, however, demonstrates that brains can overcome impossible odds. It is Ender's strategy and ingenuity that turns the tides when his fleet is outnumbered and all seems lost.

Lethal, long-range weapons also affect how armies fight in fantasy. In an article titled "Weapons and Tactics in Fantasy Warfare," author Dan Koboldt explains:

> If there are mages or weapons on the battlefield that can throw explosions that rip up chunks of land (and bodies), no thinking army is going to stay in tight formation and wait for that to happen. If the opposing force consists of mindless drones, then sure. But if they're sentient fighters, self preservation is going to take over. Even if the leader doesn't see it, the soldiers are going to take it upon themselves to save their own lives. It would take an extremely disciplined force to continue a fight where some new horror is unleashed. Panic happens quickly. As a rule, the more lethal the weapons, the more an army will spread out. This increases the strain on leadership and communications, because you now have to transmit orders over a larger area."[2]

There will always be cause and effect in battle. If the enemy has weapons that spread your troops out, can you maintain long range communication with magic or neural links? How will your opponent try to crash those methods of communication? How effective and adaptable are your leaders in battle?

Adaptable leaders are key when it comes to responding to new and unseen threats on the field. Just like in *Ender's Game*, ingenuity can go a long way, and leaders who keep it together and make the difficult choices are often the ones who bring their troops to victory.

WEIRD WEAPONS

If you decide to break away from the traditional sword or pistol, there are some fantastic weapons you can write about instead. Atlatl (spear throwers) and spears were used for years before humans fired their first arrow. Slings and bullets are accurate and deadly at a range of up to 400 meters. Plumbatae Lead Darts —deadly predecessor to lawn darts—can be lobbed in volleys at close range. Francisca Bouncing Axes have long, arched heads that leave them unbalanced and unwieldy; they spin wildly when thrown and bounce unpredictably. One can only imagine how a volley of these axes thrown at close range could shake a formation. Quick lime, a caustic powder dropped on attackers, burns skin and eyes. Caltrops, huge spiked metal devices—think the classic game of jacks, only the jacks are huge and hooked— puncture boots when scattered on the ground. We still use similar devices today scattered across roads to flatten vehicle tires.

You can also use your imagination to come up with futuristic weaponry. Insects as bio-drones? Designer pathogens? Warrior robot dogs? Sentient spaceships? Cyberattacks? Remote control zombies? Technology and creativity open up a whole new world of weaponry.

Sound weapons actually exist now, from high decibel personal alarms to the Israeli-invented "Thunder Generator"—a sonic cannon that produces shockwaves strong enough to disable anyone within 100 meters. The company who sells them says that an optional curved barrel allows the weapon users to fire shockwaves around corners, so one wouldn't even have to see a target to stun them. In the future, non-lethal sonic weapons will likely be even more powerful and precise.

Nanoweapons, tiny drones the size of a house fly, are ideal

for infiltrating beyond enemy lines, carrying out surveillance and even targeted assassinations via poison. Smaller, self-replicating nanobots could do even more damage, as imagined in the film *The Day the Earth Stood Still*, in which the robotic defense system of an alien ship dissolves into a swarm of nanobots that devour every object in their way.

Then, there are weapons designed to recognize certain DNA. Anyone who doesn't match the approved genetics is unable to operate the weapon. In the film *District 9*, extraterrestrials arrive in South Africa's Johannesburg en masse—and severely malnourished—within a huge spaceship. They bring high tech weapons that humans are unable to operate. When Wikus's company is employed to relocate the aliens to a new camp outside of the city, he finds a canister of fuel and accidentally sprays himself with it. This sets off a mutation in Wikus, which slowly transforms him into an alien. His DNA, a chimeric mix of human and alien, is recognized by the weaponry. His former company (a weapons manufacturer) experiments on him and eventually decides to harvest his body while he's still a hybrid. Wikus is their key to accessing the high tech weapons they've been unable to operate thus far.

Perhaps the most well-known example of a unique, futuristic weapon is the lightsaber. In the Star Wars universe, these laser swords are the weapons of the Jedi and the Sith, consisting of a hilt and plasma blade powered by a kyber crystal.

There are physical rules for how a lightsaber can be used—and what it can and cannot do. For instance, a lightsaber can cut through anything except another lightsaber, some rare metals, or a weapon made of conducted energy like an electrostaff. It can deflect blaster bolts and even absorb Force lightning. In Star Wars Legends, lightsabers short out underwater (this seems to have been changed in the new canon; in an episode of *The Clone Wars*, Anakin Skywalker and Ahsoka Tano use their weapons underwater with no problems).[3] Lightsaber wounds don't cause bleeding, because the blade cauterizes the wound as it passes through.

Locating a kyber crystal and constructing a lightsaber is part of a Jedi Padawan's training. They are also used in the knighting ceremonies of the Jedi Order to cut off the Padawan's braid. Lightsabers are not just weapons to the Jedi, but they are deeply tied to the Order's culture and history. "This weapon is your life,"[4] Obi-Wan says to his padawan, Anakin. Anakin later repeats this exact phrase to Ahsoka.

MEANING AND RITUAL

In addition to combat, consider how your character's weapon might relate to history and ritual. Take these real-world examples for inspiration—an athame is a double-edged dagger used for symbolic cutting in many Wiccan and Pagan rituals; a kīla is a stake or knife-like instrument associated with Indo-Tibetan Buddhism, used as a tool of exorcism; and a Gata is a war club from Fiji, used in war but also for dances and ceremonies.

Does your weapon have any symbolic meaning? Is it only used by a particular group of people? Does it have purposes other than battle?

In *The Lord of the Rings* (and many other epic fantasies since), many weapons have names. Tolkien borrowed this idea from European traditions and norse mythology; for example, in the Old English epic poem, "Beowulf," Beowulf is given a sword named Hrunting, which he uses to fight Grendel's mother.

Tolkien was likely also inspired by King Arthur's Excalibur, Sigurd the Volsung's Gram, And Roland's Durendal, among others. Tolkien names many weapons in his epic, including Gandalf's sword Glamdring, Thorin's sword Orcrist, and Gil-Galad's spear Aeglos. Even Grond, the evil battering-ram from Minas Morgul, has a name.

The names speak to the weapons' history and the heroes who

wielded them in the past, suggesting whoever wields them in the present will also be a hero (or, if the weapon has an evil history, that legacy will be continued).

Mythology often links the fate of its sword with its wielder, which is a significant theme with Aragorn's sword. In the novel, Aragorn carries the shards of Narsil, the sword that was broken when his ancestor, Elendil, died in battle with Sauron. In the Elvish language of Quenya, Narsil translates to "red and white flame," which is fitting since it was enchanted to shine with the light of the sun and moon. Its history goes all the way back to the First Age, when it was forged by one of the greatest Dwarf-smiths. The sword's brokenness functions as a symbol for Aragorn's refusal to become king of Gondor. His reforging of the sword and renaming it Andúril, Flame of the West, demonstrates he's accepted his heritage; it points to the ending of Sauron's reign and the dawn of a new age.

Considering a weapon's history and mythology can be a great way to enrich your story. It doesn't have to be a complex history, either. Even simply a mother passing on her sword to her daughter can have significance in how the fighter views their weapon.

Of course, let's not forget that with weaponry comes armour, and we rarely see one without the other.

KNIGHTS IN SHINING ARMOUR

The first armour was a thick skull and a rib-cage wrapped around vulnerable organs. As we evolved effective ways to overcome our natural armour with weapons like maces, swords, and pikes, our armour evolved into helmets made of larger animal skulls, thick wooden shields, leather to ward off glancing cuts, and extra padding to cushion blunt blows. Every weapon comes with strengths and weaknesses and so does every piece of armour.

For example, fighters who use rapiers know the weapon's strength: its lightness. They employ nimble thrusts and stabs paired with quick movements. These fencers don't require much in the way of armour, because they value mobility over protection. Rapiers, being light, don't have a lot of driving force behind them. For heavier weapons, fighters tend to bulk up on armour. Armour should be easy to move in, as you are meant to be running around a battlefield while wearing it, but some is heavier than others, depending on what it's made of. Here are some of the options for materials, starting with medieval armour:

Boiled Leather

Boiled leather, or cuir bouilli, is one of the most common types of armour because it's cost effective. Cuir bouilli is effective against most light slashing weapons, and padding beneath will dull some blunt blows, but it hasn't a hope against direct blows from heavy weapons or projectiles like arrows. If your fighter can afford it, they'll add some metal plating over vulnerable areas like the chest and abdomen.

For those of you who love the idea of studded leather armour, alas, it has never existed outside of D&D, biker gangs, and LARPers who love decorative embellishments; it offers no extra protection unless the studs are extremely close together, in which case, it makes more sense to use mail.

Gambeson

A full body jacket made of quilted linen or wool and stuffed with horsehair, gambeson offers decent defense against slash attacks and doesn't wear out as fast as cuir bouilli—which tends to get brittle quickly.

Brigandine

What casual museum observers may mistake as studded armour is actually brigandine, armour which has small oblong steel plates riveted between thick layers of fabric. In many cases, this can be more effective than mail if high quality metal is used in the plating.

Mail

Mail armour works well against most arrows and bolts; it doesn't need to be form-fitting or sized, so can be passed down, gifted, or plundered easily. It's light with good mobility, and it is always worn with some sort of lining because, otherwise, it would pinch skin or pull out hair. Made of high-quality metal, it is costly and time-consuming to build, so not everyone has access to it. Often, it's used with some combination of padding and plate armour to defend against heavier artillery like longbows or lances.

Plate

Lastly, and most expensive on the medieval armour list, is full plate armour. This is individually fitted and highly expensive to make. It offers immunity to thrusting, stabbing, and piercing attacks. Your character wearing plate might be more likely to survive a battle because of its protection (or because their foe keeps them alive to use as ransom, as they're probably someone important). Crushing blows from maces or other blunt weapons still cause devastating, closed-flesh injuries for plate armour wearers, and most suffer from invisible internal wounds as opposed to gushing, bloody ones.

Plate armour is hot to wear and restricts mobility, but on the whole is not as cumbersome and immobilizing as some people believe. A museum curator of arms and armour, Dirk H. Breiding, addresses this in an essay for *The Met* titled "Arms and Armor—Common Misconceptions and Frequently Asked Questions."

> An entire suit of field armor (that is, armor for battle) usually weighs between 45 and 55 lbs. (20 to 25 kg), with the helmet weighing between 4 and 8 lbs. (2 to 4 kg)—less than the full equipment of a fireman with oxygen gear, or what most modern soldiers have carried into battle since the nineteenth century. Moreover, while most modern equipment is chiefly suspended from the shoulders or waist, the weight of a well-fitted armor is distributed all over the body. It was not until the seventeenth century that the weight of field armor was greatly increased in order to render it bulletproof against ever more accurate firearms."[5]

Shields

Shield usage, size, and material will depend on your character's fighting style. Some warriors prefer to go shieldless, carrying secondary weapons into battle instead. Formation fighting requires large, unwieldy shields, whereas hand-to-hand combat may call for smaller blockers, perhaps with sharpened edges. Often, your fighter's shield will carry their family crest or their lord's colours. What does your shield—or lack of one—say about your character?

EVEN NOW, in our day of firearms, people still utilize armour. Helmets, riot shields and ballistic vests are common, and we're starting to creep into the territory of semi-autonomous armoured drones, active denial systems which use non-lethal short wavelength radiation to scald skin, and powered exoskeletons.

A lot of science fiction features cybersuits as augmented armour that bolsters strength and ability. This type of armour inspires many questions: What is its weak points? How is the suit powered? Does it have A.I. programming that can override operator input, like accident avoidance systems on cars? What if people become overly-dependent on them or too integrated into the suits and unable to operate without them? All intriguing paths to explore further.

In *The Expanse*, a TV series based on the novels by James S.A. Corey, marines from Mars and Earth use power armour, the most dangerous weapon a soldier can go up against. The Goliath suits worn by Martian marines are two and a half meters tall and weigh 400 kilograms. They function as both armour and spacesuit, the titanium and ceramic-composite exterior providing impressive shielding. They're equipped with weaponry and a sensor package that feeds data to the wearer.

The show does a remarkable job of showing us how powerful this armour is when Bobbie Draper, a member of the Martian Marine Corps, uses it in various situations to accomplish impressive feats and fight off enemies. The show never bothers to tell us how much the suits weigh or what it's made of—it doesn't need to. It simply shows us the suit's capabilities by what Bobbie does with it. Viewers are filled with dread when a group of antagonists gets their hands on several suits of Goliath armour, because, by that point in the story, we're aware of how dangerous it is.

As the author of your story, you might know how much your soldier's armour weighs and the exact length of their sword, but your reader might not need to know those details. Striking a balance with your worldbuilding is key.

Weapons and armour are tools that can demonstrate a character's class and rank, and they be imbued with meaning through history or ritual. They can even be characters themselves (who doesn't love a talking sword?). As with all worldbuilding, thoughtfulness and research are key to realistic and interesting weaponry. If your characters need to go to battle, they might as well do it in style.

Chapter 20

Bow Ties Are Cool

Clothing and Costumes

Just like we judge books by their covers, our first impressions of people are often influenced by how they're dressed. S.W.A.T. teams armoured in medieval chain mail wouldn't seem realistic. Darth Vader chilling out in yoga pants and a stained rock concert t-shirt wouldn't feel threatening—although we're definitely curious about the concert Vader crowd surfed at. Galadriel in a fuchsia pantsuit doesn't fit her character or setting.

Use clothing to your advantage, and you can elegantly convey much about your characters and their world.

One of the first things a writer should consider when choosing clothing is practicality—or lack of—in regards to climate, occupation, and availability of material.

LET'S GET MATERIAL

What are your characters' clothes made of? The material will usually be defined by climate, local textile materials, occupation, and status. Silk might be a common fabric if your story happens to take place somewhere like China, but not so easy to procure in climates unsuitable for silkworms and their sole source of food, mulberry trees. Silk is time consuming to make, takes dye well, and is both insulating and breathable, so it will likely be relatively expensive.

What is an abundant, cheap fibre in your locality? Cotton? Linen? In areas too cold for cotton and flax to grow, wool, leather and fur will be more common—not just because they are insulating, but also because they are more readily available.

The poorest among your population will dress in the cheapest, most accessible fabric available. So, in your world, if silk is dirt cheap for some reason, that's what the impoverished would wear.

Those with wealth tend to display it. The elite will wear difficult-to-obtain fabrics shipped from afar, coloured with rare dyes and accessorized with prized jewellery. The evolution of the humble button is a fascinating example of an accessory that rose to prominence among the wealthy in the middle ages. During the medieval period, when clothing styles became more form fitting, buttons were a status symbol, worn by the wealthy.

After the Renaissance, wealthy fashion sported so many buttons that wearers often needed assistance. Around this time, clothing was made with buttons on opposing sides. Men usually dressed themselves so their buttons were on the right, but women wore their buttons on the left to make it easier for their servants to work with while facing them.

In 1789, on George Washington's inauguration, the button became a political symbol. Made of brass, copper, or Sheffield plate, these buttons could fasten a coat and announce the wearer's political stripes at the same time.

The poor wore buttons as well, but they were painstaking to craft by hand. Working class families were lucky if they owned a button-mold, which could be heated and then filled with molten lead or pewter and set into a circular shape.

During the Industrial Revolution, buttons became cheap

enough to produce in bulk. Since they had been so long considered a sign of wealth, they accessorized tight-fitting clothes by the hundreds.

While you don't need to get this in-depth with your clothing and accessories, ask yourself what underpins hierarchies, political affiliations, and fashion trends in your world.

YOU CAN TELL BY MY OUTFIT

Clothing isn't just dictated by available material and manufacturing processes. Like people, most outfits have a job to do, so what your characters wear will depend on their occupation. Suitable clothing is required for different tasks, such as the following:

- **General physical labour.** These clothes should be loose-fitting enough so that the wearer has an uninhibited range of movement, but not loose enough to get caught on things. Durable, cheap fabrics are usually well-suited for physical labour.
- **Ranching/riding.** Pants are usually more suitable than skirts for horseback riding, though women in the Victorian era wore divided skirts for this purpose—they were basically pants with ruffles or panels to hide the divide. Riding clothes might also include many layers and perhaps some oil-skin or waxed outer layers, so that the wearer is dressed for any weather they might encounter on a long journey.
- **Fishing/sailing.** Sailors tend to wear short pants with waterproof footwear and outerwear. Inner layers that dry quickly, and clothing with loops or lanyards to secure tools while going aloft, are useful.
- **Urban Life.** Wealthy city people wear clothing that displays their status and the latest trends in fashion.

Hidden pockets to hide valuables are common. Poor people wear whatever is cheapest and readily available.
- **Travel.** Light-weight, wrinkle-free clothes that are easy to maintain and wash are common. Travelers might carry a small sewing kit for repairs while on the road.
- **Fighting.** Fighting clothes have to balance mobility with protection. Do your fighters display their rank with badges, crests, or armbands? Do upper ranks avoid advertising their high standing so as not to become targets? The wealth of your fighters will greatly determine what they wear.
- **Spacewear.** Perhaps this type of clothing is made with advanced fabrics that can cool or heat the wearer as needed. Most will be somewhat form-fitting so that clothes don't float around a person in zero gravity situations.

Some wealthy people display their status by wearing clothing that's utterly impractical. Dresses with acres of fabric make it impossible for women to sit or even walk properly while wearing them. Bustles and long trains are a tremendous pain to navigate in, but the excess of unneeded fabric means money. Highly impractical clothes also suggest they pay someone else to do mundane tasks for them.

Effie Trinket from *The Hunger Games* by Suzanne Collins demonstrates this impracticality with her colourful wardrobe. In an interview with *The Collider*, Elizabeth Banks, who plays Effie in the movie adaptation, talks about how she couldn't function well with her false nails:

I had ladies-in-waiting that did everything for me. I couldn't type on my phone. I couldn't go to the bathroom. I couldn't get in and out of [the costume]. By the time I got to the lunch line, everybody was back in their trailers, done with lunch. I was like, 'There's no one to eat with! I just got here!' It took me 25 minutes to get in and out of my costume. My lunch hour was a full 10 minutes of eating, and that's it."[1]

How do the affluent in your world use impracticality to show their status? Ridiculous shoes? Large collar ruffs? Delicate, elaborate hairstyles? How can you tell, at a glance, that this person is most certainly not a commoner?

NOBLES AREN'T the only people who can stand out because of their clothing. In *Shadow and Bone* by Leigh Bardugo, the Grisha of the Ravkan Second Army wear keftas—long robes that resemble coats and represent their position in the army as mages. Silk kefta are worn in summer, wool kefta are worn in winter, and corecloth kefta—made of a material that can withstand bullets—are worn during combat. Not only are these coats practical, but they are also status symbols. The colour of the kefta conveys the Grisha's rank and magical ability. Blue is for Etherealki, who can manipulate wind, fire, and water; red is for Corporalki, who can manipulate the human body to kill or heal; and purple is for Materialki, who can manipulate materials like glass, wood, stone, or chemicals. Only the Darkling, a Grisha with the unique ability to manipulate shadows, wears a black kefta.

Colours are a useful way to differentiate rank or status, because passersby are going to notice a bright red coat before they see a badge or insignia.

In *Star Trek*, characters wear uniforms to represent that they are part of Starfleet. The colours vary depending on the show, but convey whether an officer is part of the command, operations, or sciences division. The common reference to redshirts being expendable refers to security officers from *Star Trek: The Original Series* who wear red uniforms and frequently die during their duties.

Uniforms can serve several purposes in your story. They may provide physical protection, such as the corecloth keftas. They allow for instant recognition, which might translate to respect, disrespect, or a variety of attitudes depending on the individual. They may allow characters to access certain areas they couldn't otherwise. And they may promote a sense of team building or unity within the group—which can be a good thing (yay to camaraderie!) or a bad thing (boo to people who abuse their authority and think they are better than others). The bigger the organization is, the more variety of attitudes and behaviours you'll see from both the people wearing the uniforms and the "commoners" who interact with them. Uniforms are status symbols that can be almost as powerful as magic, weapons, or knowledge, depending on the situation.

THE FUTURE IS NOW

Common tropes in science fiction include explorers who wear white, lower class workers who wear earth tones, troops who wear uniforms, and villains who wear black. But you can always break the mold.

If your world is futuristic, what do the clothes look like? Knee high boots and miniskirts? Unfortunate red shirts denoting expendable ranks? Gothic? Victorian Steampunk? Road warrior? It might depend on whether your future is a dystopian collapse, in which people have regressed to whatever materials they can cobble together from fashions past, or a progressive society with technology facilitating every aspect of their day-to-day lives.

Science changes the way we make clothing. Textiles can now be manufactured as a tube of fabric, allowing for seamless garments. *Fabrican Ltd.* has already invented a spray-on fabric that can be redissolved into a solvent and used over and over again—not just for clothing, but for bandages and casts too.

How can you think outside the box regarding your futuristic clothing? Have materials been invented that can control temperature? Change texture or thickness as needed? Camouflage?

Modesty standards change with time and culture. What body parts are acceptable to reveal and what are taboo? What is allowable exposure in some societies may be considered near nudity in others. Depending on the time and civilization your story is set in, it may be off-limits for a woman to expose her ankles, hair, shoulders, or arms. Many cultures mandate the covering of genitalia and breasts, but there are regulations regarding situations when they can be exposed—such as breastfeeding in public or topless beaches. How much skin do costumes reveal in your world? What do they accentuate and draw attention to? What must people cover up at all costs?

LEARN FROM THEIR CLOTHES

Readers will infer things about a character's personality by the way they dress. Whether or not their assumptions prove true is up to you, but clothing is an easy way to show something about a character rather than tell it.

For example, three characters show up to a job interview—the first is in a full suit, complete with tie and jacket; the second arrives in a sweatshirt and jeans; and the third shows up wearing all black and goth makeup. What might your readers infer about their personalities? How will they compare these three characters in their minds?

Every time a new actor takes on the role of the Doctor in *Doctor Who*, their outfit changes to match their personality. As a result, the Doctor's clothing choices are iconic (and ripe for cosplay!). The first iteration of the Doctor in 1963, played by William Hartnell, wears an Edwardian-style coat, trousers, and a ribbon tie, occasionally accompanied by an Astrakhan (wool hat), cape, and monocle. His outfit speaks to mystery and eccentricity—which is a perfect fit for the Doctor.

The Fourth Doctor, played by Tom Baker, wears what is perhaps their most iconic outfit—a brown coat, fedora, and ridiculously long, multicoloured scarf. While the previous Doctors' clothing is ornate and impeccable, Baker's look is shabby and fits his mop of curly hair, awkward nature, and maniacal stare.

When the series was rebooted in 2005 with Christopher Eccleston's Ninth Doctor, he wears a leather jacket over a v-neck shirt and black pants. All the fancy coats and ties are exchanged for a simple, modern look that matches Eccleston's Doctor to a tee—he's a much more down-to-earth version of the character.

The costume designers faced perhaps the most pressure with the thirteenth Doctor because, for the first time, the character is played by a woman (Jodie Whittaker). Women's clothing is often more scrutinized than men's, and there was already a sexist uproar about Whittaker taking on the role, so there was pressure to get it right. The Doctor's colourful look—complete with rainbow t-shirt, long jacket, and suspenders—pays homage to previous iterations of the character while embracing the new. In a BBC interview, Whittaker's costume designer, Ray Holman, says:

> The possibilities are endless when designing a costume but you start with the script, which will paint the world you're designing for, it could be now, period or future. Landscape, locations and weather are also a big factor... You also have to consider fabrics and technology in order to deliver the perfect idea that makes and helps the script tell the story."[2]

What do your characters' clothing choices say about them? Do the materials and colours have meaning? How do people perceive them based on the way they are dressed? The sci-fi and fantasy genres allow you lots of creativity with your materials, colours, and styles. A dress made of stars? A bullet-proof cloak? A temperature-adjusting sweater? No problem. You can even make up fabrics and their properties. So get material and have fun dressing your characters.

Chapter 21

Mae Govannen, quSDaq ba'lu"a'?
Languages and Communication

Mobility is not the first thing children try to learn; language is.

By the age of six months, most infants are already experimenting, watching speakers' faces when talked to, making noises to get attention, or, if exposed to it, starting to understand sign language.

And once we've learned it, we often take language for granted—its complexities, how it evolves, where it came from, and even what it might look like in other sentient species. Unless you study linguistics—or write fantasy or science fiction—digging into your language's origins may never have occurred to you.

Wherever people flourish, language does too, whether spoken, gestured, or more recently, written. And there is an incredible variety to the languages we speak. You don't have to travel far to experience changes in dialect, tone, and even common gestures. Nodding your head doesn't mean "yes" everywhere in the world, and shaking it isn't a universal "no." Subtle facial expressions and changes in tone can completely change the meaning of a phrase as well.

You don't have to be a linguist in order to craft a language for your novel. Not all of us have the stamina to spend decades crafting multiple languages like J.R.R. Tolkien did. But there are some decisions you can make about language that will help your fiction feel authentic.

There are currently about seven thousand living languages worldwide, and twenty three of these account for more than half of the world's population.[1] With that in mind, it's likely that the beings inhabiting your world don't all speak the same language. So, how do your characters understand each other?

If your fiction covers a lot of geographical ground and your characters aren't isolated, chances are you are going to deal with several different languages and even more local dialects. Here are some options for how to do so, organized by low to high effort.

1. Characters use the same universal language.

There's a tongue-in-cheek example of this in *The Simpsons*, when aliens invade Springfield:

> Kang: "Greetings Earthlings, I am Kang. Do not be frightened. We mean you no harm."
> Marge: "You... you speak English."
> Kang: "I am actually speaking Rigeliah. By an astonishing coincidence, both our languages are exactly the same."[2]

This episode pokes fun at how writers ignore language barriers in hopes that readers won't notice, or simply because they want to get on with the story and aren't concerned with realism. If this is your preferred method, no judgement here. Realism shouldn't necessarily trump entertainment. If your story is well-written and interesting, readers probably won't care.

However, if realism is your thing, a universal language won't just naturally occur. It will have to be enforced in some way.

According to many of its novelizations, the universal

language in the Star Wars universe is Galactic Basic Standard, enforced by the Empire. Even so, there are aliens who, due to their physiology, are unable to speak Basic (such as Wookiees like Chewbacca). Are there situations in your world where certain life-forms are unable to speak a prevalent language due to physical differences?

If you choose a universal language, consider *why* it persists in a geographically vast story.

2. Characters use different languages, but everyone can understand each other through translators.

Star Trek characters use universal translators, technology that scans the brainwaves of the speaker and translates them into English. Kirk uses a handheld unit, while future Federation members have their translators installed as implant modules near their ears. In *The Hitchhiker's Guide to the Galaxy* by Douglas Adams, a Babel fish inserted into your ear allows instant communication in any language. In the *Farscape* series, a microbe injection flocks to the language centres in the brain and has the same effect.

These shortcuts aren't limited to science fiction, either. In *Magic Kingdom for Sale—Sold!* by Terry Brooks, a magic medallion allows Ben Holiday to speak, write, and understand the language of Landover.

If you don't want to be concerned by language barriers, creative shortcuts like these might be the route for you. This method also introduces opportunities to play with the subtleties of language. For example, how often do translators malfunction, break down, or simply do a sub-par job in your world?

Being able to understand a language doesn't mean you'll comprehend unique turns of phrase, either. English is full of those, and it stands to reason that fictional languages would be too. Would an alien understand the meaning behind "bite the bullet," "cat got your tongue," or "the apple of your eye"?

3. The main characters speak the same language, but other developed languages are also present.

This method presents an existing or a fictional language, complete with functioning grammar, rules, history, and perhaps even dialects.

For J.R.R. Tolkien, the fictional languages came first and the story came after. By twelve years old, Tolkien knew Latin, French, and German, and he went on to learn Middle English, Old English, Finnish, Gothic, Greek, Italian, Old Norse, Spanish, Welsh, and Medieval Welsh. He also understood the grammar and writing systems of several other languages and became a philologist by profession, studying how languages develop over time.

It's no wonder the languages of Middle-earth are so complex! They took him decades to create, and he continued revising and polishing them throughout his lifetime. On the specifics of the two major Elvish languages, Quenya and Sindarin, English teacher Olga Polomoshnova from *Middle Earth Reflections* writes:

> Quenya has a complex morphology and is, thus, a very inflected language; possesses ten cases of noun declension and four numbers alongside having several types of verbs, to name but a few grammar aspects. Some Sindarin grammar features include many vowel changes when forming plural nouns and an article in a plural form, which is absent in Quenya. Concerning communication, it is known that Sindarin was the spoken language used by the Elves in Middle-earth while Quenya remained the language of lore. Tolkien also thought about such a vital aspect of language as a writing system. Quenya and Sindarin were written with tengwar — the alphabet created by Fëanor. There was also cirth

by Daeron of Doriath, but it was adopted by the Dwarves and rarely used by the Elves."[3]

While Sindarin and Quenya are fully developed, other Middle-earth languages, like Dwarvish and the orcs' black speech, are much less refined, with only a few words sprinkled in here and there.

WHILE YOU DON'T HAVE to spend your entire lifetime to develop a language like Tolkien did with Elvish, here are some questions you can consider if you do want to dip your toes into creating a fictional language.

1. What does your culture talk about?

Like we mentioned in our chapter on dialogue, people have common words and phrases they use in their day-to-day lives. What does your society's life revolve around? Are they arctic northerners, coastal mariners, long distance traders? A culture dealing with cold climates will likely have a robust number of words describing different types of snow and ice. Mariners might have a wide vocabulary for types of waves, cloud formations, or navigation. Traders dealing in currencies, weights, and volumes will have more words to describe those things.

For the *Game of Thrones* TV series, David Peterson of the Language Creation Society was hired to create Dothraki—an invented language for a society of people who largely depend on horses in their day-to-day. It has many different words to describe horses, and the people's reverence for the animal is woven into common phrases. For example, *hash yer dothrae chek asshekh?* means "how are you today?" But, more literally, "Do you ride well today?"[4]

2. How large does vocabulary need to be?

How deep into this invented language do you want to dive? If you are just using it to colour dialogue and add authenticity, you don't need a *whole* language—a simple root language will do.

Try learning the most common words in your language and go from there. Make a list of common words, places, animals, and phrases and then translate them to another language.

Are you looking for soft, lilting cadences? Guttural, clipped rhythms? Nasal tones? Click languages? Listen to the plethora of beautiful natural languages out there and choose one for inspiration that reflects your imaginary world well, but don't appropriate it. Change things up and make your language fresh. Perhaps you could use a prefix from one tongue and a suffix from another or build onto root words.

If you choose to invent a language—even for just the odd phrase—try to avoid writing gibberish on the page. Remember, humans are wired to learn language from birth and readers are likely to spot the difference between word vomit and a simple phrase that actually utilizes grammar and syntax. Even if your readers don't understand the meaning, they'll recognize a thought-out language over nonsense words.

3. Does your language include spoken words, gestures, or something more?

Language is not just words. Look at how often meaning gets misconstrued when people text each other. So much of our oral language is tied to subtle tones, facial expressions, and hand gestures, and many of these aren't universal. In India, shaking your head has a different meaning depending on your facial expression and how slow or fast you're moving your head. In some societies, giving a thumbs up is akin to flipping someone the bird.

What about the sounds in your speech? Some noises carry

further than others. Is that important to your culture? South African click languages are some of the oldest living languages left. They tend to stem from hunter/gatherer societies. Clicking sounds carry well over longer distances, which would be advantageous in group hunting scenarios. Do your people whistle, clap, or snap?

Aliens and non-human races can have languages that are vastly different from ours, as well. Subtle changes in face shape and throat physiology impact the sound of a speaker's voice.

Sandra Martelli, a researcher in biology and anatomy at the University College London, has been using CT scans and computer models to study Neanderthal vocal tracts. Neanderthals, like humans, possess a hyoid bone in the throat, which is an anchor point for all the muscles and ligaments involved with speech and swallowing. According to Martelli's models, Neanderthals had larger voice boxes and may have pronounced vowels differently as a result. Using computer simulations to emulate speech through a Neanderthal larynx yielded some interesting results. *Oo* and *ee* sounds are similar to ours, but *ah* sounds like a hybrid between *ah* and *uh* that is hard for modern humans to pronounce.[5]

What if your story is populated with creatures wildly different from humans? How does physiology, mouth, or face shape change how they speak? Do they even *have* faces? In what other ways could they make sounds to communicate? What if they can't produce sound at all? The rachni, an insect-like species from the *Mass Effect* video game series, perceive speech and thought as forms of music and communicate using pheromones. A rachni queen speaks with Commander Shepard by taking over the body of a corpse and speaking through it.

4. What are the grammatical rules?

Even if you are using an invented language sparsely in your fiction, it helps to know some of the basic rules of language, including the following:

- **Phonology**, the sounds (or signs) of a language.
- **Morphology**, the structure of words and their relation to other words.
- **Syntax**, word order and construction in sentences.
- **Semantics**, word meaning and how this can change over time.
- **Pragmatics**, how context affects meaning.

How do plurals, possessives, and articles work in your language? Do you use gendered language or compound words? If grammar and structure of a fictional language fascinates you, check out the work of linguists and language-enthusiasts. (Mark Rosenfelder's website, *The Language Construction Kit*,[6] also available as a book, is a great place to start.)

WE COULD DIG into language for a lifetime and still not cover it all, but here are a few more questions to ask:

Will your language have its own written alphabet? Are there different languages for different classes in your society—a "high" tongue and a "common" one? What are some of your society's cliches and where did they originate? What are some of their slang words? Are there noted differences in how one speaks among formal peers and more familiar conversation partners?

Since languages aren't just oral, what about touch? Is a friendly pat on the arm while conversing acceptable in your culture? Should people make eye contact while talking, or is that rude in some situations? Do they embrace when they greet or keep their distance out of respect?

When Allison visited Romania, she was informed that the "bubble" of space people respect in social situations is much smaller than in North America. People would get right up in your face, almost standing toe-to-toe, when talking with you, and this was normal there, but it felt awkward to her because she was used to a bigger bubble.

If your characters aren't human, look to nature for inspiration on how other creatures communicate using posture, gestures, or even colour changes. And with sci-fi and fantasy, you also have otherworldly options like telepathy, energy, light waves, or magic.

Forget what you know, and think about what you take for granted where languages are concerned. This will help you get creative and bring your cultures to life with realistic languages on the page.

Chapter 22

The King is Dead

Politics and Economics

We're going to come right out and say it: politics and economics are confusing. There are so many varieties and many areas where they overlap in our world. We're breaking things down into bite-sized chunks to feed your worldbuilding.

TEN POLITICAL SYSTEMS

Below are ten types of governments to get you started when brainstorming your culture's leadership. Note that these systems can blur together, and you can have more than one of the following present in a single political system (for example, a democratic monarchy).

1. Democracy

People either vote on legislation and decide laws together (direct democracy) or they choose their political leaders by voting (representative democracy).

When building a democracy, consider who gets to vote and who gets to be in leadership—does your class, race, gender, age, wealth, or identity matter? Do some people's votes count more than others? Are voters educated and able to make informed choices? How long do government officials serve for?

Examples: Elendel (*The Alloy of Law* by Brandon Sanderson), United Earth (*Star Trek*)

2. Monarchy

Laws are dictated by a single monarch, such as a king or queen. In an absolute monarchy, the sovereign has supreme authority and can rule how they see fit; succession is often hereditary and limited to the sovereign's family. In a constitutional monarchy, the monarch's authority is restrained by laws, and leadership may involve a council.

When building a monarchy, consider your rules for succession—can only blood heirs become monarchs? Do they have to be a certain age, have a certain education, identify as a specific gender, or follow a particular religion? Does the monarch have a council of advisors or heads of state? What powers does the monarch have? Are they merely a figurehead?

Examples: Kingdom of the North (*Game of Thrones* by George R.R. Martin), Naboo (*Star Wars*)

3. Theocracy

Religious ideology determines leadership and laws. Religious clergy will typically claim positions of rule, and they are often considered appointed by God (or gods). Worship is often mandated and non-believers are persecuted.

When building a theocracy, consider who interprets scripture and whether laws are based on the text or if the scripture itself is law. What happens to nonbelievers—are they ignored? Frowned upon? Outcast? Killed? How are religious leaders treated—are they deified?

Examples: New England (*The Handmaid's Tale* by Margaret Atwood), Arrakis (*Dune* by Frank Herbert)

4. Magocracy

Rule by magic-users. Government positions are limited to those with magical abilities. Sometimes, people who can't use magic are considered second-class.

When building a magocracy, ask yourself how hierarchy is structured. How does your magic system fit into the political system? Are certain powers revered more than others? Are some people simply *more* powerful than others? How are people who can't use magic treated, and what is the general public attitude towards mages?

Examples: Earthsea (Earthsea Cycle by Ursela K. Le Guin), Tevinter Imperium (*Dragon Age*)

5. Technocracy

The leaders of government and policymakers are technical experts, scientists, and engineers. Scientific advancement is often prioritized, and science is usually elevated above religion.

When building a technocracy, consider how your society might be affected by valuing efficiency and progression over anything else. How are non-experts treated? What about people with disabilities? What about artists and creatives? Is education free or highly subsidized? How do leaders get their positions?

Examples: The Institute (*Fallout 4*), *Brave New World* by Aldous Huxley

6. Dictatorship

Rule that has been taken over by force, and the government is led by one person. The rule of a dictator can occur through military might, rebellion, or a leader refusing to step down from office. Dictators can remove corruption (need to execute that traitorous advisor? No problem!) and demand economic equality. Lots of problems can be solved quickly when you've got overwhelming force behind you, but benevolent dictatorships are rare.

When building a dictatorship, consider how the dictator came to their position and how the public feels about their rule. What are your dictator's goals? Do they use intimidation or bribery (or both) to get what they want? Are political ranks the same as military ranks? What does your dictator demand of its citizens?

Examples: Earth (*Samurai Jack*), the Empire (*Star Wars*)

7. Totalitarianism

The government has no limits to what they can do, and attempts to rule every aspect of its citizens' public and private lives. Individualism is discouraged or prohibited.

When building a totalitarian government, consider *how* the government controls people. What happens to people whose goals don't align with the state's? What are the goals of the government? What media is censored and propaganda spread? Is there a secret police and mandatory military sign-up? Are specific religious or political affiliations prohibited? How are jobs and housing assigned?

Examples: Britain (*Nineteen Eighty-Four* by George Orwell), Panem (*The Hunger Games* by Suzanne Collins)

8. Anarchy

There is no governing body, and societies function without laws or authorities. The term *anarchy* can also refer to a revolt against the current governing body.

When building an anarchical society, ask yourself what would happen without a government. Would currency exist? How are disputes and injustices handled? How are material, social, and spiritual needs of the people met? How does the society celebrate individuality and freedom?

Examples: Anarres (*The Dispossessed* by Ursula K. Le Guin), San Francisco (*The Fifth Sacred Thing* by Starhawk)

9. Feudalism

The government grants land to nobles in exchange for service or labour. Working relationships are a hierarchy, usually with a monarch on top; then the nobles (such as Earls, Dukes, and Barons) who are granted land; then their vassals, who swear loyalty to the nobles in exchange for their (usually military) services; then serfs, servants who have to get the noble's permission to do just about anything (leave the land, get married, etc.); then slaves, who have no rights whatsoever.

When building a feudalistic society, consider how people become nobles. What happens if people don't pay their taxes? How are contracts between nobles and vassals enforced? Who educates the nobles? Is there a widespread religion that provides moral and philosophical guidance?

Examples: Cottman IV (*Darkover* by Marion Zimmer Bradley), Alera (Codex Alera series by Jim Butcher)

10. Tribalism

People are organized into small, cultural groups and laws are based on customs, ceremonies, and traditions. They may be self-governed, or be part of a larger, governing body. Loyalty to the tribe's ideals is key to membership.

When building a tribalistic society, determine what the tribe's customs are and how they originated. How do they feed themselves (farming? Raising animals? Hunting? Fishing? Trading?). Are they nomadic or stationary? Do they have religious beliefs that inform their daily life? Is there a tribal leader?

Examples: Unnamed land (*Under the Lesser Moon* by Shelly Campbell), Chicago (*Divergent* by Veronica Roth)

AS YOU KNOW BY NOW, one of our favourite brainstorming methods is asking "what if?" Check out the political questions that inspired these published stories:

- What if your social and political rank was determined by a board game? (*The Player of Games* by Iain M. Banks)
- What if women had no rights? (*The Handmaid's Tale* by Margaret Atwood)
- What if private property didn't exist? (*The Dispossessed* by Ursula K. Le Guin)
- What if a monarch was deposed in the attempt to set up a republic? (*Promise of Blood* by Brian McClellan)
- What if an exiled, half-goblin son of the Emperor had to take the throne? (*The Goblin Emperor* by Katherine Addison)

Brandon Sanderson's Mistborn trilogy explores some fascinating political questions, particularly with the character Elend Venture and his desire for democracy in place of the Lord Ruler's feudal dictatorship. After the Lord Ruler's death, Elend establishes himself as king of the Central Dominance and drafts democratic laws. He creates a council, which includes nobles, skaa (slaves), and merchants. The council holds elections for king, and Elend loses the vote.

Things fall into chaos with corrupt people on the throne, a battle occurs in which Elend takes control of several armies, and he ends up establishing a New Empire with himself as Emperor. Elend becomes the leader of the very type of government he abhors, because he feels like there is no other choice. It's not surprising that his attempt at democracy fails, because he tries to establish a completely new form of government in the middle of a crisis. Though he doesn't get to see it, the ideals he strives for do come about in the sequel books.

Philosophical ideals and the theories behind political systems often don't play out the way they should, because humans are, well, human. There are always people who abuse power, and every system has its flaws. Keep that flawed nature in mind when creating your societies.

FOUR ECONOMIC SYSTEMS

Economic systems are the methods societies use to organize and distribute resources, services, and goods. Currency is almost always involved, but economics is less about money and more about how people's basic needs are met. Here are four basic types of economies that you can use to inspire your fictional societies:

1. Traditional Economy

The oldest of the four systems, anthropologists believe all economies start out this way. Traditional economies are rural-based, hunter-gatherer societies, and they rely on bartering rather than money. Tradition and/or elders dictate economic decisions. Once a society settles down, starts farming, and a surplus is possible, the economy is likely to change.

The advantages of a traditional economy include a lack of waste (generally, only what is needed is produced), that members of society understand their roles (as hunter, gatherer, farmer, weaver, etc.), and sustainability.

The disadvantages of a traditional economy include a vulnerability to nature and weather, a lack of growth (when the conditions aren't right, people starve, keeping these populations small), and a vulnerability to other economic types/societies stealing their resources.

Examples: *Under the Lesser Moon* by Shelly Campbell, *The Clan of the Cave Bear* by Jean M. Auel

2. Command Economy

The economy is largely controlled by a central authority (usually the government). They control production and societal goals, distribute resources for projects, and set quotas and prices with the goal of meeting its citizens' basic needs, food, and housing. Theoretically, this system works well as long as the government has its people's best interests in mind.

The advantages of a command economy include job security for citizens, a focus on society as a whole rather than individuals, and efficient use of resources.

The disadvantages of a command economy include a lack of creativity and innovation, an inability for the government to predict demand (so resources often require rationing), and an inability to react quickly to economic crises or changes.

Communism is a type of command economy that promotes a classless society in which property and wealth are shared, and the government controls all land, goods, and economic activities, including people's jobs.

Socialism is a type of command economy in which the government controls most aspects of production, distribution, and price of goods and services, but it does not mandate where people work.

Examples: *The Dispossessed* by Ursula Le Guin, *Anthem* by Ayn Rand

3. Market Economy

The government doesn't interfere much in the market, exercising little control over resources or the economy. Instead, supply and demand is what dictates the economy, and the people regulate the production of goods and who buys them. A pure market economy with no government interference whatsoever doesn't exist in our world, as governments will still regulate fair trade and monopolies.

The advantages of a market economy include the incentive for entrepreneurship and innovation, competition between businesses (which often results in efficient production and consumers not over-paying—though you'll still see certain brands dominating the market), and a society in which (ideally) no one is forced into a specific role or job.

The disadvantages of a market economy include a lack of consideration for disabled, poor, sick, and disadvantaged people due to a focus on economy over societal needs; exploitation of workers; monopolies; and basing people's value on what they "do" or how financially successful they are.

Capitalism is a type of market economy in which wealth is owned by individuals, and they keep the profits of their labour and accept their losses without intervention from a governing body.

Examples: *Iron Council* by China Mieville, *Making Money* by Terry Pratchett

4. Mixed Economy

A cross between market and command economies. Most industries are privately owned, but some things, such as public services like transportation, are run by the government. The government will often regulate private businesses and promote general welfare.

The advantages of a mixed economy include that private businesses can run efficiently; there is opportunity for creativity and innovation; the government can intervene in situations like market failure, when companies abuse their power, and to tax harmful products like cigarettes; the government can create programs like free access to healthcare; and the government can create tax policies to redistribute wealth and reduce inequality.

The disadvantages of a mixed economy include too much or too little interference from government (and public opinion on this varies) and the difficulties of finding a balance that truly promotes equality and meets the needs of the people.

Examples: Murderbot series by Martha Wells, *Accelerando* by Charles Stross

THE FUN PART about creating fictional economies is imagining systems that are drastically different from the ones we're familiar with. Here are some "what if?" questions some sci-fi and fantasy authors asked about their worlds' economies:

- What if magic regulates the trade of goods and services? Spoiler: if you don't pay off your debt, you'll

slowly turn into a bird. (*In an Absent Dream* by Seanan McGuire)
- What if a computer algorithm can predict what products people want even before they want them? (*Accelerando* by Charles Stross)
- What if calories become currency? (*The Windup Girl* by Paolo Bacigalupi)
- What if, when you can't pay off your debts, you're indentured and have to give up your citizenship? (*Autonomous* by Annalee Newitz)
- What if magic is currency, so people automatically achieve social and economic status based on what powers they're born with? (*Radiant* by Karina Sumner-Smith)

In Martha Wells' Murderbot series, the Corporate Rim is a powerful political entity composed of many private companies that trade with each other, and they own a lot of territory across the galaxy. There's no overarching government and a lot of competition between the corporations. The Corporate Rim represents an extreme form of capitalism, in which everything can be bought and sold. Even humans are assets, often indentured to corporations for generations.

This is the world Murderbot, a sentient A.I. and the protagonist of the series, is familiar with. It's used to be treated as an object (as robots have even fewer rights than humans do in the Corporate Rim). So when Murderbot meets people from the Preservation Alliance, a system of independent worlds with a very different political ideology and economy than the Corporate Rim, it's surprised by the way they treat it (like a person whose feelings and preferences matter). Preservation is communitarian, meeting people's basic needs for free. In *Network Effect*, Murderbot describes how strange Preservation seems:

> Humans in the Preservation Alliance didn't have to sign up for contract labor and get shipped off to mines or whatever for 80 to 90 percent of their lifespans. There was some strange system where they all got their food and shelter and education and medical for free, no matter what job they did. It had something to do with the giant colony ship that had brought them here, and a promise by the original crew to take care of everyone in perpetuity if they would just get on the damn thing and not die in the old colony."[1]

It's unclear exactly how the economy on Preservation planets works—there's a barter system, families operate farms, and everyone seems to be prosperous. Martha Wells uses these contrasting economies to comment on individual rights vs. corporate rights and critiques capitalism for dehumanizing people.

In an interview with Brookfield Institute, Wells says:

> I think [science fiction] lets us look at these possibilities. When you're reading them, you experience them through the point of view of the characters. That's a more real experience for our brain than just thinking what might or might not happen. You're getting all these different viewpoints from different people, and different types of people, that let you see the problem from different angles. It's kind of like any fiction, it's what we do when we read storybooks when we're children, and why we read dystopias. It's looking at worst case scenarios and seeing how people survived them and building empathy and stretching that to scenarios that we wouldn't see in contemporary literary fiction but

we might actually be coming toward in the future."[2]

At its heart, fiction is all about empathy: seeing the world from someone else's eyes and considering how people might react to unfamiliar worlds. Use your world's politics and economics to explore questions about your characters and drive the plot forward.

Chapter 23

Spitting on Tables is a Compliment
Society and Culture

Society and culture shape who we are on such a subliminal level that we often don't even notice. What we believe in, cherish, respect, or hate is influenced by our surroundings. Society and culture are also the backbones that support our fictional worldbuilding.

WHY ARE A VARIETY OF CULTURES IMPORTANT IN FICTION?

In our world, societies range from small clubs to whole countries. In sci-fi and fantasy, societies often expand to worlds, planets, galaxies, and even universes. This means, naturally, that people are members of many societies at once. Society is also tied directly to culture—the beliefs, values, customs, and behaviours that a group of people share. Both society and culture are keys to realistic worldbuilding that can draw readers into your story.

Many fantasy authors are inspired by medieval Europe settings and Tolkienesque races for their stories. This often translates to fair-skinned elves who live in a polytheistic, monogamous, heteronormative society and who commune with nature; stocky dwarves who also live in a polytheistic, monogamous, heteronormative society, and whose chief occupation is mining; and humans who live in a monotheistic, monogamous, heteronormative society, and who are known to be power hungry and impatient. All of these people fight with bows and arrows and swords, maybe the odd axe. When they go to war, they fight as regimented infantry and cavalry. Women have no place in power and are often damsels in distress.

Science fiction authors have more history of playing with different types of governments and societies, imagining what our world would look like if it was run differently. However, the market has still been dominated by cisgender, white, male authors for years.

Mainstream publishing and much of the entertainment industry in Western society has been dominated by a narrow portion of culture—mostly cis white men of European descent. Thankfully, that's slowly changing, and more diverse voices are being published.

A prevailing culture can seep into every facet of our lives, including the fiction we read for entertainment. If everything a reader picks up mirrors only one culture, this gives them a narrow view of life, and separates the "normal people" from the "outcasts."

One of the amazing things about sci-fi and fantasy is that you don't have to be beholden to the cultures you know, or even the cultures that already exist in this world. You can explore what a completely different perspective and world might look like. Take advantage of that opportunity by looking beyond your own culture when creating your world!

WHAT IS CULTURAL BIAS?

Humans pull our beliefs from what we are taught and what we see around us. We often believe something because the people around us believe it, too. Our cultures tell us what is "right" and what is "wrong," what is acceptable and what is inappropriate, regardless of whether it's a provable fact or not.

At one point, most of the world's cultures believed the world was flat and the cosmos rotated around Earth. Even when proof pointed otherwise, there was a huge resistance to changing that belief.

These days, many people view the world through social media. Since we hand-pick who we follow and block those we find offensive, our news reaches us in an echo chamber where our beliefs are reinforced.

Here are some things you might not have thought about if you don't belong to that people group:

- If you're a man, you may have never clutched your keys while walking alone at night, wondering if the man behind you is speeding up so they can assault you.
- If you are heteronormative, you may have never questioned what public washroom you should use.
- If you are white, you may have never considered why crayons, Band-Aids, or ballet slippers in "flesh colour" are all the same pale beige.
- If you are able-bodied, you may have never faced the anger of someone demanding you prove your disability because you parked in a disabled space, but you don't "look" disabled.
- If you are wealthy or middle-class, you may have never wondered where your next meal will come from.
- If you're not from Switzerland, you might be shocked at how Swiss farmers sell produce via unattended, roadside stands and rely on the honour system for payment.
- If you're visiting Japan or South Korea, you might not realize that tipping your waiter is an insult.

- If you think complimenting someone's clothing or home is a nice way to break the ice, you might be surprised at how some Africans will interpret this as a desire to own the item in question. They may even feel obligated to give it to you.

> Often we think that the way we live is normal and not cultural," writes anthropology specialist Christine Folch in an article for *The Atlantic* titled "Why the West Loves Sci-Fi and Fantasy: A Cultural Explanation." "This is what anthropologists call *tacit ethnocentrism*, when we are not trying to be prejudiced, but we have unquestioned assumptions that somehow we are the normal human baseline and others somehow deviate from that."[1]

Being human implies a universal commonality and sameness regardless of where we live or what our background is. And we do share *some* universal similarities, but we're also part of numerous, diverse and ever-changing smaller cultures that shape us on a more local level. This is what anthropology is all about and what science fiction is about too.

SCI-FI AND REAL SCIENCE

In the article "The Necessary Tension between Science Fiction and Anthropology," anthropologist Matthew Wolf-Meyer writes:

> I started my academic career in literature. SF was a curiosity, a genre that everyone seemed to accept the presence of, but that not many scholars took seriously.
>
> "It came as a surprise when I moved into anthropology and was surrounded by people who took SF very seriously. Everyone wanted to tell me

that Ursula Le Guin was the daughter of anthropologists, yet no one wanted to talk about Doris Lessing's postcolonial Canopus in Argos sequence of novels. What was going on here? Why, in literary studies, was SF so trivial, while in anthropology it seemed so vital?"[2]

Science fiction often explores questions about what life would look like in a different setting or how humanity would survive after a catastrophic change. Anthropology asks similar questions. What is human life like in different settings and times? How are biology, culture, and language affected by big changes?

While anthropology is a social science grounded in reality, science fiction uses imagination to press *beyond* the limits of current reality. It gives us a glimpse into how our universe might respond to alternate or future realities. It has been used as satire or commentary on how technology might affect civilizations.

There have even been instances where science fiction has inspired or predicted real science. Research into warp technology is happening right now. Dick Tracy's wristwatch from the 1940s comics has similarities to today's smartwatches. *Star Trek*'s universal translator is no longer fiction, as translator apps and products become more common. Luke Skywalker's bionic hand might become reality as researchers develop a way for amputees to control prosthetic fingers using ultrasonic sensors.[3] How amazing is that!

FANTASY AND CULTURAL COMMENTARY

Fantasy fiction is no stranger to cultural commentary either. In Tolkien's *The Lord of the Rings*, Isengard's transformation from forest to factory is a commentary on industrialization. Terry Pratchett's *Making Money* tackles economic theory and *Small Gods* is a commentary on organized religion. George Lucas was inspired by the Vietnam War and imperialism when he created Star Wars.

Children of Blood and Bone by Tomi Adeyemi, a novel about oppressed magic users in an African-inspired setting, has some obvious parallels between magic use and race. It demonstrates how misunderstandings and assumptions can feed prejudice.

Fantasy also asks "what if?" questions with its alternative history stories. For example, Justina Ireland's *Dread Nation* asks: what would happen if zombies appeared during the Civil War era? Her answer—black and indigenous people would be forced to stand on the frontlines; laws like the Native and Negro Reeducation Act would require these children to learn combat; and rich, white people would still have dinner parties and pretend like everything was normal (even when one of their members goes full zombie and attempts to bite his neighbour during high tea).

Culture is a powerful tool that you can use in your stories to empathize themes and question the status quo.

HOW TO CREATE A FICTIONAL SOCIETY

Your fictional culture can certainly take inspiration from real-life cultures, including your own. If you are looking at cultures other than your own, this should be approached with great care and the use of sensitivity readers to make sure you aren't misrepresenting, appropriating, or making one melting pot of numerous peoples.

If you want to start from scratch, there are a variety of areas you should consider. First, the things that outsiders can clearly see or access, such as language, dress, cuisine, and literature. Second, the less visible areas of culture, such as family roles, manners, body language, and definitions of modesty.

If we take the time to explore some of the deeper subjects of culture—even if we don't reveal all of them in our story, the culture will *feel* more authentic to our readers. When brainstorming a fictional society, try starting with the following eight topics.

1. Geography

Location impacts culture in a variety of ways. If water is key to your people's life (as is the case with lifeforms we're familiar with), they will likely be located near a water source; if not, how are they getting water? Geography will have a vast effect on culture in other ways too. Are your people isolated, or do they have complex trade partnerships? This will affect their language. Traders are more likely to speak several languages, while isolated people probably only know their home tongue. Intermarriage with trade partners is more common if cultures are neighbours, and you'll start to get some cultural cross-pollination happening here. This cultural merging happens slowly among friendly neighbours, but rapidly during war if one culture overtakes another, imposes its beliefs and customs, and tries to erase the loser's culture.

Geography also affects food, textiles, and natural resources. Does your society have access to wood, copper, iron, flint, jade, or gold? What about spices? For a huge chunk of history, cultures only used whatever spices grew locally. Global spice trade is a relatively recent phenomenon.

Speaking of phenomena, do your people witness any special weather elements, like Aurora Borealis, tidal waves, glaciers, tornados, or volcanic activity? These powerful marvels can also impact your culture's religious beliefs in addition to other behaviours.

For example, a Sami legend says the Aurora Borealis are caused by a magical fox running across the sky and sweeping his tail over the ground to stir up the snow and send up a trail of sparks.

Inuit culture believes the light comes from torches held by their ancestors to light the way for the dead. Some parents warn their children not to whistle at the Northern Lights to make them dance, because, if the lights sweep too low, they'll snatch you away—or in more gruesome versions, behead you.

See how a natural phenomena, like the Northern Lights, can influence a people group's beliefs and mythology?

General weather patterns will also determine how your people dress. Is agriculture feasible or do your groups hunt and gather in nomadic tribes? What survival skills do they need to thrive? Are they long-ranging sea-farers? Boat builders? Mountaineers? Shepherds? Weather forecasters? Water dowsers? What latitude does this group live at? If they've always lived near the equator, their skin will be a different colour than if they originated in polar climates.

2. Physiology

A species' physiology can also impact its culture. For example, most humans have two hands and ten fingers that allow us to deftly manipulate objects. Many cultures have developed hand motions that carry meaning (e.g. sign language, high fives, thumbs up, giving the middle finger, etc.). Our physiology also determines how we ingest food, how we get stinky when we don't shower, how we look at people when they're talking to us —and all these things have cultural connotations.

In *Project Hail Mary* by Andy Weir, scientist Ryland Grace befriends an alien (whom he dubs "Rocky") whose physiology is extremely different from a human's. Rocky is a five-legged being with a stone-like shell, about half the size of Grace. He breathes ammonia and lives in an atmosphere 29 times denser than Earth's. Instead of sight, he uses echolocation to understand his surroundings, and he communicates in music-like tones.

Grace names Rocky's people "Eridians," since they come from the Eridani star system, and you can probably already imagine how their culture might differ from humans' just because of the way their bodies work.

For one thing, Rocky likes to watch Grace sleep. This seems weird to Grace, but eventually he learns that when Rocky sleeps, the Eridian's body is completely immobile and he can't wake up until his body finishes the sleep cycle. Thus, Eridians watch each other sleep to make sure nothing bad happens to their bodies while they're unconscious.

For another, Eridians don't eat in public. Rocky reluctantly allows Grace to watch him eat once, "for science," and it's a disgusting endeavour where the Eridian opens up his carapace to reveal his squishy insides and shove food inside.

If a race or alien species in your world has vastly different physiology than humans, consider how that affects how they interact with the world, what is acceptable behaviour in their culture and what is taboo.

3. Language

Does your culture speak multiple languages? How is their vocabulary a product of their environment? Are they influenced by trade?

Are there words that cannot be directly translated into similar words in other languages—like the German words *erklärungsnot* (when you are at a loss for what to say) or *treppenwitz* (how you come up with the perfect thing to say after it's too late)? Are there multiple words for things that are important to them? Are there words they would never use?

For example, speakers of Guugu Yimithirr in North Queensland, Australia, use the four cardinal directions—north, east, south, and west—when referring to location. *Left* and *right* do not exist in their language. They have an internal compass that orients themselves around these directions at all times.[4]

Your alien race does not need to use speech at all, either—look at how *Project Hail Mary*'s Eridians communicate using musical tones.

4. History

History is almost always written by the winners of wars. As the author of your society, you can play with that concept. What do people think happened in the past? What *really* happened? What caused past conflicts between territories? Why did the invaders conquer? What were their needs? What gave them the leg-up over the society they bulldozed? What else did these colonizers bring? Disease? New technology or resources? How do hidden pockets of the losing culture survive or resist?

Europe had a favourable latitude for growing certain crops and domesticating work animals that gave them the technological advantage over many other cultures in the past. Do some of your societies have specific advantages over others?

Past events that affect cities, territories, continents, or entire worlds will shape the culture. Did a disease sweep the world, and now everyone wears masks whenever they are out? Did a wizard curse a city so no one could speak, and sign language became their method of communicating? Did aliens enslave all of humanity?

5. Education

Widespread education was not common until the advent of the printing press. Before that, only those who could afford to be educated were taught. Who receives education in your world? The wealthy? Royalty? Magic wielders? If you have mass education, how is it passed on? Verbally? Written? Apprenticeships? Who are your society's teachers? Elders? Scholars? Warriors? Tradespeople? Religious leaders? Are there schools or educational guilds?

6. Religion

Who do your people worship and why? What is their religion's message? Are they peaceful or do they seek war? Do they worship many gods and goddesses or just one? How do they treat those who don't share the same religious beliefs?

7. Social Constructs

Does your society have hierarchies and classes? Are they ruled by royalty? What roles do they value—warriors? Blacksmiths? Mages? Time travelers?

What are common customs that are considered "normal" or polite within your story's cultures? For example, North Americans often shake hands when meeting new people. This custom goes all the way back to 5th century B.C. where it was a symbol of peace, meant to show that neither person was carrying a weapon.

Frank Herbert's *Dune* takes place on a desert world in which water is an important commodity. The Fremen are a people group that values frugal use of energy and resources—water in particular. One character spits on a table as a sign of respect for another (giving up some of his precious moisture). What your society values most will have an impact on social constructs, customs, and behaviours.

8. Artwork

What is the role of art in your world? Practical? Satiristic? Does it serve to preserve history or celebrate events? Can everyone be an artist or is it reserved as a special role and forbidden to others? What is the most popular art style—visual, performing, costume, architectural, musical?

Consider this real-world example: the kobyz is a Turkic bowed string instrument used by Kazakh and Kyrgyz shamans.

It is carved from a single piece of wood due to the belief that this preserves the singing soul of the tree.[5] Music, culture, and religion are represented in this single item.

In Elizabeth Lim's *Spin the Dawn*, being a tailor is a high-status career and only men are allowed to be tailors. The protagonist, Maia, proves that she is a true artist in the field by creating dazzling embroidery, shawls, shoes, and dresses throughout the novel. Inspired by Chinese culture, it's clear why men are elevated above women in this society, though not why being a tailor is such an esteemed position. However, we don't need to know the *why* of it for the story to be interesting, just like we can accept shaking hands as a greeting without understanding its origin.

CULTURES ARE EVER-CHANGING. As our societies are influenced by others, or as their environment and situations change, their cultures will adapt. Take, for example, the evolution of the samurai: due to the relative peace during the Edo Period, they changed from elite warriors to teachers and artists. How do your societies adapt their culture as the world around them changes?

If developing a culture feels overwhelming, you can start with your protagonist and move outward instead of starting with the culture. What are your character's core values? How do they see the world? Do they hold a position of power in their culture or are they of lower status? Are they immigrants and outsiders within an unfamiliar society? Do they believe in the same values as the majority of their peers, or are they outcasts and rebels?

Then start asking *why* to these answers, and think about how their culture might have impacted their ideals, beliefs, and behaviours.

In *Hollow Heart* by Viola Di Grado, protagonist Dorotea is an outcast in life *as well* as the afterlife. Dumped by her boyfriend via text, she dies by suicide and is shunned by the society in the afterlife, who frowns upon suicide. Dorotea is an outcast—a ghost navigating a culture where she doesn't belong.

Consider what your culture values to determine whether your characters fit in or not.

An effective way to create instant tension and conflict in a story is to set up two vastly different cultures on a collision course. For example, perhaps one culture thinks it's polite to lower their gaze while speaking to someone in authority, but a neighbouring culture sees eye contact as a sign of respect. Or, perhaps, one greets newcomers by kissing them on both cheeks, but the other believes physical contact with acquaintances is invasive. And these aren't even major cultural differences.

In *The Orville* episode "About a Girl," Second Officer Bortus and his mate have a newborn daughter. But Bortus is a Moclan, a humanoid species that is almost entirely male. Female newborns undergo conversion surgery so they will be accepted into their society. The other species onboard the *USS Orville* are appalled at the idea of the surgery and that females are considered inferior and unwanted in Moclan culture. The ship's doctor refuses to perform the surgery on principle. The crew wrestles with the lines between culture and morality, questioning whether they should interfere or not. It's a moral quandary, and the episode leaves us with more questions than answers.

If you put some time and effort into creating diverse societies with deep and varied cultures in your stories, you'll hook your readers with experiences that feel authentic.

Conclusion

I'll let you in on a secret. I'm terribly disorganized. My office contains dog-eared papers filed in an order no one can decipher. My computer folders have multiple versions of drafts and copies of files spread haphazardly across my desktop. I write on napkins and the backs of envelopes and then promptly lose said notes. My world is often tattered around the edges. Who am I to give advice on worldbuilding and organizing your novel?

Yet, writing is such a satisfying way to gather up random bits of words into something with defined order, isn't it? I love making seemingly unrelated ideas and chapters into an organized whole, and I had so much fun researching and writing this book with Allison—who did the lion's share of organizing it!

Let me tell you, I'll be referencing my own copy of *Making Myths and Magic* until its pages are well-loved and worn. What a treasure to have all these worldbuilding ideas under one cover instead of scrawled on random napkins! What an adventure it's been researching the fantastic array of existing fiction out there for inspiration. I hope, in some small way, this book will fuel your adventures.

I can't wait to read about your new worlds. Keep feeding

your imagination, and thank you so much for letting us be a part of your writing process.

—Shelly Campbell

Endnotes

1. At Dawn... We Plan

1. Harmon, Dan. "Rick and Morty Dan Harmon Story Circle," YouTube, uploaded by Ryan Bose, 23 Jun 2018, https://www.youtube.com/watch?v=urd3MYV3RqE

3. In a Hole in the Ground

1. Sanderson, Brandon. *Elantris*. Tor Fantasy, 2006.
2. Palmer, Ada. *Too Like the Lightning*. Tor Books, 2016.
3. Palmer, Ada. *Too Like the Lightning*. Tor Books, 2016.

4. I Have a Bad Feeling About This

1. *Star Wars: Episode V - The Empire Strikes Back*. Directed by Irvin Kershner, Lucasfilm, 1980.
2. Demchick, Harrison. "The Best Way to use Conflict and Tension in your Narrative." *The Writer's Ally*, 24 Mar 2021, https://thewritersally.com/articles/tag/cause-and-effect/
3. "The Rains of Castamere" (Season 3, Episode 9). *Game of Thrones*. HBO, 2 Jun 2013.

5. We'll Make a Gonnagle Out of Ye

1. Dickens, Charles. *Bleak House*. Penguin Books, 2006 (first published 1853).
2. Rowling, J.K. *Harry Potter and the Philosopher's Stone*. Bloomsbury, 1997.
3. Rowling, J.K. *Harry Potter and the Goblet of Fire*. Scholastic, 2002 (first published 2000).
4. Pratchett, Terry. *The Wee Free Men*. HarperTrophy, 2004 (first published May 1st 2003).
5. Ondrušeková, Judtia. "Narrative Function of Language in Terry Pratchett's *Wee Free Men*." Constantine the Philosopher University, https://files.eric.ed.gov/fulltext/ED603463.pdf
6. "Family Ties" (Season 1, Episode 22). *Farscape*. Debmar-Mercury, 28 Jan 2000.
7. "Rhapsody in Blue" (Season 1, Episode 13). *Farscape*. Debmar-Mercury, 23 Jul 1999.
8. "Exodus from Genesis" (Season 1, Episode 3). *Farscape*. Debmar-Mercury, 14 May 1999.

9. Skrovon, Jon. "Guest Post: How to Build a Fantasy Language, from Slang to Swearing, by Jon Skovron." Barnes & Noble Sci-Fi & Fantasy blog, 28 Jun 2016, https://www.barnesandnoble.com/blog/sci-fi-fantasy/guest-post-how-to-build-a-fantasy-language-from-slang-to-swearing-by-jon-skrovon/
10. Hansen, Essa. *Nophek Gloss*. Orbit, 2020.
11. Mass Effect 2, Windows PC version, BioWare, 2010.
12. Butcher, Jim. Storm Front. Penguin, 2000.

6. Our Princess is in Another Castle

1. Stockholm syndrome is a psychological phenomenon in which hostages and victims develop emotional ties to their captors as a survival strategy. They develop loyalty and affection for their kidnapper, excuse abusive behaviour, and distrust authorities or potential rescuers; they even start to assimilate their captor's beliefs and goals. Stockholm syndrome requires an uneven power relationship, that the captive is held under threat of death or injury, and that they are unable to take initiative to escape even if the opportunity comes up.

7. I'm Afraid I Can't Do That, Dave

1. Once known as the soul of Cape Town, District Six was home to a population of 55,000 predominantly coloured people who suffered displacement and the demolishment of their homes and businesses. This event culminated when District Six was declared a white-only area under the Group Areas Act in 1966.
2. "Jaynestown." *Firefly*. Directed by Joss Whedon. 20th Television, 2002.

8. It is a Great Misfortune to Be Alone

1. Verne, Jules. *The Mysterious Island*. Modern Library, 2004 (first published 1865).
2. Not everyone agrees on the definitions of high and low fantasy. Some define high fantasy as having fantastical elements (like magic) and low fantasy as having minimal or no magic. By this definition, George R.R. Martin's *Game of Thrones* would be low fantasy, as magic doesn't play a big part in the story. But by our definition, *Game of Thrones* would be high fantasy, because it takes place in another world. Due to this confusion, we recommend choosing one of the other, more specific subgenres to define your novel.

9. We All Know I'm the Funny One

1. Brioux, Bil. "Firefly series ready for lift off." *Jam Showbiz*, 15 Jul 2012, https://archive.is/20120715154524/http://jam.canoe.ca/Television/TV_Shows/F/Firefly/2002/07/22/734323.html.

11. To Be Human Is to Be Complex

1. Butler, Octavia. "In 1980: Octavia Butler Asked, Why Is Science Fiction So White?" *Garage Magazine*, 4 Sep 2018, https://garage.vice.com/en_us/article/d3ekbm/octavia-butler
2. @MaryRobinette. "It's not about adding diversity for the sake of diversity, it's about subtracting homogeneity for the sake of realism." Twitter, 17 Dec 2014, 10:01 p.m., twitter.com/MaryRobinette/status/545428674812465152
3. Szalavitz, Maia. "Why do we think poor people are poor because of their own bad choices?" *The Guardian*, 5 Jul 2017, https://www.theguardian.com/us-news/2017/jul/05/us-inequality-poor-people-bad-choices-wealthy-bias
4. Johansson, Emil. "Middle-earth in Numbers." *LOTR PROJECT*, http://lotrproject.com/statistics/
5. Tilley, Cristen. "Book week: Analysis of bestsellers suggests kids' bookshelves are on a lean." ABC, 21 August 2018, https://www.abc.net.au/news/2018-08-22/kids-book-top-100-analysis/10042904
6. Elliott, Kate. "Writing Women Characters Into Epic Fantasy Without Quotas." TOR, 23 Mar 2016, https://www.tor.com/2016/03/23/writing-women-characters-into-epic-fantasy-without-quotas/
7. Berlatsky, Noah. "In Ann Leckie's Imperial Radch trilogy, gender isn't just different, it's irrelevant." *ABP Culture*, 30 Nov 2017, https://abeautifulperspective.com/2017/11/science-fiction-lot-teach-us-changing-gender-norms/
8. Shurrens, Skye. "Our Friend is Here! Asian Heritage Month Edition – An Interview with Xiran Jay Zhao, Author of Iron Widow; On Feminist Fantasy, Giant Robots, & Diaspora Worldbuilding." *The Quiet Pond*. 7 May 2020, https://thequietpond.com/2020/05/07/our-friend-is-here-asian-heritage-month-edition-an-interview-with-xiran-jay-zhao-author-of-iron-widow-on-feminist-fantasy-giant-robots-diaspora-worldbuilding/
9. Handyman, Wren. "Diversity in Sci Fi Is Important. Here's How We Write That Future." *We Need Diverse Books*, 30 Jul 2020, https://diversebooks.org/diversity-in-sci-fi-is-important-heres-how-we-write-that-future/
10. Nittle, Nadra Kareem. "Understanding the Difference Between Race and Ethnicity." *ThoughtCo.*, 13 Mar 2021, https://www.thoughtco.com/difference-between-race-and-ethnicity-2834950
11. @saladinahmed. "dear writers: your white characters have race and skin color too. write like you know that. otherwise you make them the default." Twitter, 7 Dec 2017, 6:36 a.m., https://twitter.com/saladinahmed/status/938749041751543808
12. Ifueko, Jordan. *Raybearer*. Amulet Books, 2020.
13. Brown, Roseanne A. *A Song of Wraiths and Ruin*. HarperCollins, 2020.

14. Badger, Darcie Little. *Elatsoe*. Levine Querido, 2020.
15. Benson, SF. "SF Benson: Writing Diverse Characters." *We Write Fantasy*, 1 Jul 2020, https://wewritefantasy.com/2020/07/01/sf-benson-writing-diverse-characters/
16. Boyce, Michael. "The Uncomfortable Racism of C.S. Lewis." *Area of Effect* Issue 10, Sep 2017.
17. Price, Fran and Halli Gomez. "WRITING FEATURE Neurodivergent Characters, Part 1." *Words & Pictures*, https://www.wordsandpics.org/2021/02/writing-feature-neurodivergent.html
18. Author Unknown. "a guide to writing tourettic characters." Tumblr, 18 Nov 2018, https://tic-loud-tic-proud.tumblr.com/post/180245940663/a-guide-to-writing-tourettic-characters
19. Bartmess, Elizabeth. "What Good Representation of Autistic Characters Looks Like, Part I: Interiority and Neurology." *Thinking Person's Guide to Autism*, 28 Feb 2018, http://www.thinkingautismguide.com/2018/02/what-good-representation-of-autistic.html
20. Hoffmann, Ada. "Towards a Neurodiverse Future: Writing an Autistic Heroine." TOR, 24 Jul 2019, https://www.tor.com/2019/07/24/writing-an-autistic-heroine/
21. Neufeld, Kyla. "Monstrous Bodies: Fat Shaming in Geek Culture." *Never Split the Party (and Other Wisdom from Geek Culture That Changed My Life)*. Mythos & Ink, 2019.
22. Onyx, Fay. "How Do I Describe Fat Characters Respectfully?" *Mythcreants*, 15 Jun 2020, https://mythcreants.com/blog/how-do-i-describe-fat-characters-respectfully/
23. Anders, Charlie Jane. "Never Say You Can't Survive: When Is It Okay To Write About Someone Else's Culture or Experience?" TOR, 6 Oct 2020, https://www.tor.com/2020/10/06/never-say-you-cant-survive-when-is-it-okay-to-write-about-someone-elses-culture-or-experience/
24. Kirabo, Sincere. "Muggles' Magical Thinking: Why J.K. Rowling's Cultural Appropriation is a Problem." *The Humanist*, 14 Mar 2016, https://thehumanist.com/arts_entertainment/books/muggles-magical-thinking-j-k-rowlings-cultural-appropriation-problem/
25. Scalzi, John. "The Big Idea: N.K. Jemisin." *Whatever*, 2 May 2012, https://whatever.scalzi.com/2012/05/02/the-big-idea-n-k-jemisin-3/
26. Alderman, Naomi et al. "Whose life is it anyway? Novelists have their say on cultural appropriation." *The Guardian*, 1 Oct 2016, https://www.theguardian.com/books/2016/oct/01/novelists-cultural-appropriation-literature-lionel-shriver
27. Garcia-Navarro, Lulu and Amélie Wen Zhao. " Amélie Wen Zhao On 'Blood Heir'." *NPR*, 17 Nov 2019, https://www.npr.org/2019/11/17/780231746/am-lie-wen-zhao-on-blood-heir
28. Zutter, Natalie. "We Need Diverse Books Talks True, Political, Global Diversity in Sci-Fi and Fantasy." TOR, 1 Jun 2015, https://www.tor.com/2015/06/01/we-need-diverse-books-sff-panel-bookcon-2015/

12. Hey, Listen!

1. Saghir, Isra Aemen Saghir. "'Torrent and Tempest and Flood.' An Analysis of the Flood Myth Across Cultures." *Young Anthropology*, 2019, https://jps.library.utoronto.ca/index.php/ya/article/view/33362

13. We Will Shake the World for Our Beliefs

1. Ambrosino, Brandon. "How and why did religion evolve?" *BBC Future*, 18 April 2019, https://www.bbc.com/future/article/20190418-how-and-why-did-religion-evolve
2. "The Global Religious Landscape," *Pew Research Center*, 18 Dec 2012, https://www.pewforum.org/2012/12/18/global-religious-landscape-exec/
3. de Waal, Frans. *The Bonobo and the Atheist: In Search of Humanism Among the Primates*. W. W. Norton Company, 2013.
4. *Rogue One: A Star Wars Story*. Directed by Gareth Edwards. Lucasfilm, 2016.

14. Even NASA Can't Improve on Duct Tape

1. Sofia, Maddie, host, and Jessica Coon. "What *Arrival* Gest RIght — And Wrong — About Linguistics." *Science Movie Club*, NPR, 21 August 2020, https://www.npr.org/transcripts/901705799
2. Hoffmann, Ada. "How Science Feels." *Substack*, 21 Sep 2021, https://adahoffmann.substack.com/p/how-science-feels

15. Higitus Figitus Migitus Mum

1. Sanderson, Brandon. "Sanderson's First Law." *Brandon Sanderson*, 20 Feb 2007, https://www.brandonsanderson.com/sandersons-first-law/
2. Sanderson, Brandon. "Sanderson's Second Law." *Brandon Sanderson*, 16 Feb 2012, https://www.brandonsanderson.com/sandersons-second-law/
3. Sanderson, Brandon. "Sanderson's Third Law." *Brandon Sanderson*, 25 Sep 2013, https://www.brandonsanderson.com/sandersons-third-law-of-magic/

16. What Has it Got in Its Future, Precious?

1. Watson, Galadriel. "Why solving puzzles feels so satisfying, especially during a quarantine," The Washington Post, 4 May 2020, https://www.washingtonpost.com/lifestyle/wellness/why-solving-puzzles-feels-so-satisfying-especially-during-a-quarantine/2020/05/03/b87ac636-8bda-11ea-9dfd-990f9dcc71fc_story.html.
2. Rodda, Emily. *The Lake of Tears*. Scholastic, 2001 (first published 2000).

3. Nix, Garth. *Aenir*. Scholastic, 2000.
4. Nix, Garth. *Aenir*.
5. Tolkien, J.R.R. *The Hobbit*. Houghton Mifflin, 2002 (first published 1937).
6. Cooper, Susan. *The Dark is Rising Sequence (The Dark is Rising, #1-5)*. Simon & Schuster, 1986.
7. Tolkien, J.R.R. *The Lord of the Rings: The Fellowship of the Ring*. Ballantine Books, 1973 (originally published 1954).
8. Bujold, Lois McMaster. *The Curse of Chalion*. Voyager, 2003 (first published 2001).
9. Gaiman, Neil and Terry Pratchett. *Good Omens: The Nice and Accurate Prophecies of Agnes Nutter, Witch*. William Morrow, 2006 (first published 1990).
10. Kyla Neufeld, "How to Write a Poetic Prophecy, Mythos & Ink, 04 July 2019, https://www.mythosink.com/how-to-write-a-poetic-prophecy/.

17. So Sing We All

1. Tolkien, J.R.R. *The Lord of the Rings: The Fellowship of the Ring*. Ballantine Books, 1973 (originally published 1954).
2. *The Lord of the Rings: The Fellowship of the Ring*. Directed by Peter Jackson. New Line Cinema, 2001.
3. Collins, Suzanne. *The Ballad of Songbirds and Snakes*. Scholastic Press, 2020.
4. Ifueko, Jordan. *Raybearer*. Amulet Books, 2020.
5. *Dragon Age: Inquisition*. Windows PC version, Bioware, 2014.
6. Jordan, Robert. *A Crown of Swords*. TOR, 1997.
7. *The Legend of Zelda: Skyward Sword*. Wii version, Nintendo, 2011.
8. Rothfuss, Patrick. *The Wise Man's Fear*. DAW Books, 2011.
9. Valente, Catherynne M. *Mass Effect Andromeda: Annihilation*. Titan Books, 2018.
10. Hobb, Robin. *Fool's Fate*. Spectra, 2004.
11. *Star Wars: Republic Commando*. Windows PC version, LucasArts, 2005.

18. Avoid the Gaze of the Ravenous Bugblatter

1. Lisa O'Kelly, "Philip Pullman: "My daemon is a raven, a bird that steals things'," The Guardian, 22 Oct 2017, https://www.theguardian.com/books/2017/oct/22/philip-pullman-my-daemon-is-a-raven-la-belle-sauvage-interview-questions.
2. Trout, Paul A. "Why We Invented Monsters," *Salon*, 2 Dec 2011, https://www.salon.com/2011/12/03/the_evolution_of_monsters/
3. Athans, Philip. "Writing Monsters: What Makes a Monster Scary," Writer's Digest, 27 Oct 2017, https://www.writersdigest.com/write-better-fiction/writing-monsters-scary-qualities
4. Albrecht, Karl. "The (Only) 5 Fears We All Share." *Psychology Today*, 22 Mar 2012, https://www.psychologytoday.com/ca/blog/brainsnacks/201203/the-only-5-fears-we-all-share

19. This Weapon Is Your Life

1. Jordan, Robert. *The Dragon Reborn.* TOR, 1991.
2. Koboldt, Dan. "Weapons and Tactics in Fantasy Warfare." *Dan Koboldt*, 23 Jul 2015, http://dankoboldt.com/fantasy-warfare-tactics/
3. "Water War." *Star Wars: The Clone Wars.* Season 4, Episode 1, Lucasfilm, 2011.
4. *Star Wars: Episode II - Attack of the Clones.* Directed by George Lucas, Lucasfilm, 2002.
5. Breiding, Dirk H. "Arms and Armor—Common Misconceptions and Frequently Asked Questions." *The Metropolitan Museum of Art*, Oct 2004, https://www.metmuseum.org/toah/hd/aams/hd_aams.htm

20. Bow Ties Are Cool

1. Radish, Christina. "Elizabeth Banks, Lenny Kravitz and Wes Bentley, The Hunger Games Interview." *Collider*, 12 Mar 2012, https://collider.com/elizabeth-banks-lenny-kravitz-wes-bentley-hunger-games-interview/
2. Holman, Ray. "Ray Holman - Costume Designer Q+A." BBC, 11 October 2018, https://www.bbc.co.uk/blogs/doctorwho/entries/3cfd7b93-2e89-4fec-a7b9-8de903f454f5

21. Mae Govannen, quSDaq ba'lu"a'?

1. "How many languages are there in the world?" *Ethnologue Languages of the World*, https://www.ethnologue.com/guides/how-many-languages
2. "Treehouse of Horror." *The Simpsons*, created by Matt Croening, season 2, episode 16, Fox, 1990.
3. Polomoshnova, Olga. "On linguistic creation: what makes Tolkien's invented languages special." *Middle-earth Reflections*, 6 January 2019, https://middleearthreflections.com/2019/01/06/on-linguistic-creation-what-makes-tolkiens-invented-languages-special/
4. Eldrige, Alison. "6 Fictional Languages You Can Really Learn." Encyclopaedia Britannica, Inc., https://www.britannica.com/list/6-fictional-languages-you-can-really-learn.
5. Goldfield, Anna. "The Neanderthal Throat—Did Neanderthals Speak?" *Sapiens Anthropology Magazine*, 12 June 2019, https://www.sapiens.org/column/field-trips/did-neanderthals-speak/
6. Rosenfelder, Mark. "Grammar." *The Language Construction Kit*, http://www.zompist.com/kitgram.html

22. The King is Dead

1. Wells, Martha. *Network Effect*. TOR, 2020.
2. Wells, Martha and Diana Rivera. "Surviving the Corporate Galaxy: An interview with Martha Wells." Brookfield Institute. 2 July 2020, https://brookfieldinstitute.ca/surviving-the-corporate-galaxy-an-interview-with-martha-wells/

23. Spitting on Tables is a Compliment

1. Christine Folch, "Why the West Loves Sci-Fi and Fantasy: A Cultural Explanation," The Atlantic, 13 June 2013, https://www.theatlantic.com/entertainment/archive/2013/06/why-the-west-loves-sci-fi-and-fantasy-a-cultural-explanation/276816/.
2. Wolf-Meyer, Matthew. "The Necessary Tension between Science Fiction and Anthropology." Society for Cultural Anthropology, https://culanth.org/fieldsights/the-necessary-tension-between-science-fiction-and-anthropology
3. "The Force is Strong: Amputee Controls Individual Prosthetic Fingers." *Georgia Tech*, 12 Nov 2017, https://www.ic.gatech.edu/news/599762/force-strong-amputee-controls-individual-prosthetic-fingers
4. Maria Diment, "Does the language we speak shape the way we think?" ALTA Language Services, Inc. 20 Nov 2019, https://www.altalang.com/beyond-words/language-shape-thought/.
5. Aslanova, Amanova Roza. "Sacred Functions of Musical Instruments in the Creative Syncretism of Shamanistic Ritual," *ResearchGate*, May 2018,

Acknowledgments

So many people had a hand in encouraging us to write this book, and we want to thank everyone!

Thanks to Christiana, Emma, and Kyle for proofreading the book, supporting us, and cheering us on.

Thanks to Sunyi, Antoine, Trudie, Bharat, Giles, Julie, C.R., Mur, and Dakota for reading an early copy and saying such lovely things about it.

Thanks to Arina, Christiana, and Kayla for sensitivity reading.

Thanks to our families for letting us read chapter drafts to them, listening to our rants about fantasy tropes, and supporting our writing careers.

Thanks to Kyla for always being willing to chat about why Tolkien named a bunch of swords in *The Lord of the Rings*.

Thanks to everyone who supported this project that we forgot to mention because our brains are sludge after writing a 370-page book.

And thanks to you, dear writer, for picking up this book, for appreciating sci-fi and fantasy, and for sharing your creativity with the world! You rock.

About Shelly Campbell

At a young age, Shelly Campbell wanted to be an air show pilot or a pirate, possibly a dragon and definitely a writer and artist. She's piloted a Cessna 172 through spins and stalls, and sailed up the east coast on a tall ship barque—mostly without projectile vomiting. In the end, Shelly found writing fantasy and drawing dragons to be so much easier on the stomach.

Shelly's tales are speculative fiction, tending toward literary with dollops of oddity. She enjoys the challenge of exploring new techniques and subject matter, and strives to embed inspiring stories in her writing and art.

facebook.com/shellycampbellauthorandart
twitter.com/ShellyCFineArt
instagram.com/shellycampbellfineart

About Allison Alexander

Allison is a writer, artist, nerd, and 400 other things. From her home on Hoth (a.k.a. Canada), she builds fantasy worlds with a keyboard and a drawing tablet. She makes up for the shocking absence of cats and coffee in her life by spending time with her supportive partner and drinking tea. From her experience as an editor at a small press, she shares insights about publishing and writing on her blog, and in between art posts, she  occasionally rants about living with a chronic illness on social media. You can find her at **aealexander.com** or chasing otter penguins out of the Normandy.

goodreads.com/authoraealexander
twitter.com/allisonexander
instagram.com/allisonexander

Also by the Authors

By Shelly Campbell

Under the Lesser Moon (The Marked Son #1)
Voice of the Banished (The Marked Son #2)
Gulf
Knowledge Itself

By Allison Alexander

Super Sick: Making Peace with Chronic Illness

www.ingramcontent.com/pod-product-compliance
Lightning Source LLC
Chambersburg PA
CBHW070734170426
43200CB00007B/522